ARMSTRONG'S FIGHT
FOR
FM BROADCASTING

ARMSTRONG'S FIGHT FOR FM BROADCASTING:

One Man vs
Big Business and Bureaucracy

by
DON V. ERICKSON

THE UNIVERSITY OF ALABAMA PRESS
University, Alabama

CONTENTS

A VERY PERSONAL
OPENING

In a legal sense it is difficult to prove innocence or guilt. Acceptable evidence in court must be of a certain kind and must conform to certain rules for its acceptability. It is equally difficult to "prove," outside a court, that a person or firm has perhaps broken the written and unwritten rules of normally acceptable conduct. It is the intent of this book to prove that the government's regulatory commissions, in this case the Federal Communications Commission, consciously do exactly what they were intended not to do. They protect the industry to be regulated instead of protecting the public.

The regulatory agencies of this country such as the FCC, the Federal Trade Commission, the Interstate Commerce Commission, the Federal Food and Drug Administration, the National Maritime Commission, the National Railroad Commission, the Airline Commission, the Securities Exchange Commission, the Federal Housing Administration, the Federal Power Commission, and the commissions created in 1971 to regulate prices and wages were created, in theory, to regulate certain industries in the public interest. They were sometimes created because those industries not only could not regulate themselves, but because abuses in the industry were so rampant and serious that some greater power had to step in to protect the public.

The broadcasting industry asked the government back in the 1920's to step in to clear up the chaos on the air and

bring some sort of order to the growing industry. This fact
of history is often forgotten or overlooked by present-day
broadcasters who find regulation a possible and real danger
to more or extra profits. As a general rule, beware of any
radio or television executive who speaks of government interference and free speech in any situation. If one digs a little
deeper he will often find the executive has found a method
to cover up his own greed or obvious lack of public responsibility (perhaps not so deep—just lift off the thin veneer
of "principle" and see the profit-and-loss statement peeking
boldly through). The method is simply to talk a lot about
government interference (which, in fact, does not exist in
broadcasting to any significant degree) so as to raise fears
and doubts about such inteference (which, in fact, do exist)
in order to keep people worried and fearful. Meanwhile,
back at the till, the money continues to flow into the broadcasting coffers. But the immense size of the money flow is
carefully shielded from the public by the broadcast industry's continual barrage of alarm over supposed government interference and/or censorship. The industry keeps up
a smokescreen of fear and publicly wraps the smokescreen
in appeals to and about the American Flag, the Constitution,
and their rights under the law. There is a general and subtle
public relations campaign that suggests that any criticism
against, say, RCA or CBS or Metromedia or Paramount
or ITT is somehow un-American. To criticize the Bell
System must be the most mortal sin of all and only an avowed
Communist or "weirdo" could possibly be capable of such
heresy. Such a critic must be dismissed or made to seem
irrelevant.

I will try to take the story of FM radio broadcasting and
prove that the broadcasting lobby and the Federal Communications Commission did (and do), indeed, work together for
each other's mutual (usually "mutual" may be read "financial")
benefit and the public be damned. If the reader is convinced
at the end of the book that I have documented the charges

that such agencies are run, and such decisions are reached by these under-the-table methods; always have been and (unless some major and minor miracles are wrought) always will be. If the reader needs extra reinforcement or proof, he is urged to read all of the Ralph Nader investigations and any number of books written about the history of American industry (oil, forests, railroad, journalism, shipping) provided the books were not written by or financed by that industry!

Mass communications and the media by which these commercial and entertainment messages reach millions have become the single most important influence on our society. Obviously that statement is a personal one, though shared by many, many others. I do not choose to argue its validity here. I do feel, however, the mass media have more power—financial, political, impact, authority—than any other modern institution including the family, the church, the military, education, government, and even the business institution. This mass media power derives from the fact that they are often the voice of these other institutions and therefore usually support them, justify them, and make their living from them. That is my belief and bias. If you are looking for an unbiased account, forget it. The FM story cannot be told without bias or emotion. Do not despair altogether those of you who demand objectivity in all you encounter. There has been a very conscious effort to carefully research and interpret "facts" (whatever those are), events, and results. My personal concern is over the fact (that word again!) that mass media, especially the electronic media of radio and television, are so important and influential in our lives and that they are operated by the kinds of men, companies, and government agencies that make up the cast of characters of this story.

When one finally understands completely the power and importance of all mass media and realizes the kind of conglomerate/corporate/profit-oriented thinking that goes into the running of the media, then the shock hits home. For the media are becoming the substitutes for and/or the equal to the functions of the family, church, education, and the primary groups of a person's lifetime.

I am not here concerned with the more shallow criticisms of media that may come to one's mind quickly, such as carping over too many commercials on radio, or decrying a television ad in bad taste, or arguing the fruitless problem of whether a book is obscene or a movie too boring. That kind of discussion is for neophytes in communications. Sunday-supplement articles are to be engaged in by somebody's uncle, after dinner, on a rainy Sunday when there's nothing left to talk about and the television set is broken.

I'm more concerned about the media's effects (I often use media in the singular) on people in a society over time. My concern, therefore, is about the kinds of things that Marshall McLuhan, Harold Innis, Wilbur Schramm, Jack Gould, Robert Louis Shayon, Pauline Kael, Marya Mannes, Nicholas Johnson, John Kenneth Galbraith and dozens of others of similiar ilk are concerned about. They often equate media effects with survival. And that's realistic.

Since I, and they, are concerned, I'd like to assume all should be concerned with the media and how they are run. How are decisions made? What kind of men make them? For what reasons? What are their qualifications? It is an interesting sidelight that working in mass communications often requires no previous professional commitment to any kind of value or moral responsibility. However, to be a hairstylist or barber one must go to school and then get a permit to practice. I am aware that to be an engineer in broadcasting you must have a license, but I am thinking of the vast number of people who work in media (executives, white collar workers, advertising people included) whose jobs needed no real professional or required demands. Yet the mass media are "weapons" in the most serious meaning of that word. And turning over this persuasive/semantic/visual/audio weapon to the kinds of men and organziations that make up the FM story is my personal horror and concern.

I regard the regulatory commissions of our country on an equal—if not higher—level with the Congress itself. Congress may pass or kill a bill, make laws, give itself a lot of tax-supported vacations, but the commissions *run* things. I'd like to be a Commissioner at Christmastime. You don't understand? Think about it! But lest anyone put all the blame for evil doings on this shadow government I call the regulatory commissions, it is a President who puts the men on these commissions. So, like the Supreme Court, one can change the feeling and actions of a commission simply by putting the right men on it.

Most of us have heard the phrase "the Nixon Court" or "the Roosevelt Court" or "the Johnson Court." It is obvious what is meant by that. A President (and his political party) can change—in fact reverse—the entire complexion of the Supreme Court or the Federal Communications Commission by putting men on the court or commission who know what is expected of them. The FCC is a 7-man commission (term of seven years) and the normal method of getting on such a commission is usually patronage. What did he do for the party in the last election campaign. Often the men who serve on these commissions know nothing of the industry they are to regulate (that may or may not be a good thing), often they are lawyers or know law (that also may or may not be good for the public, as will be shown). But they do share one common interest that gets them into the job—they are members of a political party. Loyalty to our particular two major parties (their names need not be mentioned, I assume) is hardly a useful or legitimate criterion for service to the public. There are some, myself included, who feel blind loyalty to a political party is reason enough to bar a person from any job that requires service to the public!

After a President appoints a man to a commission, the Congress must approve the appointment, as is the case with the Supreme Court. In the case of commission appointees, the approval is almost always a rubber stamp procedure. I know of no celebrated case where the Press was filled with the controversy over such a commission appointment. That sort of thing is saved for appointments to the Supreme Court (witness the sensational news made during the Nixon administration over several Supreme Court candidates) where it is treated with all the glamor and coverage we give to a Miss America Contest or the Kentucky Derby.

It may be no accident that the role of our regulatory commissions is simply not part of Press coverage in depth or even school courses in depth. The less the public and the student know about what these commissions really do from day to day, the more the status-quo boat is likely not to be rocked. And both the management forces and the labor forces who lobby before these commissions want to keep things the way they are.

I am not a political expert concerning my own country. Still, over the years, I am vaguely aware that the guts of our government operations and its decisions lie deeply within Congressional committees and regulatory agencies. And that the "performance" of the Congress itself and the President in public view is more of a giant fashion show. The interviews on television with Senators, Congressional 4-day trips to foreign war areas, Army Day at your favorite military base, Presidential jaunts here, there and everywhere all are part of the show—the outer garment, seen by all, marvelled at, discussed and criticized. Meanwhile, under the dazzle are the undergarments that hold it all together with paste, glue, blood, bobby pins, and guts so it really works and looks good. But never, never lift the lady's skirt to get too close a look, for then the magic and myth are gone.

Behind the pleasures that an FM listener may get from his or her stereo broadcast system lies such a skirt-lifting story.

ARMSTRONG'S FIGHT
FOR
FM BROADCASTING

I

THE INVENTOR:

EDWIN HOWARD ARMSTRONG

In the spring of 1968, Motorola, Inc., settled the last of twenty FM patent infringement court cases and, in settling, paid the last of some ten million dollars to the widow of Major Edwin Howard Armstrong, the inventor of present-day FM. The Supreme Court had refused to hear an appeal by Motorola, which had lost this case in a lower court some years earlier. The Supreme Court's refusal to review the case brought to a close a legal struggle which had plagued FM broadcasting since its invention in 1933.

The legal battle was over the infringement of the FM patents. Some two dozen companies, over the years, had produced FM sets without paying royalties to the inventor or to his estate. The companies contended that they had invented FM (or controlled the FM patents). Or they maintained that there had been no invention to begin with, that FM was simply an outgrowth of the radio art, a natural development not assignable to any one person. These legal arguments cover a period of roughly from 1948 to 1968.

The technical obstacles facing FM's acceptance were caused by the radio engineering society into whose unbelieving lap it was dramatically dumped in 1935. Though FM has a half-dozen decided advantages over AM, its ability to suppress extraneous electrical noises (static) was the hoped-for goal of many electrical engineers in the 1920's and 1930's. Therefore, in November, 1935, when Armstrong demonstrated noise-free radio reception at a meeting of this country's leading engineers, they refused to believe what they had heard. And, in fact, they would not believe it for some time to come.

The economic future of FM broadcasting seemed doomed until the late 1960's. In 1966, the industry figures still showed a loss of $3,300,000. That the FM economic picture was so bleak during its first thirty-five years of existence had nothing to do with its ability to perform a superior broadcasting service.

During these years, in addition to the radio engineers, the federal government, as represented by the Federal Communications Commission, played a major role. Recognizing FM's superior service, the FCC, first on an experimental basis (1936) and then on a commercial basis (1940), authorized FM broadcasting. Subsequently, in a series of strangely conflicting decisions, the FCC both encouraged and thwarted any real commercial growth. One decision alone was catastrophic in its results: the 1945 decision to move the FM broadcasting band from one position in the radio spectrum to a much higher position, made obsolescent every FM radio receiver, every FM transmitter, and a major part of all FM equipment and tubes. Thus, with no new FM equipment on the lucrative postwar market and no advertisers to purchase time on the new band of frequencies, FM, in its first ten years of existence was brought close to the brink of commercial death. It is, and was, believed that this was not entirely accidental—that this was the result of a loosely planned campaign by various interests in industry and government.

Armstrong invented FM toward the close of his career. Prior to that, his inventions in the radio field were of such a magnitude that he is considered, along with Marconi, as the major contributor to the radio art. *Fortune* magazine states:

Wide-band frequency modulation is the fourth and perhaps the greatest, in a line of Armstrong inventions that have made most of modern broadcasting what it is. Major Armstrong is the acknowledged inventor of the regenerative "feedback" circuit, which brought radio art out of the crystal-detector headphone stage and made the amplification of broadcasting possible; the superheterodyne circuit, which is the basis of practically all modern radio receivers; and the super-regenerative circuit now in wide use in... short wave systems.[1]

Esquire magazine called Armstrong " . . . America's greatest electronic genius."[2]

Critic and author Edward Tatnall Canby states: "Armstrong . . . was the father of modern radio and TV broadcasting, inventor of the major circuits that made the whole enormous broadcast development possible."[3]

In the FCC's own history of broadcasting, only one individual name appears in the section on FM—"Largely as a result of . . . extensive FM development work by Edwin H. Armstrong, in the 1930's . . . ,"[4] FM was made possible.

In May, 1966, in a Chicago magazine, there appeared a story titled, "Genius Vs. the Cartel—the Tragic Story of FM's Father." It opens as follows:

> This story is written in anger and dismay.
>
> Anger, for the manner in which we radio listeners have been deprived over the years of the signals we were rightfully entitled to: Static-free, wide-ranging, powerful, high-fidelity signals which only recently, while still limited (by law limited), now come to us as FM.
>
> Dismay, because of the manner in which the envious, the cartel, and government alike treated the man who, with Guglielmo Marconi, might have shared the title, "A parent of radio."[5]

The allusion to conscious and planned manipulation to hold back the use of FM is not confined to this one regional magazine. It was made by whole segments of the communication industry and appears in print as early as 1939. An article, "Revolution In Radio," describes the struggle to launch FM commercially as " . . . the biggest and bitterest behind-the-scenes fight in radio's career,"[6] and sums up the then current FM situation as regards the attitudes of the radio industry and the government:

> . . . the observer cannot help remarking that the industry has been infuriatingly reactionary in its attitude toward Major Armstrong's development. This criticism falls against all set manufacturers except General Electric, Stromberg Carlson, and a few smaller manufacturing units, but it leans with particular emphasis on RCA, which brooded for nearly five years . . . the Commission's [FCC] failure to understand frequency modulation, and to place the proper estimate on its technological importance, is just as

deplorable as the industry's failure to push it. Instead of encouraging ... the Commission has acted as a deterrent.[7]

Eighteen years after this *Fortune* article, *Esquire*, in discussing
the brighter FM picture, reminded the reader that "to get
where it is today, FM ran a course so full of obstacles it
resembles a steeplechase."[8] In discussing just what some of
these obstacles were, the article included the FCC. Comment-
ing on the 1945 FCC decision to move FM from one part
of the broadcast band to a higher part, *Esquire* continued:

> The FCC, in a series of rather murky moves, invoked potential
> "ionospheric" interference for the move—reassigned the band
> to government safety and emergency communications services
> (luckily for safety and emergency, the predicted interference was
> a myth).[9]

In 1946, a privately published labor booklet made sweeping
indictments against both industry and government:

> This study and report tells the full story of how the Big Business
> interests—the monopoly corporations, the old-system standard
> (AM) broadcasting giants, and the big money publishers and news-
> paper owners—aided and abetted by the Federal Communications
> Commission, have taken FM from labor and the people, from
> small business and the veterans.[10]

Packed in the booklet's forty-eight pages is a fairly well-
documented (though emotional) diatribe against these monopoly interests. Singled out, by the author, as a major villain
is RCA.

> We may note here, too, report of a recent request of the Depart-
> ment of Justice to investigate a conspiracy to restrict production
> of FM radio sets in 1946. RCA which is a mammoth among the
> radio trust giants issued a denial of such conspiracy. But this
> is not the first time RCA and other radio trust members have
> been under fire for monopoly malpractices. In 1941 the FCC was
> forced to conduct an investigation of monopoly in radio. In 1930
> the Department of Justice filed suit against RCA and 13 other
> radio companies for violation of anti-trust laws. In 1942 Thurman
> Arnold indicated, relative to this suit, that the monopoly practices
> of RCA and its associates embraced FM and Television. In 1937
> Representative W. D. McFarlane of Texas called for investigation

of the FCC itself to ascertain to what extent it was controlled by Big Business.[11]

The booklet's main relevance to this book is to show that the AM/FM conflict and the public charges of questionable methods appeared early in the history of FM broadcasting. Of the Federal Communications Commission's role, the booklet states:

> It is not necessary to establish that the majority of the members of the FCC *consciously* or *deliberately* followed the dictates of the monopoly interests or directly took orders from them. That question is as irrelevant to the issues as the question as to whether Paul A. Porter, while acting as Chairman of the FCC, abandoned personal integrity in rendering service to reactionary interests.
>
> The outstanding and irrefutable fact is that, had the FCC consciously, deliberately and dishonestly set out to serve the radio commercial monopoly and the monopoly interests as a whole, they could not have done a much better job than they did.[12]

Certainly that language seems to suggest out-and-out bribery.

From the date of patent in 1933 until the final money settlement with Motorola in 1968, FM had been in a continuous struggle for survival. The testimonies concerning FM in hearings before Congress, before the FCC, and before all levels of courts make it a contender for constituting the longest and most expensive legal problem of its kind in the world.

During most of this time the average American citizen was unaware of what was going on. Brief flurries of publicity (mostly in the Northeast) accompanied only FM's invention and some of the more outstanding Washington hearings. Even less was written about its inventor.

Curiously, and tragically, the history of FM, and of this most unusual period, is closely tied to Armstrong's personal history. Even after his death, an FM legal battle wore on with millions of dollars at stake. An excellent biography came out shortly after Armstrong's death in 1954.[13]

To understand the history of FM, the reader must understand something of Armstrong's life and of the times in which he lived—times which covered the period from horse-and-buggy to satellite days.

Edwin Howard Armstrong died during the night of January 31, 1954. His body was found the next morning by a worker in the building where he lived. It is generally agreed that he ended his own life by jumping from the thirteenth floor. He was sixty-three years old and had been one of the rare phenomena of our time—a millionaire inventor. Yet his wealth never gave him the leisure and glamour one normally associates with the very rich.

His radio inventions had brought him some fifteen million dollars. To that figure can be added the ten million paid after his death to his widow as a result of her suits against the major radio manufacturers of this country.

Armstrong's credentials for inventing include forty-eight patents. Among these are patents for the regenerative or feedback circuit, the superheterodyne circuit, the superregenerative circuit, and wide-band frequency modulation.

His last patent had a most ironic aftermath. With his assistant, John Bose, Armstrong in 1954 patented an improved system of multiplexing—a very useful fringe benefit of frequency modulation broadcasting. Multiplexing is the ability of the FM radio wave to carry with it, piggyback so to speak, more than one signal. It is useful in that it allows one transmitting source to put out several signals at the same time over the same frequency. A radio station can program FM music into a regular home receiver and a different musical program into special receivers in stores and offices. But more glamorously, this ability gives us stereo broadcasting. The irony concerning this invention is that FM stereo broadcasting has pulled many FM stations out of the red, has given great impetus to new FM stations going on the air, has caused the manufacture of much new equipment and components for transmitting and receiving, and has been credited with the revival of certain music (baroque via long-play records) and yet Armstrong never lived to see his own frequency modulation system freed from economic restraints.

Armstrong's interest in electronics stemmed from an early boyhood interest in inventors and their lives. His own life has all the elements of a Horatio Alger story: pleasant and strong family ties, close and loyal friends, youthful enthusiasm over the new radio art, distinguished military career in two wars, experience with the madness of the 1920's, charming girl, romance and marriage, inventions, and status as a millionaire. It is hard to imagine a believable story emerging from such a mixture—of Metro-Goldwyn-Mayer, Walt Whitman, Huck Finn, and Wall Street.

Yet the story becomes believable—and dramatic—as we see it unified by the very human properties of grief and disappointment which run through Armstrong's life from the onset of adulthood to death. Armstrong is often described as one of the last of the "attic" inventors, in the tradition of Edison. His interest in wireless telegraphy began in his early teens and he set up his own hand-made wireless set in the attic of his parents' Yonkers, New York, home. He became proficient at using the telegraph key and soon was communicating in Morse code with a number of similarly inclined youths. It was this group of amateurs, and others like them, who became the radio "hams," who would sit, transfixed for hours, waiting to hear the click-click-click of some fellow enthusiast, or the faint emissions from a distant ship or distant transmitter.

Why nighttime was so much better than daytime for wireless communications was not known then, but it was obvious that stations came in clearer and louder at night. So amateur telegraphy developed as a "night" hobby. And when, in 1906, Professor R. A. Fessenden of Harvard sent out the first broadcast of music, it was the "hams" who embraced the new service and who later pioneered and led the way to improvement and innovation.[14]

Armstrong, the "ham," became Armstrong, the college student, in 1909, when he entered Columbia University to study electrical engineering. At his graduation in 1913, however, he had much more than a normal college degree—he had demonstrated his first invention, which was to revolutionize broadcasting.

To appreciate this revolution the reader of today must also

know something of the radio art of that time. Millions of older Americans may have already forgotten that radio during its infancy had all of the defects and few of the charms of an infant. Radio squalled with crackling noises; voice and music signals were of a primitive fidelity. Today, a novelty phonograph record may, by electronic gimmick, recreate the scratchy, tinny, and nasal characteristics of early radio for the sake of nostalgia. The 1914 reality, however, was worse, since there was no way to amplify the weak signals that coursed through the dark and unknown ether.

The only answer seemed to lie in attempts to increase power at the transmitter (which was also in a primitive state and problematic), or to develop more sensitive receiving devices (earphones). Then, if the hour was late enough and if the listener was in a very quiet room, he was rewarded with snatches of talk or music barely above whisper level.

Many scientists were attempting to figure out a way to hear the signals better. One path was to try and build up the signal when it reached the receiver. If the signal could be amplified greatly, then need for greater and greater power at the transmitter would not be important. It was the Columbia undergraduate Armstrong who solved the problem. He did it by a method that was to become a trademark with him; that is, in order to arrive at a useful conclusion, one ignores all accepted current theory and goes in an opposite direction, often embracing a rejected theory. In this case, Armstrong refused to accept another inventor's explanation of his own invention.

The most sensitive detector available at this time was the De Forest audion tube. Lee De Forest had developed some refinements of the vacuum tube. The vacuum tube began with Edison (1883), whose work with his electric lamps led to basic principles in this field. J. A. Fleming, in England, later applied Edison's principles and used an early tube for detecting wireless signals. But the tube, or valve as it was called, did little more than "detect."

Lee De Forest was able to add to the make-up of the tube. His device did strengthen, somewhat, the incoming signal, but *how* was an open question. Armstrong set out to answer it. His tinkering with the tube led him to reject De Forest's explanation as to how the tube worked and to experiment until he himself knew how it worked and why. Then Armstrong made his contribution—the regenerative circuit. It became the basis for almost all world-wide radio communications and enabled radio receivers to detect and amplify sound. Further, Armstrong found the audion tube capable of performing two tasks; not only could it receive, but also it could generate high frequency waves. With this, the crystal sets and headphones became part of America's past.

Armstrong's first invention has been included here to help explain events that were, as yet, some forty years in the future. In 1934 the Supreme Court decided, in a patent interference suit that lasted almost twenty years, that De Forest had invented the regenerative circuit. The decision was not popular with the radio engineers. They knew too well that De Forest had given lectures in 1913 in which he rejected Armstrong's version of the tube and that De Forest had never claimed for his own tube any of the powers then being demonstrated by Armstrong to the electronic world. That is, he never claimed them until six months after he saw an Armstrong demonstration at Columbia in the fall of 1913.

In March, 1914, De Forest put in his first claim for a similar invention. For the next twenty years, patent problems plagued Armstrong, and, though he held the only legitimate patent on the regenerative circuit (which the courts upheld for ten years), the episode ended with the 1934 decision against him. Today, Supreme Court or no, major engineering societies throughout the world recognize Armstrong as the inventor of the regenerative circuit and he has been given numerous awards (never retracted) by these organizations. A number of these awards came after the Supreme Court decision while De Forest was alive and a member of the awarding organizations.

A certain bitterness was bound to creep into Armstrong's personality, but, during these twenty years, so many other things happened that the final defeat in 1934 was an anticlimax.

A world war, two more major inventions, marriage, and the beginning of FM (in 1933) were all highlights of this period.

However, this particular legal battle was to make Armstrong more sophisticated about legal matters, patents, and business life. Armstrong had some rather rare attributes which are attested to by scores of friends and intimates. He was extremely honest, unusually generous, and an individualist in the largest sense. Indeed, his independence is given as a partial (if not full) explanation of the events leading up to the tragedy of his suicide in 1954.

A serious psychological blow to any inventor is to be denied recognition for his invention. And though Armstrong's contemporaries always gave him recognition for the regenerative circuit, the legal denial was unjust to him. This same legal battle and denial was to take place all over again with frequency modulation. Only this time, his personal fortune would also be dissipated. Had he lived, he would have had to endure the FM struggle until 1968—another twenty years in the courts, a total of forty years in legal arguments. The economic struggle of FM at every level (inventor's economic problems, individual FM station's economic problems, and the FM industry itself) began with its invention and is still going on today.

Armstrong's second major radio invention took place during World War I. Shortly after his arrival in Europe as an army captain in 1917, he was told of a major radio problem. To escape interception, the Germans were transmitting their military radio signals in the high frequencies. The British were not able to detect these signals. The French also were stymied: in some cases it was known that the German transmitters were only four miles away from French receivers and yet the signals escaped detection.

A series of unrelated events suddenly made sense to Armstrong while he was watching a bombing raid over Paris in 1918. He was able to bring together from his experience, memory of technical facts, and ability to synthesize, a method by which the elusive signals could become audible; it was called the superheterodyne principle.[15]

The war ended before this new radio receiver circuit could be used, but in the 1920's this circuit became the standard circuit in radio because of its powerful detection and amplification features. Further, this same circuit in a highly advanced form was used in World War II to convert the very high frequencies of radar beams into workable signals on radar receiver scopes.

At war's end in 1918, Armstrong, now a major, returned to the United States to find himself in the midst of legal litigation involving De Forest and the regenerative circuit. The litigation had begun earlier, but had been interrupted by the war. Armstrong accepted, reluctantly, an offer from Westinghouse for his regenerative circuit patent. He needed money badly. With this money he was able to pay off many debts and carry on the De Forest court battle. In 1922 he won an important victory over De Forest in the U.S. Circuit Court of Appeals. Though the patent now belonged to Westinghouse, Armstrong still felt it necessary to battle for recognition.

In this same year, Armstrong developed his third major invention, the superregenerative circuit. Strangely, he came upon it while running an experiment to disprove some remarks made by a De Forest lawyer during the patent trial. The superregenerative circuit eventually turned out to be a lesser invention: it had technical limitations that made it unsuitable for broadcasting as it was then developing.[16] But since this was not known at the time, RCA bought it for $200,000 and 60,000 shares of common stock (which made Armstrong the largest individual stockholder in the corporation and later led to a most unusual situation, when he was fighting RCA and selling this stock to gain money for the fight).[17] At the time of these negotiations for the patent, Armstrong visited the offices of RCA president David Sarnoff. They had met in 1913 and became close friends. Both had been enthusiastic radio "hams" and Sarnoff had been a continuous admirer of Armstrong and his accomplishments.

The personal friendship and the business association that Armstrong had with Sarnoff and RCA took him to Sarnoff's office many times. It was there that he met Sarnoff's secretary, Marian MacInnis. In what can be truly termed a "whirlwind," they met, courted, and married within a few months. The new Mrs. Armstrong, secretary in a leading radio company, was able to appreciate fully and understand much of what was to come in a stormy and richly varied life with Armstrong.

Having just consummated the deal with RCA and married, so to speak, "the boss's daughter," Armstrong took off on his honeymoon in a newly purchased-in-Italy Hispano-Suiza to Florida. But the personal and financial honeymoon ended about the same time. Although his marriage continued on successfully, Armstrong found himself back in the courts over both the regenerative circuit and the superheterodyne.

The next ten years were filled with legal squabbles and trials. They began in 1924, with Armstrong considered as the inventor of both circuits, ended in 1934 with the Supreme Court decision in favor of De Forest as the inventor of the regenerative circuit. The other patent interference suit concerning the superheterodyne was settled in Armstrong's favor. But in 1934, Armstrong and RCA, after years of amiable association, were at a breaking point, and FM was about to burst on the scene. To understand the unusual actions of the companies involved at this time, it is important to know something of the birth and history of the Radio Corporation of America.

Immediately after World War I, the U.S. Navy began negotiations to develop an American communications industry. During the previous fifteen years, many of the world's communications advances and patents had been centered in Europe—most significantly in England. In this country, the Navy had a vital and natural interest in such techniques as ship-to-shore communications, especially in time of distress. However, many basic patents were held by British Marconi, which refused to supply equipment except on a rental basis:

> The formation of an industry rarely bears any resemblance to the enterprising legend later built up in the popular mind. The formation of the radio industry in 1919 resembled nothing so

much as an uneasy consolidation of Balkan States. The government, and particularly the Navy Department, was increasingly concerned at the end of the war over the fact that all wireless communications out of the country were more strongly dominated than ever by a foreign concern, British Marconi. When the Navy's Admiral William H. G. Bullard heard that the British Marconi was attempting to buy wireless generating equipment from General Electric on an exclusive basis, he set about through all channels to urge General Electric to buy out British Marconi's U.S. subsidiary, American Marconi, and reorganize it into an all-American company. General Electric's Chairman Owen D. Young accepted the task with alacrity and with great skill began a series of intricate negotiations.[18]

To achieve its ends, the United States commercial and government interests could not overlook the American Telephone and Telegraph Company—the largest single power in the communications field, owned or controlled practically all the patents in telephony, and had bought out the major De Forest patents in electronics. Many more patents and improvements were held by General Electric:

Thus it was thought that an agreement between these industrial states would pull together all important techniques and put an end to the patent conflicts that blocked swift development of wireless. During the war the government had discovered that no wireless equipment could be put together without inviting endless postwar claims, counterclaims and suits. Well over 2,000 patents had grown up in the wireless art, many of a minor or merely nuisance value.... The consolidation of all the dispersed patents in wireless was only second in the government's view to getting rid of foreign domination in the field.

Nowhere, however, in all the sections, articles, clauses, codicils and cross-licensing arrangements of the elaborate Agreement that was finally drawn up by the negotiating corporations was there any provision for radio broadcasting as it was soon to develop. It was not even remotely contemplated. All that was arranged for was an extension of wireless services as they had been known, for the assembled dignitaries could not see any way to make money except in point-to-point communications for which tolls could be charged. The idea of spraying the air with "free" music, instruction and entertainment occurred to no one. No one, that is, except American Marconi's young assistant engineer and by then commercial manager, David Sarnoff, who in 1916 and again in 1920 wrote two important memoranda, promptly turned down but destined to become the vehicles by which he later rose to power, urging his company to get into the sale of what he called radio "music boxes."[19]

Late in 1919, General Electric purchased American Marconi from the British for a sum in excess of three million dollars and transferred its assets in exchange for stock to the newly formed Radio Corporation of America, which was incorporated on October 17, 1919. A few months later, AT&T joined the so-called Radio Group, by purchasing some two and a half million dollars worth of this RCA stock.

Ironically, for the first two years of its life this corporation was to have nothing to do with radio as we know it.... All patents of the participating companies were to be freely available to one another for ten years. AT&T was to have roughly as its exclusive field all radio-telephony associated with its telephone service, plus the manufacture of transmitter apparatus. G.E. was to have roughly all wireless telegraphy and the manufacture of receiver apparatus. RCA, with no manufacturing rights, was to operate the trans-Atlantic service of the old Marconi Company and act solely as a sales and service organization for the group....

Thus was the stage set for the almost spontaneous and unforeseen explosion of radio broadcasting in the Twenties. The Radio Corporation of America was born as a quasi-governmental instrument of national policy. Into its hands was put, by cross-licensing agreement, the administration of all important wireless patents as they applied to radio use, eventually giving this one company enormous power and control over the new industry. Perhaps there was no other way in a laissez-faire economy to create the industry, for the commercial development of electronics was to require the concentration and engagement, by one means or another, of very large technical and financial forces. In a rough and ready way the Agreement of 1919 created the largest and most vigorous industry of its kind in the world. But a high price was to be paid in chaos and in abuse of power for lack of sufficient government foresight and control. More than a quarter of a century later the government would still be trying to undo some of the more baleful consequences of the 1919 Agreement.[20]

In 1921, Westinghouse had joined the elite Radio Group. The new arrangement gave Westinghouse 40 percent of the manufacture of whatever radio receiver equipment RCA sold, while General Electric retained 60 percent. AT&T continued to make all equipment for telephone use.

Meanwhile, amateur or "ham" radio had exploded across the nation. To satisfy the vast demands for equipment, nearly 200 set manufacturers were deluging the market with sets, and, in doing so, were completely ignoring the carefully created patent structure of RCA and the Radio Group. At the same time over 500 radio stations were on the air—all ignoring AT&T claims that it, alone, could build transmitting equipment. Within the law and outside the law, "A raggle-taggle mob of free enterprisers were running away with the business."[21]

> During 1922, RCA sold 1,583,021 tubes.... But apparently most of the tubes sold ... were finding their way, through one channel or another, into sets assembled for sale by the two hundred companies ... they were ... taking the major share of the receiving-set market away from RCA, GE, and Westinghouse. Of almost 600 stations on the air in 1923, only 35 had bought Western Electric transmitters, (supposedly the only legal patented equipment).[22]

At the same time the members of the Radio Group began fighting among themselves and the Agreement of 1919 seemed more a financial prison than a protected patent road to financial success. The so-called "exclusive" areas of manufacture and sales were no longer exclusive, what with AT&T entering radio broadcasting, and GE beginning to build transmitters. "Finally, the members of this historic Balkan entente were attacking one another for violating, of all things, the anti-trust laws."[23]

It was not until 1923 that RCA was able to get a radio set on the market. Since RCA was still tied to the agreement with GE and Westinghouse, it took the next ten years of patent side-stepping, and waiting for the original ten-year patent agreement to expire, for RCA to begin to catch up with the manufacturing aspects of radio broadcasting. In 1926 AT&T, by mutual agreement with the Radio Group, left the radio broadcasting field (selling its key station, WEAF, to RCA for one million dollars), and the Radio Group (RCA, Westinghouse, GE) set up the National Broadcasting Company with 50 percent owned by RCA, 30 percent by GE, and 20 percent by Westinghouse. So RCA, which was set up almost by government command, grew in true Topsy form, until in 1932 (as a result of a government anti-trust suit started in 1930) it remained alone and with all its patent force intact. RCA had become a completely self-contained organization with wholly-owned subsidiary companies operating a broadcasting business, a communications business, a marine radio business, a radio school, and a manufacturing and merchandising business. In 1934 the tube business was augmented by the purchase of certain patents from the defunct De Forest Radio Company. This brought about the beginning of transmitting tube manufacturing by RCA.[24]

By 1967 RCA had grown to exceed 120,000 in total employment here and abroad. Diversification led RCA into publishing (Random House, Inc., became a wholly-owned subsidiary in 1966), into operation of Job Corps training centers, into development of electronic medical equipment, into computer development and installation, into acquisition of the Hertz-Rent-a-Car system—all in addition to broadcasting, radio/phonograph/television manufacture, recordings, and tapes. RCA is deeply involved in government contracts having to do with space and military electronics. Total annual sales for 1966 stood at $2.5 billion.[25]

By 1922, chaos was the order of the day in broadcasting, with stations interfering with each other by broadcasting on the same, or on an adjacent channel. Very few broadcasters followed any of the legal rules set up, let alone any unwritten rules. As early as 1923, Secretary of Commerce Herbert Hoover had found the chaos in the air "simply intolerable."[26] By 1924, the public investment in equipment had reached

$358,000,000. New stations sprang up and died weekly, but others were always ready to take the place of the fallen. There were literally no restrictions on gaining a license. "The stations ranged from well-financed to quaint and primitive . . . emerging from attics and shacks. . . ."[27] With just so many channels available and with more broadcasters than channels, Congress set up the Federal Radio Commission in 1927 to bring about some order and regulation (which it did only to some degree). In 1934, the Federal Communications Commission superseded the FRC.

The Communications Act of 1934 set up the FCC to license and police in the public interest, not only radio broadcasting stations, but also wireless and wire communications, including telegraphy, telephony, television, and facsimile:

In the broad and somewhat indistinct powers delegated to the seven-man FCC there was to be an endless source of friction and uneasiness for the private interests thus regulated. But as with all regulatory bodies, there were compensating loopholes. The commissioners were political appointees of various tenure and shifting complexion, generally without technical or practical knowledge of the industry they were set up to regulate. Power, therefore, devolved largely upon the Commission's engineering and legal staff, which like most such staffs in government service, was ill-paid and inadequate. Finally, the issues the FCC was called upon to decide were generally of such a nature as the public found hard to understand even if it was adequately informed or interested, which it rarely was.

Under these conditions the communications industry was never to find itself severely hampered by the FCC in getting its own way. Indeed, it found ways to use the FCC to further limit competition and increase its own powers. Whereas the industry's trade associations and leading corporations were constantly dealing with the FCC from day to day, the public rarely if ever had so intimate a contact with, or representation in its workings. All such governmental regulatory bodies over the years tend to take on the coloring and viewpoints of the industries they are set up to regulate. The means of fraternizing with and influencing such bodies are many and varied, not the least being the dangling of such tangible rewards before [FCC] staff members as a better

job at higher pay in the industry being regulated. The new FCC
was barely two years old when RCA hired away its chief engineer
Dr. Charles B. Jolliffe, eventually to be vice-president in charge
of all RCA research.[28]

RCA, by 1935, had become the largest and most potent
force in radio. It bought out major radio set manufacturing
plants to become the biggest manufacturer of radios. Through
NBC, it developed the largest radio network and, through
its unique patent arrangement with GE and Westinghouse,
it controlled all key radio patents. Under a consent decree
resulting from a government anti-trust suit, GE and Westinghouse had to divest themselves of all stock in RCA, thus giving
RCA full control of all previous arrangements, including NBC.

Radio manufacturing was a most lucrative business at this
time. In 1929, for instance, 4,500,000 radio receivers were
bought at an average cost of $162 a set. Whoever held the
patents on the basic radio circuits, therefore, stood to make
millions of dollars. During the seventeen years that a patent
is in force, the amount of money involved, in the case of
radio manufacturing, is staggering.

Thus it is very important that a basic patent be held legal,
and, indeed, identify clearly the inventor and invention. It
seems part of the game that when a basic invention comes
along, others will then purposefully set out to find some
loophole that will put the original patent in "interference."[29]
Often there is no real question as to who was the actual inventor. It is simply a matter of economics. If an individual or
a firm can somehow show, through legal or technical loopholes,
some discrepancy, some error, or by clever (but often dishonest) presentation of "fact," that a similar invention came
first, a court may find against the original patent holder.
It is usually no surprise to an inventor, then, if he finds his
invention being challenged—especially if it is worth a lot of
money. So it was with Armstrong more than once. AT&T
brought such a patent interference suit against Armstrong challenging his superheterodyne circuit. With their French patent

they hoped to void Armstrong's patent and be free of royalty obligations to him. The courts found in Armstrong's favor.

At this time, AT&T was part of the Radio Group and the patent they used in their unsuccessful attempt against Armstrong was part of the great pool of patents available to all the members of the Group. Westinghouse had bought the superheterodyne patent and the regenerative patent from Armstrong in 1919; they were also part of the Radio Group. The Group controlled many De Forest patents. With these conflicting patents controlled by the Group, it made no difference to them which patent came first. When De Forest won his first interference suit (claiming he was the inventor of the regenerative circuit) in 1924, a more serious situation arose.

This 1924 decision in favor of De Forest gave him his patent on this basic circuit beginning with that year. Armstrong's patent on this same circuit had been issued in 1913, and would soon terminate. Since this patent of Armstrong's was now being challenged successfully by De Forest, Westinghouse (who bought the patent from Armstrong after World War I) decided not to pay Armstrong the last installment of their 1919 agreement, which was $100,000. Even more serious was the loss of the Radio Group as a champion for Armstrong. Since they had owned three of his patents, they had been both a legal and a moral friend. Now, with his most basic and potentially greatest money-making patent being questioned by the courts, they found it expedient to drop Armstrong and champion De Forest.

The Radio Group was far more interested in seeing that De Forest continued to win until his patent, and his patent only, was legal. As it stood, the radio manufacturing industry faced a most unusual case—two people holding patents on the same things. It was not a question of who invented the regenerative circuit at all, for that was a matter of personal pride and historical significance. Since the Radio Group owned both the De Forest and the Armstrong patents, they stood to make millions of dollars from U.S. radio manufacturers for seventeen additional years if the De Forest patent could be held as the legal one. The De Forest patent issued in 1924 would extend to 1941. The Armstrong patents covering this circuit were not as valuable; they would soon expire. In 1928, and again in 1934, the Supreme Court upheld the lower court decision in favor of De Forest.

From a business point of view, the episode did not involve poor business decision-making. The companies were not dealing with human reputation and pride, or even with justice. The decision to back De Forest was considered good business and the companies did gain the extra seventeen years of profit. That there was, perhaps, an ethical or moral issue at stake is another matter and one about which each individual must come to his own conclusions.

Armstrong took this setback unusually well, though he never did forgive RCA's part in it. The engineers and scientists who made up the electronic and general scientific world were appalled by the Supreme Court's decision:

> Misled by the biggest corporations in radio and telephony, pressing arguments clearly contrary to scientific fact, the Supreme Court froze into legal precedent the fallacy that two things are identical because they can be described in the same words.[30]

The Court had decided in favor of De Forest by accepting his uncorroborated word that he had invented the regenerative circuit on August 6, 1912. It is very unusual (almost unheard of) in a patent trial to accept as legal evidence a statement made by one witness as proof of a date of invention. Usually, notes, documents, experimentation data, and other witnesses all go to make up acceptable proof. De Forest's notebook not only showed no regenerative circuit (also called the "feedback" circuit) but indicated that no such thing as "feedback" was occurring in the tube.[31]

> ... the decision of the Supreme Court ... [has] aroused the scientific world, which has expressed the unanimous opinion that the Court has made findings of fact which are contrary to accepted scientific knowledge. The dean of electrical and radio engineers, Professor Michael Pupin, in an article in the New York Times,[32]

asserts that the Court's decision is due to a "misunderstanding" of the scientific principles underlying the audion experiments of the two inventors.

After the publication of Professor Pupin's article a distinguished mining engineer addressed a letter to the New York Times advancing the Supreme Court's decision as grounds for a Congressional investigation to determine whether the Courts, as now constituted, are competent to decide scientific questions, or whether separate courts for these matters should be created.[33]

Professor Hazeltine of Stevens Institute, himself a distinguished radio inventor and scientist, has also publicly taken exception to the decision of the Supreme Court.[34] He points out... that Mr. Justice Cardozo found that the De Forest circuits produced currents whose frequency could be altered at will.... This, says Professor Hazeltine, proves the opposite of what the Court thought it proved.... Professor Hazeltine also points out that De Forest himself found that he did not have a controllable device since, in his August, 1912 notebooks, he himself recorded the fact that the frequency of the singing note which he observed was independent of the... circuits.[35]

It was the extraneous "singing" that led Armstrong to investigate the workings of the audion tube to find out just what was going on. The Supreme Court declared De Forest the inventor because he had heard this singing in a telephone amplifier system. The Court said that this was the invention. The scientific world asserted that this plainly and demonstrably was not the invention.

In May of 1934, a few weeks after the De Forest decision, Armstrong attended a national convention of the Institute of Radio Engineers. In 1918, this same body had awarded him their highest Medal of Honor for his work in regeneration. At that time they had investigated the whole problem of just who had invented the circuit. Now Major Armstrong had come to give the medal back and to make a speech, which he was not allowed to make.

The president of the Institute interrupted Armstrong's opening and made his own speech before the assembled group of almost 1000 engineers. He said that by unanimous opinion of the Board, Armstrong was to keep the medal; that nothing had happened to change the Institute's judgment as to the facts of the case; that they wanted to reaffirm their stand. Most interesting is the fact that half of the Board membership were engineers employed by RCA and AT&T or their affiliated companies.

During the twenty-year period of this regenerative patent struggle, twelve separate court decisions were made prior to the Supreme Court's final reversal. Six found in favor of Armstrong (the early decisions) and six found for De Forest: even the legal box-score seems less than decisive. American and international engineering societies continued to honor Armstrong for this invention, even after the Supreme Court found against him. In 1941 he received perhaps the highest award the U.S. scientific world can give—the Franklin Medal. This award honored all of Armstrong's achievements and mentioned the regenerative circuit as one of them, stating further that De Forest was not aware of the regenerative qualities of his own invention.

All this litigation over regeneration ended in the spring of 1934. Armstrong was not only engaged in it, but was, at the same time, experimenting with FM at the top of the Empire State Building, sending out static-free messages by a system of broadcasting said to be unworkable, and sending them out farther than believed possible, and with less power than utilized by AM stations in the same area.

Frequency modulation, however, does not begin with these experiments in 1933 and 1934. FM, as a method of broadcasting, was known even before Armstrong began experimenting with it.[36] In fact, it goes back to 1903 when Armstrong was only thirteen years old:

> It was a tranquil, genteel, late-Victorian household into which Edwin Howard Armstrong was born, December 18, 1890, in a neat brownstone house at 347 West 29th Street in the old Chelsea district of New York City, the first child of Emily and John Armstrong.[37]

It was hardly such a world he left sixty-four years later.

NOTES

[1]"Revolution in Radio," *Fortune*, October, 1939, p. 116.

[2]Ivan B. Berger, "HI-FI," *Esquire*, November, 1967, p. 18.

[3]Edward Tatnall Canby, "A Study in Greatness and Tragedy," *Audio*, June, 1967, p. 10.

[4]*Broadcast Primer*, FCC Information Bulletin No. 2-B, February, 1966, p. 12.

[5]John Stofa, "Tragedy of FM's Father," *Omnibus* (Chicago), May, 1966, p. 30.

[6]"Revolution in Radio," p. 86.

[7]*Ibid.*, p. 121.

[8]"HI-FI," p. 18.

[9]*Ibid.*, p. 21.

[10]Eugene Konecky, *Monopoly Steals FM from the People* (New York: Pamphlet published by Provisional Committee for Democracy in Radio, 1946), p. 2.

[11]*Ibid.*, p. 3.

[12]*Ibid.*, p. 10.

[13]Lawrence P. Lessing, *Man of High Fidelity: Edwin Howard Armstrong, A Biography* (Philadelphia: J. B. Lippincott Company, 1956).

[14]Erik Barnouw, *A Tower in Babel: A History of Broadcasting in the United States: Volume I—to 1933* (New York: Oxford University Press, 1966), p. 115.

[15]Lawrence Lessing was a science editor for *Fortune* magazine and is now on their Board of Editors. In his biography of Armstrong, he often explains some of the more technical details of broadcasting in fairly simple language. The following is his account of what he calls Armstrong's "superheterodyne feat" at a level the reader can appreciate: "The superheterodyne was not quite as basic an invention as the regenerative circuit, but it was a fundamentally new manipulation of electromagnetic waves so deft as to appear almost a feat of sleight-of-hand.... The essence of his idea was to build a four-stage receiver that would reach up and bring down the weak high-frequency waves to a level where they could be amplified and detected by ordinary means. In the first stage, a tube would simply take in the signal from the air at 1,000,000 cycles, say, and mix or heterodyne it with a local current of 970,000 cycles, supplied by an oscillator tube, to bring the signal down to an inter-

mediate frequency of 30,000 cycles, the difference between the two currents. This heterodyned signal would still be weak and undetectable, but it would now be at a frequency that the tubes could work on. In the second stage a fixed-frequency amplifier would magnify the signal several thousand times. In the third stage the greatly amplified signal would finally be detected and converted to direct current. In the last stage this current would be amplified still further to actuate headphones or loudspeaker. In this ingenious, roundabout way, the new receiver was made to take in weak signals of almost any high frequency, beat them down to a pre-selected intermediate frequency and then amplify them to a level never heard before.... This piece of legerdemain, which now underlies ninety-eight percent of all radio receivers, embodies a large part of the essential, if oftentimes tarnished, magic of radio (Lessing, *Armstrong*, p. 106).

[16]Lessing explains why superregeneration was not suitable for general broadcasting: "Not only did superregeneration give tremendous amplification, but it was simple. Two tubes did all the work. In fact, even down to the present day, it is the only method ever discovered by which only two tubes can be made to receive weak signals of 800 kilocycles or higher at loudspeaker volume.... Despite its spectacular amplification and other virtues, it had one bad drawback, apparent as more and more stations crowded the air: it was not able to separate stations cleanly from one another when they were close together in frequencies, and nothing could be done to make it more selectable. Superregeneration was to be used later for such special purposes as police radio, ship-to-shore and emergency mobile services, where as a powerful, light receiver it could operate on well-spaced high-frequency channels. It also found use in World War II radar known as IFF (Identification, Friend or Foe) (Lessing, *Armstrong*, p. 144 and 146).

[17]Carl Dreher, "E. H. Armstrong: The Hero as Inventor," *Harper's Magazine*, April, 1956, p. 61.

[18]Lessing, *Armstrong*, p. 120.

[19]*Ibid.*, p. 121.

[20]*Ibid.*, p. 122.

[21]*Ibid.*, p. 134.

[22]Barnouw, *Babel*, p. 115.

[23]Lessing, *Armstrong*, p. 134.

[24]J. C. Warner, "Radio Corporation of America: Part I—The Years to 1938," *The Radio Corporation of America: Four Historical Views* (New York: RCA, 1967), p. 7.

[25]*Ibid.*, pp. 21–27.

[26]Barnouw, *Babel*, p. 121.

[27]*Ibid.*, p. 125.

[28]Lessing, *Armstrong*, p. 215.

[29]An *interference* suit can be brought against any patent if another inventor feels he has actually made the invention earlier. Also, the United States Patent Office may institute such an interference action if it feels two patents are in conflict. The interference suit may be settled in court or out of court, whichever the two parties decide.

[30]Lessing, *Armstrong*, p. 187.

[31]Armstrong's regenerative or feedback circuit was the result of his working with the De Forest audion tube. While experimenting with this primitive vacuum tube, Armstrong discovered he was able to bring in signals from unheard of distances. In the autumn of 1912 his investigations led him to discover how the tube actually worked and how to improve on it. "He found that if he took the radio signal as it came from the audion and fed back part of it to reinforce the signal coming into the tube, this reinforced signal, in turn, would be amplified further by the audion—a process that, repeated over and over, increased the output volume of the tube to several thousand times that of the input signal. This, in essence, was the regenerative or "feed back" circuit. It made possible the reception of transoceanic, transcontinental, and all other signals that were too weak to be detected with reliability by existing, insensitive equipment. It was, in fact, the development on which the whole of commercial radio hinged.... When Armstrong approached his father for $150 to cover the costs of patenting his discovery, he was firmly refused. The important thing, said John Armstrong, was to get one's college degree. When this decision stood despite weeks of promises, protests, and an appeal to an uncle for cash, Armstrong did the only other thing he could do—he had the paper with his original drawing of the circuit notarized on January 31, 1913, and filed it away.... At just about this time, Armstrong made another, equally important discovery about regeneration. He found that when the amount of the signal fed back into the audion reached a certain level, the tube ceased merely to amplify current and began to oscillate on its own—i.e., generate periodic high-frequency waves. Whereas Armstrong's first use of the circuit had resulted in increasing the strength of the signal at the *receiver*, this new principle of oscillation was to turn the tide from the spark-system to the continuous wave system and lead to the vacuum tube transmit-

ter. The fact that these two different uses of the circuit were discovered by Armstrong at two different times led him to file separate patent applications instead of one cover-all application—a move that . . . cost him heavily in the end" ("Armstrong of Radio," *Fortune*, February, 1948, p. 89 and 91).

[32]*New York Times*, June 10, 1934, sec. 4, p. 1, col. 1.

[33]*New York Times*, July 8, 1934, sec. 4, p. 1, col. 7.

[34]*New York Times*, July 1, 1934, sec. 4, p. 1, col. 2.

[35]Alfred McCormack, "The Regenerative Circuit Litigation," *Air Law Review*, V, July, 1934, p. 293 (The 1934 Supreme Court action was not in the form of a "trial" in which the seven judges did, in fact, review the case and then give *their* verdict. The judges decided *not* to review the lower court's decision in awarding De Forest the patent. All seven judges concurred in the decision to let the lower court's verdict stand. In essence, they did affirm the verdict as they had no wish, evidently, to go into the evidence. To a person who has appealed to the Supreme Court for help, therefore, this kind of decision is far from what they would want for they are never allowed to present their side of the case to our highest court.)

[36]As a method of transmitting intelligence, frequency modulation was known to exist during the first three decades of this century. However, as used by the scientists of that period it never worked well and the performance was well below that of amplitude modulation. Armstrong did not invent frequency modulation. He did invent a system by which frequency modulation could work and this system had within it the ability to eliminate static, plus the other technical superiorities of present-day FM.

[37]Lessing, *Armstrong*, p. 21.

2

THE INVENTION:

FREQUENCY MODULATION

Today's frequency modulation is not an invention in the sense that it is a brand-new thing. Armstrong's work was largely an improvement over an existing method of broadcasting. However, the improvement was so great and the way it was done is so unique (as compared with the method in use in 1933) that the system itself could be patented. It should be understood that Armstrong's wide-band frequency modulation system is just that—a system. For it to work, it must include the transmitter and receiver as part of the description of the invention.

To appreciate the contribution Armstrong made, the reader must have some details as to the state of pre-FM radio art and the problems besetting it. The technical background of readers from radio and electronics will be varied, and so the details will be presented in the simplest and most general terms. Indeed, it is assumed that the majority of readers of this book will have no technical background whatsoever.

Radio broadcasting is done by electromagnetic radiation, wave propagation. These waves travel at the speed of light (186,000 miles a second).[1] On a completely calm body of water, we can set up various sorts of waves simply by starting them in various ways. Some of the tops or peaks of waves will be higher if more force is used to initiate the waves. The distance between peaks will vary depending on the initial force also. The stronger that force (say, a rock), the closer one wave peak will be to the next. So we can get two major differences in waves; the height of the wave, and the distance between waves. The faster the wave travels, the closer the peaks. Thus the number of waves passing any given point can be described by the *frequency* at which waves go by that point. Frequency means the time lapse between wave peaks. When viewed from the side (a "cut-away" view), a series of waves will show the top of the wave, the peak, to be at a certain height above the normal water level and also a valley where the waves dip below this level. In broadcasting, the name given to this up and down measurement (normally thought of as height) is called *amplitude*.

In broadcasting the terms frequency and amplitude are used in conjunction with a third term, *modulation*. This is simply the technical name given to the *method* by which human intelligence is added to an already existing natural phenomenon—radio waves. Just as lakes and oceans have water waves on them, so the atmosphere has invisible radio waves in it. These waves were always present—long before broadcasting. Inventors and men of science discovered their existence, and then learned how to harness them. So the term modulation can be thought of as the way of changing one thing (the natural radio wave) to another (the addition of speech or music to that wave). A modulated radio wave carries intelligence.

There are three ways to add intelligence to these waves; amplitude modulation, frequency modulation, and phase modulation. In this book phase modulation will not be discussed, since it is not used in our broadcasting system to any great extent (and it is more similar to frequency modulation than it is to amplitude modulation).

It may be easier to think of communications in terms of a comparison to transportation. To transport (communicate), we can walk, ride a bicycle, drive a car, ride a train, fly a plane, or sail a ship. These are all methods of transportation and all of them are useful, but some are faster, some more comfortable, some more economical.

In communications we also have various methods available: telephone, telegraph, television, radio, personal conversation, smoke signals. Again, they can all do the job of communicating with varying degrees of efficiency, speed, economy, and reliability.

We can further the analogy in the following. If we decide to fly, we can choose either a propeller-driven plane or a jet-driven plane. Both share an advantage over all other ways of transportation—they are faster. However, there are minor differences between them. Jets are faster than propellor driven planes. Jets need fewer moving parts. Jets can be more economical.

AM and FM are like the planes. Both are the same method of communicating, radio broadcasting, as are the planes the same method of transportation, flying. FM might be compared to the jet, in that FM has a number of distinct advantages over AM (though AM has some natural advantages over FM which will be discussed).

This is how one hears any radio broadcast in a home or car:

1. An announcer speaks into a microphone. The *natural* sound waves coming from the announcer are travelling in the air at the normal speed of sound, 1,100 feet per second.
2. These natural sound waves enter the microphone and, by a method beyond the scope of this book, are changed into electrical impulses.
3. The transmitter (represented by a radio tower) takes these electrical impulses and sends them out as electromagnetic waves at the speed of light in all directions (there are antennas capable of "directing" these waves in a concentrated direction).
4. The radio receiver, in home or car or portable, picks up the electrical waves through its antenna.
5. The equipment in the radio, by a reverse process, changes the electrical waves back to normal, slower moving, natural sound waves and sends them out as the original speech.
6. The human ear picks up these normal waves and the speech is heard normally.

From the inception of radio (a German term), the method used to carry these electrical sound waves was amplitude modulation. In the earlier days of wireless or wireless telegraphy, modulation was accomplished simply by interrupting the normal radio wave so that short and long pulses occurred. This resulted in the bursts of noise and the silences that occurred at the telegraphy key; and the Morse code was the means by which a message was sent.

Improved equipment allowed a continuous source of energy to be used for power and made possible the carrying of human speech. The natural radio wave is known as the *carrier wave;* the wave which will carry the message. AM (amplitude modulation) is one of the methods used to superimpose intelligence on this carrier wave. From the earlier definition of amplitude (the distance up and down of the wave from peak to valley), it will be seen that AM broadcasting is accomplished by electronically changing or varying this distance. How this is done is a subject far too technical for this book and one superfluous to an appreciation of the difference between AM and FM. (It is not necessary to know how a jet engine works in comparison to a piston engine to appreciate the qualities of the jet plane.) But AM carries with it certain advantages and disadvantages. The disadvantages have a rather serious side affecting what the listener hears.

Built, by nature, into amplitude modulation is the basic disadvantage of static. The frequency modulation system of broadcasting, as developed by Armstrong, overcomes this, and several other disadvantages. Five hundred years from now scientists will, no doubt, view the electronic art as practiced in the 1970's as an early primitive period. In this case, they will have to view as Paleolithic the art as practiced in the 1930's.

Experimenting equipment in the 1930's was often scarce, inefficient, and expensive. The radio manufacturing companies were slowly building up great equity in AM transmitting and receiving equipment. Some of this was designed to try to get rid of static, which was *the* major problem in radio broadcasting for the first thirty years of its existence (and still remains a problem in AM broadcasting).

For purposes of simplicity, in this book static will mean all forms of natural and man-made electrical disturbances.

These include noises caused by electrical storms, lightning, automobile ignition systems, X-ray and diathermy machines, airplanes, elevators, electric razors—almost any electrical appliance. It also includes the relatively little known static caused by the radio tubes themselves. All these electrical sources send out electric signals which are similar in character and behavior to the signals sent out by the AM radio station—as if they were all in the same family. The AM radio receiver works in such a way as to be incapable of separating all the signals which reach it. It allows the regular radio wave signal carrying the message—plus all the parasitic "friends" and "relatives" of the same family of waves—to be heard.

Two major attempts to eliminate the static were to try to drown it out with more power, and to try to cut down its amount through special filter-type equipment. This later attempt can be compared to a door: the bigger the door, the more people can pass through at one time; the smaller the door, the fewer the people. Of course, as fewer enter, we have more control over who does enter. We can keep certain people out or arrange their entrance in a more orderly fashion.

Finally, though, if we make the door as small as possible, we begin to change the nature of the people entering. A very small door will allow only very un-average people to enter —only the thinnest, and tiniest. So the price we pay for getting rid of the unwanted (static), eventually is a very unrealistic person (a degraded radio signal).

So it was in AM broadcasting. As receivers were built to allow a signal to be heard with as little static as possible, the various components in the receiver were built to make the receiving band (or door) as small as possible. This still did not stop all the static. In addition, this method degraded the signal because the original signal (like an average person) was now forced to enter through this very small door or channel, and, in so doing, it got cut off at the top and bottom. This is loss of fidelity—the human ear is capable of hearing sounds from a low of about thirty cycles to a high of 20,000 cycles. Normal speech vibrates between 400 to 2,000 cycles a second,[2] while a symphony orchestra plays in the whole range. The accepted range of an AM radio in 1930 was about 3000 cycles; today it is about 6000 cycles. FM is capable of reproducing the entire human audio spectrum.

In order to make audible even more of this degraded AM signal, more power was often used, literally to push more of the signal through the radio (as people might be pushed through a door). That is why some local stations in large cities have such tremendous power; they must be able to overcome electrical static with force. But this force is expensive because of the cost of the equipment to make and maintain it. In addition, the extra power sends the signal out farther, and radio stations which share the same channel may find they are in interference with each other in many listening areas.

Armstrong's FM system was able to reduce the amount of static to near zero. And it accomplished this feat by going against every published and accepted radio principle of the time. It did it by enlarging the "door" to an unusual extent, thus allowing both the "wanted" and the "unwanted" to enter. It was this, among other similarly reversed scientific principles, that engineers and laymen alike refused to accept. The trouble was, in the hundreds of demonstrations given by Armstrong between 1933 and 1940, these same people kept hearing static-free radio by a principle they had long held to be unworkable. It was as if an observer, years ago, had watched two planes flying overhead; the jet and the propeller driven. He might have been heard to remark that, although he saw the jet flying with no apparent engine or propeller in operation, it still should not be up there at all!

FM is, then, a system of broadcasting in which the method used to carry the message is done by changes in the *frequency* (the distance between peaks of waves) of the radio wave. AM broadcasting is done by changes in the *amplitude* (the distance from wave top to bottom).

FM boasted a second advantage. Special FM receivers had to be built, since the standard radio accepted only the AM signal. Into these receivers went the newly developed tubes that were capable of cutting out the static, which was still being received through the very wide "door" Armstrong had built. But when the unwanted signals entered the set, they were cut out by special equipment. This did not reduce the fidelity as it had in AM. On the contrary, since the natural carrier wave was now modulated, or changed, by a different method (FM), that is, since the natural sound wave was now added to the carrier wave in a different manner from AM, the receiver could be built to filter out only noise and leave the entire original audio signal. For FM radio signals are not members of the same natural family as AM and electrical static. (This is what is called "high fidelity," the ability to reproduce sound as the ear might hear it in person.)

To the advantages of static-free and high fidelity, FM adds range. Range, here, means the ability to hear a softly played signal, or note, and a full orchestral crescendo without having to touch the volume control. In AM, this was not possible unless an engineer at the transmitter or studio end "rode gain," sat at the control panel and did the turning up or down of the volume so that a radio listener heard it as it was intended. Today electronic devices do this automatically with AM. In FM it is not necessary.

Fourth, FM has as a natural gift, the ability to be heard, literally without interference from other FM stations. This is called the "capture" effect. It means that FM stations, on the same channel, can be close together and not interfere with each other's singal. Two FM stations are never heard at the same time, as happens so often in AM broadcasting. If two FM stations are 100 miles apart, and operating at the same power over similar ground, there will be a point about mid-way where one station will be heard quite well, by moving just a matter of yards or blocks, that station will disappear and the other one come in clear. A home in this small "capture" area could, by using a movable antenna, hear one or the other without any cross-talk between. The interference problem in AM broadcasting is the major reason why radio was first regulated by the government. The entire political, social, and economic structure of radio today (and, therefore, of television also) might—almost surely would—be different if Armstrong's FM system had been invented twenty years earlier. That is simply because the interference problem led to the FRC and the FCC. And AM technically is suited to network operation and monopoly. FM is technically better suited to independent operation.

A fifth advantage of FM is its ability to transmit more than one signal at the same time—called multiplexing. It is as if the frequency modulated wave were built to handle piggy-back loads, like a bridge with one level for carrying cars, another for trains, and a third for pedestrians. That is why an FM station can broadcast at one and the same time a program to a regular FM receiver, another program to a doctor's office, and a facsimile copy of the local newspaper. Multiplexing also allows the station to send out the dual signal needed for stereo broadcasting.

Almost every major radio company was trying to eliminate static prior to 1933. An eminent mathematician working for the prestigious Bell system had delivered a number of papers on the subject of AM, FM, and static. One of his conclusions was that the characteristics of signals emanating from natural and man-made sources were so closely identified with the signals emanating from an AM station that the two could not be separated. He was right. However, he further proclaimed FM unsuitable for broadcasting, on the basis that it was an inherently inferior service. As used by the Bell system and others in the field, FM did, indeed, seem unworkable. For the narrower they made the FM "door," as they had made the AM channels, the more static occurred.

After an authority like the Bell system, backed by money and prestige, had made those statements, few researchers paid any attention to FM between 1922 and 1932. It was felt that if an expert in communications, as surely Bell was, said that static was here to stay and that FM was an inferior method of broadcasting, there would be no reason to pursue research

down a dark and unused corridor. After these pronouncements, research turned from the *elimination* of static to a
reduction of static.

FM was considered to be a poor broadcasting method
because all attempts at using it had been along the principles
laid down by AM broadcasting research. FM transmitting
was done by the "narrow door" technique. The narrower the
receiving band width, the more static supposedly was cut
out. It worked with AM; therefore, it should work with FM.
But did not. Armstrong had "opened the door" to a new world
of sound. He had begun this search as far back as his college
days at Columbia.

One of his teachers and personal friends was Michael Pupin.
Pupin was an inventor of note and a leading scientist in electronics. It was Pupin who got Armstrong interested in the
elimination of static. Over the twenty years from 1913 to
1933, when Armstrong was not busy with other inventions,
legal battles, and a world war, he tried many experiments,
most of them failures, to solve this problem. Most of his experiments during this time were in line with accepted radio thinking—narrow band.

Both he and Pupin worked on the static problem till about
1922. In that year, a business trip took Armstrong to Europe;
after his return he continued his laboratory work alone. He
had an inner revelation that led to experiments with two
receiver circuits, one to carry the static separately and siphon
it off. It was at this time, in 1922, that his idea was published
and supposedly destroyed by the AT&T scientist, John Carson. In a paper, "Notes on the Theory of Modulation," printed
by the Institute of Radio Engineers in February, 1922, Carson
states that frequency modulation "inherently distorts without
any compensating advantages whatsoever."[3]

There was further mathematical proof that this was so,
that static was a natural thing that could not be eliminated,
and that the only way to reduce static was to get as sharp
an edge as possible on the radio signal—to force high power
through a narrow wave band. Armstrong wrote in 1922 that

the presentation of frequency modulation as a means of reducing the band width required to transmit a given range of frequencies was examined mathematically by Carson:

> . . . who dispelled the illusion that a saving in spectrum could be obtained over that required by the amplitude modulation method. Carson proved that at least the same and usually greater space was required by the frequency modulation method. Other conclusions unfavorable to the frequency modulation method were reached. The principal conclusions were substantially confirmed by other mathematical treatments.[4]

The reference in the quote to saving in spectrum space needs some explanation in order to understand why Carson was objecting to FM. The door analogy is useful here also. Narrowing the receiving band width did two things: it not only helped receivers cut down the static; it allowed more interference-free stations on the air. Anyone who has ever tuned in an AM radio is aware that, as the tuning dial is turned, stations tune "in" and "out" rather rapidly. That is, the station can be heard best at exactly one point on the dial. Any slight movement of that dial diminishes the audio quality rapidly to nothing at all, in a matter of centimeters or less.

Most radio users become familiar with the radio band of numbers which (when rounded off for convenience) run from 5.5 to 16. Favorite radio stations are known to be at 1320 "on your dial" or 890, etc. They are heard at only exactly that spot. Another station may be only a fraction of an inch away. And into this band of 5.5 to 16, the nation must put all the stations it can possibly fit. A radio channel must be used over and over again, but since AM characteristics are what they are, two stations sharing this channel may interfere with each other. Therefore, AM stations are usually located as far apart as reasonable when they share the same or adjoining channels.

Let us think of each station on the receiving band as a "door" through which sound may pass. Obviously the narrower the door, the more doors can be squeezed into the band. Narrow bandwidths (even if they did cost the listener good fidelity) were therefore essential to getting many stations on the air without cross-talk interference. Since amplitude modulation does not have the particular characteristic described earlier as the FM "capture" effect, AM stations cannot share the same channel and be close together. But there are only so many usable channels and they must be able to cover the entire country.

Narrow receiver bands, over the years, became one of the accepted and indisputable facts of any broadcasting system. It was not even considered that a receiving "door" be widened—that would be wasteful of valuable spectrum space. It would both let more static in and cut down on the number of available interference-free channels.

When Armstrong's FM widened the door and got rid of static, his method seemed heresy to the engineering world. But a further horror to economy-minded scientists (and radio businessmen) was the "fact" that, even if FM did eliminate static (and there was no denying that), it did it wastefully—by using too much valuable space. It was felt that the price for static-free radio would be fewer stations and that would mean less money and service for listener and businessman alike.

What was not understood at first (and to some extent not even today) is that because FM operates up in very high frequencies, the loss of space does not occur—or, more accurately, is not important. In FM broadcasting as it has now developed, not only can the "door" be widened, but many FM stations can be fitted into this particular range of frequencies. This is because the very high frequencies give so much room to move around in that a big "door" or wide channel is an easy accommodation. And there is so much room available (though it certainly is limited) that FM can find the room for its wide-band needs, plus room in which many stations can operate.

After the Carson papers, industry progress on static elimination all but stopped. By 1925 Armstrong had decided no gadget, filter, powerful transmitter, or miracle could solve this problem:

The wild glimpse of a solution that he saw in 1925 was that the effects of static could be overcome only by employing a radio wave different in character from the electrical waves that static produced.[5]

Electrical waves produced by static, and electrical waves produced by AM broadcasting, are members of the family already discussed. They share the same characteristics and habits. What Armstrong envisioned was a broadcasting system using a different *kind* of radio wave:

Understanding began with static itself. This was not an ingredient generated by malevolent spirits to bedevil poor radio operators, but a natural phenomenon in the atmosphere in which radio operated. As early as 1915 Armstrong had conducted a series of experiments proving to his own satisfaction, and contrary to previous theory, that the bulk of all natural electrical disturbances was produced by waves varying in amplitude or power just like the modulated waves of radio itself. Hence lightning and other electrical discharges surging around the great electromagnet of the earth could easily break into and mix with radio waves to produce those crackling and crashing noises known as static. It was futile to try to blanket or exclude these discharges by brute force (i.e., more power in transmitters), for one lightning bolt could far overtop any power than puny man could put into a transmitter. It also was futile, as he laboriously found out, to try any other half-measure. On any standard broadcasting and radio receiver terms, static was ineradicable. Any device that passed amplitude variations passed static.

Here all investigations came to a dead-end, for there was little more to be done. There was only one other characteristic of a radio wave besides amplitude that could be significantly modulated or varied, and that was its frequency—the number of complete wave cycles or undulations passing a given point per second. . . . Frequency modulation had been tried many times in radio over the years, and all the text-books pronounced it useless for the transmission of intelligence. . . . By 1932 he saw a revolutionary way to employ this method of modulation not only to eliminate static, but also to provide, contrary to all the textbooks, a system of broadcasting superior in sound reproduction and in many engineering features to the system of amplitude modulation radio in use for over thirty years.

. . . . It had been found that amplitude modulated waves moved most efficiently through space, with a minimum of interference

and a maximum of clarity and economy, when they were held
to as narrow a band of fixed frequencies as possible. The dictum
was that radio waves should be as sharp as a knife, i.e., so "sharply
tuned" that stations came in at a hairline point on the receiver
dial. When, however, frequency modulated waves were held to
as narrow a band of frequencies as possible, nothing came through
but horribly distorted tones. Hence it was concluded that frequency modulation was wholly unsuitable for intelligible radio
communications.

Apparatus for producing frequency modulation had been crude
and unreliable. The Major, therefore, set out to develop, for the
first time, a transmitter and receiver system that would give as
nearly perfect, controllable and measurable a form of frequency
modulation as could be achieved. Even with this near-perfect system, however, he discovered that up to a point, the textbooks
had been right. Frequency modulated waves, treated like amplitude modulated ones, would not work. It was at this point in
1932 that he conceived his revolutionary idea, going against all
orthodoxy. Instead of transmitting his waves over a narrow band
of frequencies, he would allow them to swing over a very wide
band of frequencies. When he did so, he found that frequency
modulation became capable of transmitting intelligence with a
clarity and lack of distortion and interference unknown in
amplitude modulation. Thus by a combination of new apparatus,
without which such results could not have been obtained, and
a new idea, Armstrong created an entirely new radio system.[6]

Lessing goes on to point out a most interesting irony of
this same period; RCA and AT&T had done much FM
experimentation and both corporations had decided it was
useless. Armstrong had not forgiven either company for its
part in his losing his regenerative patent battle with the Supreme Court. With FM proved to work successfully, Armstrong, in published papers and personal comments, never
let either company (especially the Bell system and their Mr.
Carson) forget how they had missed the boat on FM. "Indeed,
if Armstrong had set out deliberately to make an invention
to annoy his corporate antagonists he could not have found
a more infuriating one than wide-band frequency modulation."[7] How FM could be so very "infuriating" will be
seen shortly. The repercussions of this invention rolled on

for years in corporate offices, secret government hearings, and the law courts. In the end, every major radio company (and most of the minor ones), almost every major radio executive, a prominent list of congressmen, respected judges at all levels, and some of the country's leading corporation lawyers would find themselves embroiled in FM problems.

Some of these people had their professional careers advanced or broken by this conflict. Indeed, it was alleged that bribes, other financial rewards, or both, were offered to top executive and administrative officials of industry and government and the Supreme Court. In many cases the charges were specific and damning. Such was the aftermath of the invention of FM, but in this book it is still to come. On December 26, 1933, Armstrong had issued to him four patents covering the FM system.[8]

With patents safely taken care of in detail (Armstrong wanted no patent problem, such as he had with De Forest), Armstrong went to RCA to offer them the invention. In fact, he went directly to his old friend, David Sarnoff, to show him his "little black box." (Sarnoff had said he was waiting for someone to come along with a little black box which would eliminate static.) The original little black box of Armstrong's, however, filled two rooms with tubes and circuitry.

It may seem strange that Armstrong brought his new FM system to RCA, toward which he harbored some emnity—after De Forest. But Armstrong was not blind to the fact that RCA was the largest radio manufacturing *and* distributing firm in the country. They had the money, scientists, and facilities to promote and market such an invention. Further, Armstrong was the largest stockholder in the company (80,000 shares eventually) and if FM were to take hold, his own earnings in the company would soar. He had also promised, back when he sold RCA the rights to the superregenerative circuit, that he would give them first look at any new invention, and he kept his word. Lastly, though he had had an argument with RCA over De Forest, he still did not blame Sarnoff, personally. It took some time for Armstrong to realize that RCA policy and Sarnoff were one and the same. So in the spring of 1934 he set up his entire system in RCA's Empire State Building laboratories.

For almost two years he and RCA engineers tested FM time and again. And time and again the result showed FM transmissions to be even better than the original claims. For one thing, FM was not limited to line-of-sight transmission as predicted. Line-of-sight refers to the characteristic of some waves to travel from their source in a straight line and then shoot off the earth on a continuous extension of that line. It means that the line of sight to any horizon is normally a very short distance and so any broadcast service using a limited method would not be the most desirable one. This fallacy exists today, even among sophisticated communications men. Actually, this is the result of a superior public relations campaign that has tried to give FM a poor commercial image. However, there is some truth to the argument: the technical aspects of FM vis-a-vis this particular part of its ability to travel over distances is covered later.

FM is limited today to smaller service areas than AM, but this limitation is made by man, not nature. It is an FCC ruling that limits FM coverage. In 1934 FM signals with very low power were heard clearly, loudly, and continuously at Haddonfield, New Jersey (a town across the river from Philadelphia), some eighty miles from New York and the Empire State Building transmitter. Recordings of these demonstrations were played, in ensuing years, before major industry groups, governmental hearings, and law courts.

It was found that to the very fringe of this test area the signals were clear and did not fade. Dr. Harold H. Beverage was an employee of RCA during this period. Many years later, in 1958, he appeared as a witness for the plaintiff (Mrs. Armstrong) in a court trial involving Emerson Radio. Dr. Beverage was the Chief Research Engineer for RCA at that time (later becoming vice-president in charge of all research and development). He appeared before the court several days after his retirement from RCA.

His testimony concerning these 1934-1935 tests is as follows:

Q. Dr. Beverage, do you recall the visits by the RCA engineers at Haddonfield for the purpose of observing Major Armstrong's experiments at Haddonfield?

A. Yes, sir.

Q. And I understand that you were among the engineers who visited Haddonfield?

A. Yes, sir.

Q. Why were you so curious as a group of engineers about what went on there?

A. Well, Major Armstrong was trying to convince all of us, I think, of the virtues of his wide-swing system. And we were naturally interested in the results he was obtaining.

. . . .

Q. Well, this may not be a fair question and if it is not please decline to answer it. After the announcement of Major Armstrong's wide band idea and of the improvement claimed for it in respect to the noise-to-signal ratio, would you say that there was a very noticeable change on the part of experts in the field of textbook writers, research engineers and others who had an opportunity to express their opinions; was there anything like a recantation by them respecting the relative merits of FM to AM?

A. Yes, indeed. I think that after Major Armstrong had made his demonstrations and given his paper that the technical fraternity was changed considerably.

Q. All right, will you explain that in detail, please?

. . . .

A. The thinking in general prior to Major Armstrong's disclosure was that you should use the narrowest band that would take the modulation that you wished to transmit and because that would give you minimum noise, and since the signal would remain the same, that would give you an improved signal-to-noise ratio.

Now that rule was not really violated by Armstrong's work because if he widens the band he does get more noise, but what he taught was that by widening the band and getting more noise you still could get a large improvement in signal-to-noise ratio when the carrier signal itself was above the threshold.[9] And as I have been testifying here in the cross-examination, the widening of the band and increasing the noise [which is then filtered out before it leaves the receiver] does cut down on the service area, but you have a better signal-to-noise ratio once you are inside of that service area.

What Armstrong taught was something that engineers at the time would have considered as contrary to the general principles that we had been accustomed to thinking about. So that he got the new result that was obtained by his method which was somewhat contrary to our thinking in the years past before that.

Q. And that was confirmed . . . in subsequent statements in scientific papers and textbooks?

A. Yes, after Major Armstrong had made the demonstrations then the mathematicians and technical people had no difficulty in explaining how he got this result.[10]

A report by Dr. Beverage during this period of experimentation with RCA, dated October 9, 1935, states, " . . . as the result of exhaustive measurements; frequency modulation with a deviation of 100 kilocycles is shown as increasing the service radius from 3 to 5 times the amplitude modulation service radius."[11]

These comparisons were with AM stations operating over the same distances, and at the same power. One other experiment was between Armstrong's experimental FM transmitter of two kilowatts and an AM station twenty-five times more powerful. The FM station did far better in every test. During this period Armstrong made what was then a most astonishing demonstration. Simultaneously, he sent from the Empire State, on a single FM carrier wave: (1) two programs from NBC, (2) a facsimile reproduction of a *New York Times* front page, (3) a telegraph message.

For two years the tests continued with the same excellent results. Armstrong could not understand why RCA was taking so long in deciding what to do about FM. RCA had kept its FM experiments a secret from the rest of the industry. In fact, in 1934, the Bell system was doing some work of its own in FM, and even though both these companies were part of the mutually protective Radio Group, neither told the other of their experiments.

In the same Emerson vs. Armstrong patent infringement trial in 1958, Raymond Heising, who was the head of one of the Bell Telephone labs, testified that since his own Bell colleague, Carson, had published several papers on FM and

static, and had said, "Static . . . like the poor, will always be
with us,"[12] Bell had had very little interest in FM after 1922.
About 1932, Bell showed renewed interest in FM when some
new type tubes were introduced:

> We were, of course, not cognizant of any of the frequency modula-
> tion work being done by Radio Corporation or by Armstrong. We
> just felt that it was something which was not usable nor of advantage,
> and really likely to be harmful.
>
> However, when we got interested in it ourselves and could not
> control our frequency variation during modulation, we figured, well,
> let's see what we can use it for; and, of course, our experiments
> were still going when Armstrong came up with his momentous dis-
> covery.[13]

Of course, Mr. Heising is speaking of 1935, when he says
Armstrong came up with his momentous discovery. But actually Armstrong came up with it in 1933. In April, 1935, RCA
asked Armstrong to remove all his equipment from the Empire
State lab. He, not quite understanding why, and miffed,
decided to release his FM data himself. It was published in
April—and then Bell and everyone else in the industry heard
about it.[14] Less than two weeks later RCA announced a million
dollar research program to bring television to the public.[15]
And in the next five years RCA never mentioned FM in their
public releases to the press. In fact, as late as 1936 and 1937,
Sarnoff, in two year-end issues of the *New York Times*,[16] speaks
of every known improvement in the radio art except FM.
He predicts the coming of television, and he had predicted
this back in December of 1935. In a statement in the *New
York Times*, Sarnoff said the most revolutionary improvement
in radio in recent years was the 1935 RCA development of
the all-metal tube.[17] There was no comment on the two years
of experiments with FM. Armstrong could not understand
the silence.

FM had been publicly demonstrated for the first time in
November, 1935, a month before the Sarnoff statement on
the new metal tube. The whole industry, especially the technical side of it, was aware of FM's existence and yet there was

silence everywhere. This silence becomes rather important much later in governmental and legal hearings on FM and patent infringement cases. Doubtless it contributed to the fact that the Armstrong estate won every FM trial between 1948 and 1968. It is this silence which opens the next period.

NOTES

[1] The concept of "electromagnetic spectrum" is a term that comprises a whole series of physical phenomena. Radio and light energy both travel at 186,000 miles per second because they are basically the same kind of energy. They share this speed characteristic with X-rays and cosmic rays. The universe is saturated with this electromagnetic energy. All these energy forces also are measured by the same yardstick—wave length. The longest wave lengths (and lowest frequencies) are radio waves, followed by infra-red rays, visible light, ultra-violet rays, X-rays, gamma rays, and cosmic rays. The radio part of this vast spectrum runs from the very low frequencies from about 30 kilocycles (one kilocycle is 1000 cycles per second) to the extremely high frequencies of 300,000 megacycles (one megacycle is 1,000,000 cycles per second). At the low end of this spectrum, electromagnetic waves are over eighteen miles long, while at the upper end the length of the waves are microscopic. Regardless of length, the waves all travel at the same speed. If the electromagnetic spectrum were represented by a normal twelve-inch ruler, the radio portion would be the first four inches or so. The part used by commercial radio and television would hardly fill two inches of this space.

[2] Sydney W. Head, *Broadcasting in America* (Boston: The Riverside Press, 1956), p. 39.

[3] J. R. Carson, "Notes on the Theory of Modulation," *Proceedings of the Institute of Radio Engineers*, X, February, 1922, p. 57.

[4] Edwin H. Armstrong, "Evolution of Frequency Modulation," *Electrical Engineering*, December, 1940, p. 4.

[5] Lessing, *Armstrong*, p. 196.

[6] *Ibid.*

[7] *Ibid.*, p. 200.

[8] Lessing has some further comments on the technical details of FM and the importance of referring to Armstrong's invention as

a "system" which the more technically oriented reader may be interested in: "In the development of wide-band FM it was frontier all the way, involving a dexterous interplay of sender and receiver to create a new radio system. Basically the problem was to send out from the transmitter a new type of radio wave, the exact opposite of the amplitude-modulated waves long in use, in which the amplitude or power, instead of being varied, was held constant while the frequency was rapidly varied over a band of frequencies 200,000 cycles (200 kilocycles) wide to carry the sound-pattern variations of the human voice or music. The FM wave, instead of being variable in crest or depth, was variable only in the number of wave cycles passing a given point per second. The transmitter which Armstrong worked out, embodied in one of the patents issued to him in 1933, was part of the earlier apparatus he had devised to produce a more precise and controllable form of frequency modulation than any theretofore. It employed a highly stable crystal-controlled oscillator or transmitter whose waves were modulated by what is known as phase shift. The wider the frequency of the waves thus produced, the less did natural static or noise, narrow in frequency, impinge on them. . . . The key to the system was the receiver which Armstrong devised to accept this new type of radio wave and translate its frequency variations into amplitude variations and thence into sound at the loudspeaker. Until this special receiver was developed, embodied in another of Armstrong's basic patents of 1933, there were no precise methods for receiving frequency-modulated waves. . . . The basis of his new receiver was the superheterodyne circuit, to which he added two special circuit stages that were the key to FM reception. In the first stages of this receiver the incoming FM waves were heterodyned down to an intermediate frequency and amplified, just as in any superheterodyne set. The amplified waves then passed to a special vacuum-tube circuit called a *limiter*, which in effect clipped off any amplitude variations (static) the waves might have acquired en route or in the receiver itself. The purified signal then went to a circuit known as a *discriminator*, which converted the original frequency variations into amplitude variations, ready for detection and amplification by the usual final stages of a superheterodyne receiver. In other words, after all possible extraneous noise was strained out of the FM wave, it was translated to amplitude modulation and then into current at audible frequencies to activate a loudspeaker. . . . From transmitter to receiver, therefore,

Armstrong invented a kind of 'closed circuit' in space for a new type of radio system. . . . The FM system eliminated nearly 99 percent of all static effects, a feat unparalleled in the history of communications" (Lessing, *Armstrong*, p. 205).

[9]The FM *threshold* is the point, at some distance, at which FM loses its signal improvement (the quality of what is being heard) over AM broadcasting. This point takes place at the fringes of the FM service area—that is, in the generally circular shape of the area served by an FM station (the actual shape and distance determined by the power the station operates on), the perimeter of that area will contain the threshold point. In this fringe area, the FM signal finally loses out to noise and static, and does so rapidly. In a different manner, AM radio may be listened to, by a motorist for example, for many miles as the AM signal slowly fades as interference gets worse and worse. As the noise increases the AM listener may still continue to listen if he wants to hear a station identification or weather report. But as the noise begins to exceed what one wants to hear, listening becomes intolerable. This process may be taking place over many miles with AM. In FM broadcasting, the man-made radio wave fades out quickly at the fringe-end of its power capabilities—that is the threshold point. Within the service range of the station, the FM signal is excellent, but at the threshold, it is like going over a cliff. In AM, there is a long, slow degrading of the signal until the noise takes over completely. Instead of going over a cliff, the AM effect is more like Alice slowly falling down the rabbit hole, hearing the voice of her sister getting dimmer and dimmer.

[10]Armstrong v. Emerson Radio and Phonograph Corp. (SD NY 1959), 179 F. Supp. 95 (all quotes in this book are taken from a reprinted transcript of the trial), pp. 1722–1727.

[11]Lessing, *Armstrong*, p. 222.

[12]J. R. Carson, "Selective Circuits and Static Interference," *Bell System Technical Journal*, IV, April, 1925, p. 265.

[13]*Armstrong v. Emerson*, p. 2097.

[14]*New York Times*, April 26, 1935, p. 21, col. 5.

[15]*New York Times*, May 8, 1935, part two, p. 1, col. 1.

[16]*New York Times*, January 5, 1936, sec. 1, p. 15, col. 3 and January 3, 1937, sec. 10, p. 12, col. 2.

[17]*New York Times*, December 28, 1935, p. 13, col. 7.

3

THE EARLY YEARS:

1935–1945

On November 5, 1935, frequency modulation was publicly unveiled. This was two years after the patents were issued—two financially valuable years out of the seventeen-year commercial life of an exclusive patent. After Armstrong removed his equipment from RCA labs in the spring of 1935 he spent the rest of the summer and fall preparing for a demonstration of FM. The transmitter was set up at a friend's home in Yonkers, New York. The demonstration was to be heard in Manhattan.

The Engineers Building, where it was to be held, was on 39th Street in mid-Manhattan. A "noisier" static neighborhood would be hard to find. The Empire State Building is on 34th Street. Times Square is just north at 42nd and Broadway. Newark, New Jersey, lies just across the river to the west and the boroughs of Queens and Brooklyn lie just to the east. Three subway lines run just under this area—along with the Pennsylvania railroad. There are thousands of apartments, in private buildings and hotels. Hundreds of cars and taxis pass by each hour.

Even today it is impossible to tune in clearly every New York radio station in mid-Manhattan on the AM band. A short test by the author on an Admiral radio (used at 28th Street) and an RCA table model (used at Columbia University) showed that only twelve stations came in clear (no static) on the RCA, and only seven on the Admiral, out of thirty-three AM stations in the greater New York area.[1]

Just before the demonstration, Armstrong presented to the assembled engineers, special guests, and some members of the FCC, his paper, "A Method of Reducing Disturbances in Radio Signaling by a System of Frequency Modulation." The demonstration itself was planned as a surprise. At the conclusion of his paper:

> The Major... received a signal that all was ready.... "Now, suppose we have a little demonstration," he drawled. For a moment the receiver groped through the soughing regions of empty space, roaring in the loudspeaker like surf on a desolate beach, until the new station was tuned in with a dead, unearthly silence, as if the whole apparatus had been abruptly turned off. Suddenly out of the silence came ... supernaturally [a] clear voice: "This is amateur station W2AG at Yonkers, New York operating on frequency modulation at two and a half meters."[2]

During the next few minutes, sound effects and the tonal qualities of music came through with a fidelity beyond anything ever heard over the air. The original demonstration had achieved a signal-to-noise ratio of 100 to 1 (as against 30 to 1 on the best of AM stations). When music and speech were absent from the signal, all that remained was the strange and new silence. But a far stranger silence was the one that emanated from industry and government. It was almost deafening.

To understand it, we must understand a curious thing about our own society: though we often seem to be very positive about progress, actually we find progress a bit frightening and not something to embrace in a headlong rush. As soon as the engineering and radio world was able to comprehend what Armstrong had actually accomplished, and how, it became evident that FM represented a revolutionary discovery. For Armstrong envisioned nothing less than the complete abandonment of all AM broadcasting in as short a time as commercially feasible. This naive pronouncement was based on the assumption that any broadcasting service so superior, and costing so much less to operate and run, than the present one, would be accepted with open arms by public, government, and industry.

What Armstrong forgot, ignored, or relegated to a minor problem, was the fact that the AM industry was a healthy, growing, somewhat monopolistically run baby, with no intention of being replaced by a new sibling. Frequency modulation, in order to be a national broadcasting service at the AM level, required the total abandonment of all AM equipment, both transmitting and receiving. It meant the end of all AM stations, the end of AM networks, and the complete reshuffling or loss of power among the AM giants. Just to get FM started on any scale would have required, first, the manufacture of FM transmitters and receivers (non existed). Second, to use this equipment, the creation and programming of new FM stations. And, last, advertisers ready to buy the time available on the new FM stations.

Advertisers, however, are interested in none of this; they are interested in listeners. Before they will buy time to sell their wares, they must have some assurance there are great numbers of people listening. But there was no FM audience then, since there were no FM stations, programs, or receivers. The situation can be compared most easily to the old chicken-and-egg dilemma: one came first, but which one?

Armstrong did understand this particular barrier to starting something new, and that is why he was so anxious to have RCA embrace his system. He knew RCA, with its size, could produce equipment, put on programs, get advertisers and audience, all at about the same time. That RCA can do this tremendous job of production and marketing is evident from their success in television, especially color TV. They produced the sets, used their own network to show the programs, sent their sales staff to get the sponsors, put publicity into every major media. Such success can be achieved best today by a big firm with a vital interest in exploiting a product.

There was an alternative means by which to force FM on the market. If Armstrong could convince the FCC that FM did, indeed, represent a superior yet inexpensive way to give a better quality radio service, they would be forced to do something about it. The FCC is, by law, guardian of the public airwaves and they are bound to serve that public. But FCC, like so many areas in our government, has been created so that it is run by a balance-of-power method. Just as Congress can overrule a president, or the Supreme Court can overrule Congress, or the states can overrule the Congress, so the FCC has this inner ability to alter position. It can do this because its internal organization includes both civil servants and political appointees. The great body of workers in the FCC, who do the daily tasks of engineers, lawyers, clerks, researchers, and the like, are salaried civil service personnel. Over them are the seven commissioners. These men are appointed by the president and approved by Congress. They, in turn, have one of their numbers serve a chariman.

As political appointees, they may tend to represent the administration which put them in office. The chairman's job has been characterized as a patronage job; that is, a job given as reward for political service rendered, such as vote getting or similar help in an election. The commissioners, who are responsible for making the many decisions that affect broadcasting (and all other electronic communications in our country), are seldom expert in the fields in which they are asked to render opinions. Since 1934 (the year FCC replaced the older Federal Radio Commission), there have been fifteen chairmen of the commission. Of these, only two have had a background even remotely akin to broadcasting.[3] The remaining members of the commission, for the most part, have non-broadcast backgrounds.[4]

The office of the chairman changes far too rapidly for most critics of the commission. Since this office is very important and requires skill and statesmanship, the critics argue that a man who becomes able at the job would do much better to serve at it for a longer period. The fact that the job changes so often (average runs from one to two years) only adds to the conclusion drawn that the commissioners at times serve only to obtain certain ends for the communication groups regulated by the commission. Indeed, if the chairman or president of a business firm were changed as often, it could be assumed something was wrong with the entire organization.

The charge had been made that a commissioner can be "persuaded" to serve the very industry he is supposed to regulate by offering him certain monetary rewards. Nothing so brash as a cash bribe is seriously charged, but a number of commissioners and high engineering officials of the FCC have left their posts to go immediately into the service of the broadcasting industry. The most flagrant example occurred in 1947 when Charles R. Denny (then commission chairman) left the FCC and went directly to RCA.[5] During the Senate investigation of FM during 1948, this move was discussed in some detail and Senator Francis J. Myers, of Pennsylvania, bitterly attacked this procedure. He was especially unhappy about the fact that when these men served as government officials, industry viewed them with suspicion and doubt; but if they could be hired away to serve industry's own ends, they became, as if by magic, valuable men:

> Senator Myers. I might just indicate that although many of these men have been condemned as bureaucrats when they work for the Government, business realizes that many of these bureaucrats had a great ability and were quite willing to take their services and pay them two and three and four times the amount they received in the Government. They were called long-haired, starry-eyed New Dealers, but business finds that they are men with ability and sound common sense.[6]

In January 1935, when Dr. Charles B. Jolliffe was Chief Engineer for the FCC, the commission published its first annual report. In this, and in each of the succeeding reports, are sections on developments in radio broadcasting. These sections discuss recent experiments and innovations in broadcasting. The content covers new equipment and new broadcasting uses and techniques. This content (especially in the early days) was seldom based on experiments run by the FCC (whose technical department was not extensive). The FCC printed in their reports material either sent to them by the industry or presented to them in their hearings or everyday contacts. Often minor advances or equipment were reported in this section. A revolutionary invention, such as FM represented, would therefore, seem important to report and discuss (especially since the FCC was aware of FM's existence both by printed media and demonstration before January, 1936).

Since, by 1935, the term "frequency modulation" had been known for many years (from at least the first decade of this century), it seems unusual that the FCC did not use the term in its annual report until 1939. In the 1935 report, the following statement is made in the section on engineering and technical developments in radio during the preceding year:

> Interest in very high frequency experimental broadcasting has continued to develop; however, the full possibilities of the frequencies for local broadcasting are developing slowly due to the very limited number of broadcast receivers that will tune to this band of frequencies. The very high frequencies above 30 megacycles have such characteristics that they serve a small area and then beyond this range no interference will be caused to other stations. This is different from the propagation characteristics of the stations on the regular broadcast frequencies (550 to 1500 kilocycles) which have a moderate primary area. Due to this characteristic of the very high frequencies it has been considered that they offer a means of supplying strictly local service to any number of centers of population with frequency assignments duplicated at relatively low mileage separations. The individual stations would serve only a few miles, probably on the order of 2 to 10 miles depending upon the power, location of the transmitter, its efficiency, and the radio propagation characteristics of the surrounding terrain.[7]

There is no mention of "frequency modulation" as a demonstrated and working development. This is in spite of the fact that Armstrong's FM system had been discussed twice in 1935—in April and November, in plenty of time for inclusion in the report.[8] But, publicly, Andrew Ring, the assistant Chief Engineer of the FCC, was very pointedly discussing FM in the mass media. His comments were anything but enthusiastic (even though he was present at the November demonstration):

> The new circuit, however, is impractical today.... Major Armstrong's new system is too complex for the final answer, according to Mr. Ring, who sees two obstacles in the way of this new radio circuit which he calls "a visionary development years in advance of broadcasting's capacity to utilize it."[9]

And from another interview with Mr. Ring, "Major Armstrong's new system is utterly impracticable—and the quest for static-elimination must go on."[10] This same Andrew Ring left the FCC shortly after this period and became a consultant to new FM stations, helping them set up their engineering standards! This was the very industry he had earlier called "visionary" and "utterly impracticable." Television, at this time, was being hailed as the coming wonder. Electronically, television is far more complex than FM, but uses the same area of the high frequency spectrum for its transmission. No one in the industry or government has, to the author's knowledge, publicly stated that television was too advanced for the 1930's.

By April of 1936, the FCC decided that it would hold an informal engineering hearing to determine the present and future needs of the higher frequencies (above 30,000 kilocycles). Since these higher frequencies had been found useful and equipment was being developed to broadcast in them, many services wanted part of them. Not only aural broadcasting (radio), but television, the police, government and military services, and emergency services were keenly interested in getting their fair share of the newer (but still limited) frequencies.

When the hearing came in June 1936, only two witnesses appeared to talk about FM. One, of course, was the inventor. The other, Paul De Mars, was destined to become a major FM pioneer and Chief Engineer of the Yankee Network in New England. De Mars was one of the witnesses called many times during the congressional hearings and court trials that were to come over the ensuing years. He discussed the June 1936 FCC hearing in the Armstrong vs. Emerson patent trial of 1958:

Q. . . . would you tell about the hearings before the Federal Communications Commission in June of 1936?

A. The Yankee Network had served notice of appearance at this
meeting, and I went to offer my testimony concerning the
experiments that we had made in the very high frequencies,
and to make such recommendations as I felt appropriate on
the basis of my experience.

. . . the results of our experiments indicated that no improvement in broadcasting service would be expected in the very
high frequencies with amplitude modulation, that at best the
range of service would be extremely poor, and I questioned
the desirability, even need, of setting up any channels for
amplitude modulation.

Q. And were you present when Major Armstrong testified?

A. I was present at that time.

Q. And you heard the recordings?

A. I heard the recordings. I also testified at this hearing and . . .
called attention . . . that our experiments disclosed . . . that
there is static in the very high frequencies, there are severe
electrical disturbances; that when all the factors . . . are taken
into consideration, very high frequencies offer no hope for
improved or even useful broadcasting service with amplitude
modulation.

Q. . . . Do you recall any of the other companies who had representatives at that hearing?

A. At the hearing there were representatives of practically every
company in the radio industry, in communications, and in
broadcasting.

Q. And what was their purpose in meeting there?

A. Well, their purpose was to give the Commission the benefit
of their experience, so that the Commission might properly
be guided in future allocation. . . .

Q. So far as you recall did any of those witnesses from these
radio companies suggest the use of frequency modulation for
any purpose?

A. No, that was to me a rather amazing thing, that with the exception of Major Armstrong and myself nobody even mentioned
it . . . although there was a great deal of discussion of the
needs . . . for television.[11]

RCA was present at this hearing, represented by its president, David W. Sarnoff, and by Charles B. Jolliffe, the newly
hired head of their Frequency Allocation Committee and recent

FCC Chief Engineer (whose job it would have to be to get the very best place in the spectrum for the RCA upcoming innovation, television). Though no mention was made by RCA of the almost two years of successful FM experimentation in these upper frequencies in their Empire State labs, Sarnoff did say, "We are pleased to place at your disposal the information and experience of RCA gained from its operation in radio research. . . . "[12] At this point the twenty-five-year-old friendship between Sarnoff and Armstrong ended.

It is not the intention of this book to judge the "goodness" or "badness" of the acts and events that make up the history of FM broadcasting. The author feels most of them speak for themselves. The reader will no doubt draw many of the same conclusions as did the author from the various events and testimony recounted in this book. However, he should not conclude that there is a "villain" or "hero" in this highly dramatic history, albeit this approach appeals particularly to those who would like to view it as a fight between individual man and corporate man. This view is discussed in the final chapter. An objective view of the whole history would have to include earlier and contemporary business. A successful businessman gains for himself and his company the best advantage possible. He must be able to deal with competition. The idealized American mystique regards competition as healthy, needed, and somehow serving the democratic process. This competition is considered good in many aspects of our life, including nature, business, and sports.

RCA is certainly part of that mystique. It is more monopolistic in makeup than most companies, but, like any company, its main purpose is to make a profit. Since that purpose is not in serious question here, we can assume that its pursuit is legitimate. Therefore, the actions of a company to secure profit, by whatever means it can lawfully use, is to be regarded in a positive light. RCA was not under any obligation (in a legal sense) to embrace FM. Certainly it was not under any obligation to do anything that might hurt itself financially. RCA did not own the patents on FM. It did own the patents on television. Nothing is solved by wondering what might happen "if"; still, it is interesting to wonder what would have happened if Armstrong had chosen a different company to demonstrate FM to in 1933. General Electric, for instance, was intrigued by FM and was one of the first really big companies, along with Zenith, to produce FM equipment and set up its own station. Armstrong had approached RCA at the very time they were experimenting with TV. Why TV and FM should have proved so competitive will be made clear shortly. But RCA did realize that FM would definitely upset their TV applecart and they, no doubt, welcomed the opportunity to experiment with it secretly for two years, and then pursue their own course with TV.

If Sarnoff and his board of directors chose to promote the product they had developed and from which they could foresee a great return on their investment, this would be considered simply a normal, wise business move. Any other move on their part might be considered poor business, especially by the stockholders of the company. Thus, in almost every overt and covert action, it can be seen that RCA (and the majority of the AM industry) was trying desperately to forestall something that would either cut down, or cut out, their operation.

FM, unfortunately for it, posed two threats to the industry. One was the loss of money and power that might come if AM were to be supplanted. Second, was the problem with TV. Why should FM, which is radio, have been such a threat to television? Why would not RCA and the rest of the industry have been happy to embrace both FM and TV and make that much more money?

At this time RCA had spent tens of thousands of dollars in television experiments. They were about to spend millions more—and they knew it. Because of their unusual and highly beneficial patent arrangement with AT&T and the other members of the Radio Group, their system of television was protected. This was a very good business position to be in. Not only could profit be derived from the sale of their own manufactured television sets, but further monies could be made by giving out licenses to other manufacturing companies to make the same product. It is not possible to manufacture a television set in the United States without dealing with RCA (while their TV patents are in force). It is that simple. Further, since much of the equipment needed in the TV set is made by RCA, other companies often must buy these parts from them.

But all these patents and all this equipment went for AM broadcasting, and television is broadcast on AM waves also (that is, the picture portion is; by FCC rule, FM is used for the audio). The NBC network, owned by RCA, was made up of scores of AM radio stations that broadcast NBC programs and commercials. And NBC, in turn, owned several key AM stations, always in the top money-making markets of the nation. Thus, the cream of the radio advertising money was flowing into NBC stations and finally, of course, into RCA. FM technically does not lend itself as well to this ability to monopolize through networks as AM obviously does. Most of the radio industry could see what would happen if FM were to replace AM.

FM was also developed in the higher frequencies, which, as pointed out earlier, have some strange characteristics of their own. But television was developed in these same frequencies (higher, here is meant to mean higher than the standard frequencies used by AM radio). Since AM radio, plus all the other services, had used up all of the lower bands, the allocation of the higher bands (which only became possible at this time because of newer equipment and experimentation) meant life or death to the success of those broadcasting services who wanted them. To get them they had to convince the FCC of their needs.

One characteristic of the entire radio spectrum is the fact that as you gain one thing you give up another. As you go up the spectrum to higher frequencies, you lose transmitting distance. That is, at some mythical figure like channel 1, a 100-foot tower operating at a power of 1, might send a signal out 100 miles. If we now move up to channel 2, same 100-foot tower, same power of 1, the signal will now travel only 85 miles. And that continues until the service area of a signal may be reduced to 10 miles at channel 9. This applies to radio and television.

If you apply for a station and are given channel 9 and you want to reach out farther than 10 miles, you have two choices; either build a 200-foot tower, or increase power to 2 or more. The FCC regulates just how much power you may use. Regulation on tower height is variable and that is why some stations build 1000-foot towers.

Both FM and TV proponents had experimented in about the same place in the broadcasting spectrum and both had developed equipment which worked best in these areas. It followed that both wanted the same high frequency channels in order to develop a commercial service. The reason there was not really enough room for both to operate here commercially (since they had both experimented here) was that in experimentation the FCC had allocated to each a small band of experimental channels. Now that each service was ready to serve the entire nation, they needed many more channels so that they could cover the country adequately. If both FM and TV were to become commercially successful, both wanted to have the best going for them. In addition, RCA knew that if NBC had a number of its wholly-owned TV stations in places like New York, Chicago, Los Angeles, San Francisco, and Philadelphia (however many stations the FCC would eventually allow one firm to own), they would reap a bonanza in advertising money. If one could own only one TV station, and that station had its transmitting tower on the top of the Empire State, the area served by the lower frequencies could be stretched (with the consumer's use of an antenna) to upwards of 70 to 100 miles. In 1967 New York City metropolitan area population was 16,325,800, including New York City and the surrounding counties in New York and New Jersey.[13] That would be a very lucrative TV channel to have indeed!

Had Major Armstrong, by some stroke of bad luck, not been able to attend the June, 1936, hearing, it seems certain

that FM would not have received any channels for experimentation. As it was, it did get five channels.[14] However, to become
a nationwide radio service, FM needed more than these (today
there are eighty commercial FM channels). It hoped to get
them in the spectrum immediately adjacent to the experimental
five. The FM proponents (and there were soon to be many
more) wanted to push TV up into the ultra high frequencies
(where it exists today as UHF). TV proponents wanted to
push FM up to these frequencies. Eventually this became
another battle that all but ended FM broadcasting.

All these technical facts concerning FM and TV, and all
the projected profits of successful TV, were known during
this period (1933-1939). That is why FM was considered a
revolution. It not only threatened to overthrow AM; it wanted
to throw out television (at least throw it elsewhere in the
spectrum). And since radio was a known art at the time, and
new FM receivers would be far cheaper than new TV receivers,
the industry knew that the FCC would be bound to favor
a commercial radio service that was of excellent quality and
past the experimental stage, over TV, which was some years
away.

During 1935, Armstrong tried to get permission to build
a high-powered FM station. He wanted very badly to prove
the worth of FM by broadcasting to the public. His idea
was to build the transmitter at the highest point he could
near New York City to gain the coverage he wanted. Then,
to use as much power as he could get permission to use.
Even though many engineers had heard his demonstrations
between November, 1935, and the summer of 1936, the industry had remained silent. When they did talk publicly it was
always with warnings about some unusual "facts" they had
discovered. Though the Empire State/Haddonfield experiments proved a range of eighty miles, public releases continued
to indicate that the high frequencies were useful for only a
few miles. In fact, the first FCC annual report carried this
low coverage information though experiments had shown this
was not true prior to the printings of that report. Why such

a serious error was included in their report can only be guessed at. However, two of the people responsible for the engineering section were Dr. Joliffe (who was shortly, thereafter, hired by RCA) and Mr. Ring.

Surprisingly, Armstrong was denied his request for an experimental station. Normally, this is a fairly simple request and procedure with the FCC. At this time, Major Armstrong may not have been well-known to the American public (even though every radio in the country was using his basic inventions), but he was well-known and respected by every major radio engineer in and out of government. Indeed it would have seemed advantageous to the FCC to grant to this radio inventor and pioneer so simple a request. Regarding this incident, Major Armstrong gave the following testimony before the Interstate Commerce Commission, which met in 1943 to investigate the needs for changes in the 1934 Communications Act. Senator Burton K. Wheeler was the Chairman:

Dr. Armstrong: That was in 1935.... I might say here that the principal objection which was raised against the system was that it could not work through the man-made electrical disturbances, such as automobile ignition, or the great variety of noises which we have in cities, electrical machinery, power lines, or the like. The obvious answer was to build a high-power station and then demonstrate that the criticism was unfounded.

When I approached the Commission... through an interview with the assistant chief engineer, he informed me that he was not satisfied I had done anything in the public interest that would warrant the granting of a license. Not even though I was spending my own money to demonstrate the principle. He suggested that I build a... lower power FM transmitter.... In other words, do exactly the same thing which I had already been doing for the past 2 years.

The Chairman: Who was that?

Dr. Armstrong: Mr. Andrew Ring, who was then assistant chief engineer of the Federal Communications Commission.

. . . .

Dr. Armstrong: About the same time also there appeared in the Boston papers an interview with Mr. Ring labelling this invention a visionary dream.

. . . .

Senator McFarland: What became of Mr. Ring?

Dr. Armstrong: Mr. Ring has not been with the Commission for several years . . . he is in private consulting practice, engineering FM stations.

Senator McFarland: That is rather surprising, Mr. Chairman, in view of the last answer by the witness. I think the interview will be of especial interest to the members of this committee.

The Chairman: Very well. It will be furnished by Dr. Armstrong when he can get the opportunity to find them.[15]

Armstrong secured the services of an attorney practicing before the commission who was able to get one of the commissioners (Mr. T. A. M. Craven) to overrule Ring. With that, Armstrong began building his new station at Alpine, New Jersey, an area about twenty-five miles from New York to the north. On July 18, 1939 W2XMN went on the air with full power. To build the station, Armstrong needed quite a bit of money to pay for the special equipment and for the land and other expenses. To get much of this money, he cashed in a large block of the RCA stock he owned, then turned around and placed an order with RCA to build the special transmitting equipment. He may have felt there was some kind of justice in using the RCA stock for this purpose.

During the time he was building his station, the only other FM broadcasting being done was by the low-powered station in Yonkers which was operated by a personal friend of Armstrong. It was this station which had been used for the original demonstration before the IRE in 1935. Armstrong continued to use this station for demonstration purposes, and the Yankee Network of New England, after hearing a number of demonstrations, decided to build their own FM station.

By the time the Alpine station went on the air in 1939, it had cost Armstrong $300,000 to prove that FM worked. Lessing points out that the Alpine station had a much greater significance than simply being the first full-powered FM station to operate:

> The historical significance of Station W2XMN has never been widely realized. Armstrong lavished on it all the care and attention to detail of which he was prodigiously capable. With this station,

the first full-scale one of its kind, many basic contributions were made to ultra-shortwave communications. In the development of an antenna to operate in this relatively untried region of the radio spectrum, Armstrong spent long days at Alpine making meticulous measurements, observations and modifications in antenna design, which added much to the sum of general knowledge in this area. In the development of power tubes and other vacuum tubes to operate at these frequencies, Armstrong acted as a goad. No tubes adequately designed to operate at high power in the ultra-shortwaves were available when the Alpine station was contemplated. Armstrong bombarded tube manufacturers with observations, criticism, and suggestion that gradually drew forth adequate tubes. All this was part of the enormous indirect influences, which, over the years, Armstrong exercised on the development of radio.

Station W2XMN had other, more direct effects on the future of radio. Armstrong went to great lengths to make it a new standard in sound broadcasting. He tested dozens of microphones to find the one most capable of transmitting the full tonal range. He sought out the best professional record-playing apparatus available. On the receiver side, he studied loudspeakers, enclosures and acoustics, and had a speaker build to his specifications in an enclosure as tall and slim as a grandfather's clock. Many of those components had been lying around for years, played with and advanced by engineers and a few amateur enthusiasts, but almost unknown to the public.... Historically, FM provided the missing link to bind all this advanced sound apparatus together. In the full-throated 15,000 cycles of the W2XMN transmission that began pouring out of Alpine on a regular schedule in the summer of 1939, the age of high fidelity in radio and sound reproduction was born.[16]

One of the economic aspects of this advance in electronics was the growth of the component business as a significant and healthy part of equipment sales. The completely enclosed cabinet, with all parts inside, is still bought today by the majority of the public. Many hundreds of thousands of buyers, however, now buy radio-phonograph/speaker/amplifier components and use them in whatever way their personal taste dictates. Component business, as separated from the complete unit, totalled fifty-one million dollars in 1965.[17]

In the summer of 1939, two more FM stations began to

operate in New England: the Yankee Network's station on top of Mount Asnebumskit in Massachusetts, and another at Meriden Mountain, Connecticut. On only two kilowatts, the Mt. Asnebumskit station found it could blanket the entire service area of three high-powered AM stations and do it with a clearer signal than any of them could achieve. To do this with equipment that would cost less and use less power (than similar AM equipment) would surely curtail greatly (or completely) the AM economic pattern. It is somewhat significant that two weeks after the Yankee Network FM station went on the air, RCA applied to the FCC for a permit to erect an experimental FM station. Needless to say, they did not have the same trouble in gaining *their* permit for this "visionary" dream as had Major Armstrong. Their application came five years after they had first heard FM demonstrated secretly in the winter of 1932.

Another serious economic upset was building up at this time. To get the FM signal from the studio in Boston to the mountaintop, the Yankee Network tried a method not normally used then. They beamed the signal the forty mile distance by a low-powered FM relay transmitter. It worked so well that two more FM transmitters on mountaintops were put under construction. The signal thus sent by relay stations would be able to blanket the whole of northern New England. Most AM radio stations, to do anything at all like this, would have to use AT&T's wire services. Wire charges were a very substantial and profitable part of radio and television broadcasting. In this field, AT&T held an undisputed monopoly. A national radio service capable of network and relay broadcasting, which was independent of the telephone company lines, would obviously bring substantial loss in profits to AT&T.

Meanwhile, General Electric had decided to try FM and put up their own station. While experimenting with their Albany, New York, station, they discovered that two FM stations on the same wavelength would not interfere with each other. Where their station and Armstrong's Alpine station over-lapped signals, one or the other (but never both) came in clearly. This helped dispel the continuous propaganda going out that FM was wasteful of wavelengths. It was true that FM needed a wider band (the bigger "door") than AM but, without interference, FM stations could be put closer together and share more of the limited frequencies available. Statistically, this has worked out so that there is room for 3,000 FM radio stations with no interference, as opposed to the 4,000 AM stations on the air with interference a continuous problem.

The public, by 1939, was evidently wondering about FM. In the mass press, articles devoted to FM began to appear. A series of newspaper clippings from Armstrong's personal files shows a most unusual negative wording and story line concerning FM at this time. A few headlines give the flavor: "Staticless Radio Still Experimental Say Officials," "Staticless Radio Remote," "New Staticless Radio Set Still a Noble Experiment," "No Radio Revolution."[18] Interesting, too, is a clipping from the trade paper *Variety*, dated October 11, 1939, with the headline, "FCC Deplores Hint It Collaborates in Retarding Technical Advance."[19] The substance of these articles is very much like the interview story with Andrew Ring four years earlier in which FM was called impractical.

At the time these articles were written, FM was a technical fact and one which had been tested for nine years by the inventor (1930–1939), tested by RCA with Armstrong for two years (1933–1935), tested continuously by RCA after Armstrong left, tested by many amateurs and professionals, and, in 1938 and 1939, tested by General Electric. GE's published findings confirmed everything that had been in the reports RCA had never released concerning their tests at their Empire State labs. By this time it had occurred to a number of critics that the silence on FM was a planned silence. Further, that the public information releases given out by industry, and to some extent government, were planned to be negative in nature. *Fortune* magazine, which can hardly be called antibusiness, published its story of FM in October 1939. It called it "Revolution in Radio." Its opening line is, "After years of battle a fighting inventor is in a position to cause replacement of 40,000,000 radio sets and $75,000,000 worth of broadcasting equipment."[20] With that, the article explains the economic problem between AM and FM in detail and lays blame on both industry and government for selfishly attempting to thwart the invention. So FM, and the alleged plan to kill it, got into print very early in its history.

During 1939, while trade and consumer press stories were, for the most part, referring to FM as a "noble experiment," the number of FM stations operating experimentally had grown to fifty-two. Most of the stations were anxious to start commercial operation and applied to the FCC for this reason. It took the FCC until December 19, 1939 to study the possibilities of commercial FM broadcasting. This was four years and one month after they had seen it successfully demonstrated by Major Armstrong:

.... In view of the growing interest in frequency modulation and filing of applications to begin broadcast service as distinguished from experimental service on frequencies above 25,000 kilocycles, the Federal Communications Commission announced today that it will inquire fully into the possibilities of this system of modulation for aural broadcasting. Accordingly, an informal engineering hearing will be held before the full Commission beginning at 10 a.m. February 28, 1940....

Before a permanent policy can be established with respect to either or both systems of modulation on frequencies above 25,000 kilocycles for regular broadcasting service, studies and investigations must be made regarding the relative values of the two systems, the patent situation, the frequency needs of all radio services, and whether amplitude or frequency modulation, or both systems, should be recognized for other services as well as broadcasting....

The frequency bands above approximately 25,000 kilocycles are sometimes referred to as "very high frequencies," "ultra high frequencies," or "ultra short waves." These frequencies possess relatively short distance characteristics as compared with the lower frequency bands. The signals are subject to rather wide diurnal and seasonal variations in signal strength at distances beyond the horizon; therefore, as a practical matter, those frequencies may be said to be useful for broadcast service up to about 100 miles only.

Major E. H. Armstrong, professor of electrical engineering at Columbia University, appeared as a witness in behalf of frequency modulation at the Federal Communications Commission engineering hearing in June, 1936. On the basis of testimony of experts who testified at this hearing, and after studies had been made jointly by the Commission's Engineering Department and the Interdependent Radio Advisory Committee, the Commission and the President adopted permanent allocations above 25,000 kilocycles for the various government and nongovernment radio services.

Amplitude modulation has long been used as the standard system for transmitting speech and music by radio. It is the only system of modulation which is used by the existing services operating on conventional frequencies, i.e., below 25,000 kilocycles.[21]

The FCC release further stated four advantages of FM: (1) lack of static; (2) FM operates on low power and gives greater service area than an AM station with similar power; (3) FM stations do not interfere with each other (an FM receiver will accept only the strongest signal when the ratio of the desired to the undesired signal strength is about 2 to 1, whereas in the case of AM, the ratio must be at least 20 to 1 for good broadcast service); and (4) FM has definite advantages (technically, economically, quality of service) in operating low power services such as forestry, police, aircraft, etc.

Considering these advantages, which the FCC itself had proved by its own engineering department, it may be wondered why there was not a sweeping legislative action to allow for an orderly changeover from AM to FM. Actually, something like this happened in 1945 when the FCC ordered all existing FM broadcasting to move substantially higher in the spectrum, and developed a plan by which the older-type FM would continue serving its audience while the newer-type FM developed slowly. So it was not that such great changes were outside of the FCC's power or desire to initiate. And, in fact, in March of 1941, 777 out of 863 AM stations had to make minor frequency shifts to comply with some new international standards set up at that time.

Armstrong was aware that history had shown that neither new ideas, nor inventions are received with universal acceptance. He and other critics of the time were worried about the fact that FM was not just "another improvement," but something so demonstrably superior that it seemed illogical to deny it every opportunity of showing this superiority. In other words, the pro-FM camp knew that there would be an attempt to keep the status quo; they complained about the methods used to do it. In the kindest of terms,they felt the methods were unethical. The FCC finally did approve commercial FM (January 1, 1941) five years after its public demonstration and seven years after its patent date. To Armstrong, that represented seven lost years as far as his remuneration from his patent was concerned. His own financial reward for having invented FM would have to come in the remaining ten years of the patent's length, and that, of course, was never fully realized either.

Part of the problem of the industry in accepting FM lay not only in their unwillingness to dump AM (with all the economic losses that would have entailed), but also in a hint given by the FCC release of December 1939. Along with studying the technical side of FM, they had also wanted to study "the patent situation." This situation can be generalized to this: for all practical purposes, the Radio Group, as controlled primarily by RCA, owned every major radio patent in the U.S. and the world, including the basic patents of Armstrong himself (except for FM, which he kept).

The patent situation is, primarily, an economic situation normally having little to do with the FCC's role in the regulation of radio and with the assigning of broadcasting licenses. In fact, by law, economics as such is to play no role in the assigning of station licenses. That is, if the person(s) applying to the FCC to operate a broadcasting facility can show he can afford it, or can raise the capital, that is all that is needed to fulfill the financial conditions. But whether a community can economically support one or more stations is of no moment to the FCC. They cannot make a judgment as to whether or not there is enough advertising money around to support one, two, three, or more stations. At least here, they feel it up to competition and the survival of the best businessman to determine that.

If the FCC were to review the AM/FM patent situation and decide that the AM interests would lose too much by being replaced by FM, it would be in violation of their own charter. In addition, it would be considered extremely unfair, as competition is supposed to work in favor of the superior service. The specific charge that RCA did, in fact, by every possible and subtle means of persuasion, influence the FCC and others in the industry to thwart FM came not only from Armstrong, but the trade papers, others in the radio industry, and, finally, the United States Senate. In 1948, hearings were held, authorized by the 80th Congress, to investigate the progress of FM radio. The hearings were to discuss certain charges involving development of FM radio and RCA patent policies. These hearings were in the same year that Armstrong and RCA also went to court over FM patent infringements. During the progress of the hearings every charge that had ever been made in print, hinted at in speech, and previously discussed in former governmental hearings was brought up in most unsubtle terms. The witnesses included Dr. Jolliffe, the former FCC chief engineer, then employed by RCA.

The committee was made up of thirteen senators. Senator Wallace White of Maine was the chairman. Some testimony from these hearings indicates just how clearly the alleged charges of conspiracy were made during this period. In speaking to one NBC witness, one senator said:

Senator Tobey: I am coming to the point. We are just laying the ground for a demonstration of the charge that I made that your organization did everything it could to hamstring and put out of business and keep under the ground and buried if possible—kill off, in other words—FM, for a long period of years. Failing to do that, when FM demonstrated its ability, as evidenced by this report, of which you gave Russia eight copies, then you did come into the ring, under pressure of men who had the wisdom to see the value then you got busy and came across. That is all to be substantiated by documentary evidence before I get through.[22]

Senator Tobey's rather sensational charge is almost made pale by his further charges against RCA:

> I think it could be demonstrated beyond question that they blacklisted the thing as hard as they could, did everything they could to keep Armstrong down. . . . They failed miserably because the values were there. They did their damnedest to ruin FM and keep it from being where it is now . . . and I make that charge very respectfully, to hamstring and keep down and subordinate FM as long as they dared to do it or could do it, within reasonable realms.[23]

Further testimony on this subject was given by Paul De Mars of the Yankee Network:

> *Senator Capehart:* Then your criticism is directed against the FCC.
> *Mr. De Mars:* Yes, sir.
> *Senator Capehart:* I gather from most of your testimony that your main criticism has been against the FCC in the way they have handled the FM matter, and I also gather that you feel that they were encouraged and aided by RCA and NBC.
> *Mr. De Mars:* That is correct. As a matter of fact, it was common knowledge in the art that the RCA was opposing FM. I agree with you, Senator, that their opposition to FM was understandable, but the manner in which they carried out that opposition on the record was not and is not in the public interest, and did not constitute meeting the obligations that apply to such an organization as RCA and NBC.
> . . . .
> *Senator Tobey:* . . . It would seem wise at this point to hark back to the testimony of one Mr. Guy, who came before us and in the course of his testimony began to state with great eclat how strong a supporter and friend RCA . . . had been for this new development of FM, and what they were doing for its propagation, and all. Because of my understanding from reputable authorities what actually happened down during the years of FM and the stumbling blocks that were put in the way of its progress by not only RCA, but the FCC and perhaps the two acting in joint account. . . .
> So I came out and said to him, in my judgment, I had been told that instead of pushing the thing, just the reverse, they had hamstrung it and done all they could to knock it down, and . . . he disclaimed that.

We called Dr. Armstrong, the pater familias of FM, and put him on the stand, swore him, and asked him if my statement would be substantiated by the facts, and he said I had told the truth....

Mr. De Mars testified the second time this morning that in his judgment the RCA and NBC had exercised undue influence over the FCC. Now he comes down specifically and points out that in these earlier days in 1939 and 1940, during a conversation in Columbus, they, the Chief Engineer and Mr. Hanson, began to sell him a bill of goods that FM was not much anyway, and they ran it down; that it was not going to be effective, trying to disillusion him and John Shepard, who was putting the cash up. After, they went to the demonstration... which showed up a sore spot in FM reception, which was supposed to prejudice the witness against FM, the thing was no good.... Mr. De Mars has not completed his testimony, but here are two episodes... where they did belittle the thing in contradistinction to Mr. Guy's testimony of how much they are doing for it.

Now apparently at last, RCA and NBC have realized that FM is here to stay; that it provides a wonderful reception. So when they have it crammed down their throats by the logic and force of events and results, then they think it is a good thing.

. . . .

.... We have a case of not only the invention being played down, but you have evidence, before we get through... that RCA and NBC did work upon the Commission or certain members of it, and in joint account tried to keep the thing down.

. . . .

Mr. De Mars: On page 19 of *Broadcasting* magazine, April 1, 1940, the column headed "RCA Attitude A Surprise" (reads) "RCA's cryptic pronouncements through Chief Counsel Wozencraft that it believes ultra high frequency broadcasting is ready for commercial use and that they think the public interest would be served by the Commission action giving FM the green light took the FCC and the assembled audience by surprise.... Taking FM proponents wholly by surprise, the RCA position was seen as one which eliminated the greatest non-official obstacle to development of the projected service. At the outset of the hearings observers anticipated a rather bitter contest with the Armstrong-Shepard group on the one side, and RCA on the other." The purpose of reading this into the record at this hearing is to show that the art was aware of the the RCA and NBC opposition to FM. It was not something that I manufactured out of my own

mind. . . . It was well known and when the RCA at the conclusion
of the hearing stated that they felt FM should go ahead it came
as a surprise to everybody.

Senator Capehart: When did you think they should have made
the statement that they did, what year?

Mr. De Mars: Well, in substance, I think that statement should
have been made in 1935, at least in 1936.

Senator Capehart: You do not think they were justified in experimenting with it for those years?

Mr. De Mars: Not in view of the fact that they had already
experimented with it prior to 1936 and the evidence has been
shown that they had correctly appraised the advantages of FM.[24]

The "John Shepard" referred to in the preceding quote was
the president of the Yankee Network. At this time both Mr.
Shepard and his employee De Mars had become interested
in FM after hearing it demonstrated. They had not been personal friends of Major Armstrong. Their initial interest lay
in trying a good business venture. In *FM*, the industry's first
trade magazine, Shepard also indicates that a strong behind-
the-scenes fight was taking place in an opening article on FM,
"The battle for adequate frequencies for the national development of frequency modulation as a superior grade of broadcast
service is behind us."[25]

The 1948 Senate FM hearings also include a discussion
of a rather philosophical point concerning whether or not a
company has any moral and/or legal duties in its relation to
the public. Senator Capehart asked De Mars if he felt that
RCA was under any obligation to publish material beneficial
to FM or to do anything at all for FM. De Mars then gave
a thumbnail review of the supposed rights and obligations
of broadcasters, by virtue of their being granted use of the
"public" airwaves by the FCC. He stated, "No, I do not
feel they were under obligation to publish that, but I do feel
that they were under obligation to at least not begin the active
campaign of talking FM down, influencing the Commission
and as a leader of the industry, turning people away from
interest in the development of the new system.[26] Then
Capehart asked:

Senator Capehart: Do we have any testimony... that they influenced the Commission?

Mr. De Mars: .... I know of my own knowledge that the FCC, and particularly the assistant chief engineer in charge of broadcasting, in the period of 1935 and 1937, looked for guidance almost exclusively upon the RCA.

Senator Capehart: What was his name?

Mr. De Mars: Andrew D. Ring.

. . . .

Senator Capehart: That is a pretty serious charge to be making against a man.

Mr. De Mars: Mr. Ring's dependence upon advice from RCA was common knowledge among the engineers, consultants, and operators in the field.

.... That does not necessarily reflect upon the character of Mr. Ring, and I think it is quite natural that one in his position, administering the technical problems of the FCC, should look to the leaders of the industry for information.... My criticism is not of Mr. Ring's dependence upon... RCA, but the fact that RCA used that to influence Commission action.[27]

After worry, fretting, fighting, FM had its delayed commercial birth. The statement announcing its birth was in language so blandly matter-of-fact that one could never guess the turmoil that led to its release. The FCC stated on May 20, 1940:

.... Hailing frequency modulation as one of the most significant contributions to radio in recent years and declaring that FM broadcasting on a commercial basis is desirable in the public interest, the Federal Communications Commission today announced the availability of the frequency band of 42,000 to 50,000 kilocycles for that purpose. This will provide 40 FM channels, each 200 kilocycles wide—35 to regular high frequency broadcast stations and 5 to non-commercial educational broadcast stations.

Frequency modulation is highly developed... it is ready to move forward on a broad scale and on a full commercial basis. On this point there is complete agreement among the engineers of both the manufacturing and the broadcasting industries. A substantial demand for FM transmitting stations for full operation exists today. A comparable public demand for receiving sets is predicted. It can be expected, therefore, that this advancement in the broadcast art will create employment for thousands of persons in the manufacturing, installation, and maintenance of transmitting and receiving equipment and the programming of such stations.... Present standard broadcasting (AM) will continue, and certainly for a number of years will render full service. The extent to which in future years the listeners will be attracted away from the standard band cannot be predicted. Testimony at the hearing indicated that manufacturers will provide receiving sets capable of receiving both services.

.... The opening of a new band for commercial broadcast will help correct defects and inequalities now existing in the standard broadcast system. These inequalities result from the scarcity of frequencies, their technical characteristics, and the early growth of broadcasting without technical regulation. There is today a lack of stations in some communities, and other communities do not have sufficient choice of program service. The establishment of the new broadcast band in the higher frequencies will enable many communities to have their own broadcast stations.[28]

The wording of this release not only praises FM, but goes so far as to assume that at a future date it will supplant AM. That AM, as *the* national broadcast service, would probably be replaced by FM is evident from the wording, "Present broadcasting (AM) will continue certainly for a number of years...." In another public release issued the same day, the FCC went even further in this prediction:

.... The hearing yielded a vast amount of information as to the use of frequency modulation in broadcasting on high frequencies. Each interested party agreed that frequency modulation is superior to amplitude modulation for broadcasting on frequencies above 25,000 kilocycles.

.... The service range of the new (FM) stations while limited (in distance served) will, in many cases, be greater than that obtained from the primary service area of comparable standard (AM) broadcast stations.

.... However, FM stations have not demonstrated the long distance coverage properties such as obtained with present high powered clear channel stations. Accordingly, amplitude modulation stations in the standard broadcast band may be required indefinitely for the purpose of giving widespread rural coverage.[29]

Thus it was very clear that FM probably would replace AM, except for those few stations thought to be needed for large rural areas where AM seemed to have propagation advantages.

Also in June, 1940, the FCC issued the new rules and engineering standards for FM. The FM system adopted was the patented Armstrong system which had demanded the wide band or "door." There had been a number of proponents for a less-wide band in order to save space, but the FCC agreed that the Armstrong specifications gave the listener the finest aural listening possible and that anything less than this seemed undesirable. They also showed some concern over monopoly:

Under the rules just approved, FM facilities are, in effect, available to every community in the land. Important in these rules is the requirement that the program service shall embody presentation particularly adapted to the high fidelity quality of the new method of broadcast. This, with its staticless qualities, assures the listening public an improved type of service.

Unlike standard broadcast stations, FM stations will be licensed to serve a specified area in square miles. In places where one or more FM stations are located, their radius of service will be made as comparable as possible. Such parity of service is feasible because FM is not subject to objectionable interference as in the case of the older long distance type of broadcasting.

The public is assured of a reasonable amount of FM program service initially by the Commission requiring a daily, except Sunday, minimum operating schedule of at least three hours during the day and three hours at night. FM stations are further obligated to devote at least one hour each day and one hour each night to programs not duplicated simultaneously in the same area, which means programs distinct from standard broadcast. The latter provision is intended to demonstrate the full fidelity of the FM system.

To safeguard the public against monopoly, no person or group can, directly or indirectly, control more than one FM station in the same area. Likewise no person or group may control more than one such station, except upon showing that such operation would foster competition or will provide a high frequency broadcasting service distinct and separate from existing services, and that such operation would not concentrate control in a manner inconsistent with public interest, convenience, or necessity. In this connection, the Commission declares control of more than six stations by the same person or persons under common control is inconsistent with the public interest.[30]

In October, 1940, fifteen pioneer FM stations were granted

their commercial licenses. The population of their combined areas was approximately twenty-seven million people, with a service area of 110,000 square miles. By December, 1940, twenty-five stations had been licensed and were awaiting January 1, 1941, at which time commercial FM broadcasting would go into effect. Only needed were the FM radio receivers in the hands of the twenty-seven million people.

Since all interested parties at the 1940 FCC hearings on FM had enthusiastically supported FM (and that included, supposedly, RCA, plus all the broadcasters and manufacturers), it would seem that they would jump on the FM bandwagon, now that it had both official and non-official blessing. If predictions of the coming end of AM radio were true, and if FM was to supplant it, then the radio manufacturing industry surely would go into immediate production in order to supply FM sets to the waiting millions. Not to produce for FM would be economic suicide. However, they did not produce and their economy continued.

The radio industry needed an economic shot in the arm (that FM might provide)—as was discussed in an article entitled, "Revolution for Profit" in the trade magazine, *FM*, in November 1940. It says that the greatest behind-the-scenes activity known to the radio industry in many years was centered around Armstrong's frequency modulation system. The greatest need, then, in the industry (manufacturers, jobbers, dealers, and service men) was a way to bring back "real profit" to the industry. "In 1929, the greatest year the radio industry has ever known, 4,500,000 sets were bought at an average retail price of $162. Then, after a sharp drop, annual production went up and up to a record high of 9,000,000 receivers built in 1939. However, the average retail price of radio sets had declined by 1939, to a record low of $32."[31] *FM* states that the lower price was not so much a reflection of mass production as of price wars and cuts in quality:

> ... The radio industry had shown itself to be doubly short-sighted ... with disastrous results. First they have lowered retail prices as fast as they could find ways to reduce costs. Then they

reduced prices further by cutting performance to the extent that broadcasting stations have had to increase their power to enable the cheapened sets to give adequate reception. Instead of encouraging listeners to own better sets, the sales promotion has been concentrated on cheapened models until today the majority of the sets bought are inferior in performance . . . to the average sets purchased in 1935.

. . . .

Finally, the owners of these sets, not realizing that they are improperly designed, blame the broadcasting stations and the FCC because they bring in mostly squeals and cross-talk.

. . . .

It is not often that an industry, having ham-strung itself by its own shortsightedness, ever gets a chance to make a fresh start. Yet this is exactly what Major Armstrong's frequency modulation system means to the radio industry.

It provides everything that manufacturers need to direct public thinking away from price, and to revive interest in high-quality performance.[32]

The article continues to explain how FM could bring good retail prices for sets, open up the tube and equipment replacement market, give merchandising departments powerful selling features, and encourage a renaissance of good engineering practices on the part of receiver manufacturers.

An equally bright economic picture was painted by E. J. McDonald, Jr., president of Zenith Radio Corporation. He felt that the FM market about to be opened was not just a replacement market for AM, but would be " . . . basically a drive on the family living room where every home regardless of what other receivers it has, should have a high fidelity instrument for special musical broadcasts."[33]

Zenith had one of the original fifteen commercial stations on the air and had been experimenting for some time. Zenith also, one of the few giants of the industry, always had recognized Armstrong as the inventor and paid him annual royalties. McDonald continued:

. . . The general effect of FM on radio dealers . . . will be to raise the unit price of sale, and no dealer, I feel, will regret that circumstance.

Zenith has already introduced FM receivers in the 1941 radio line. They are definitely developed as quality items.

FM transmitters are relatively inexpensive to erect. They cost less than our present amplitude modulated transmitter... The actual popularity of these [receiver] models will depend largely upon the sincerity with which all radio manufacturers who enter FM will devote their energies to making it a quality product that will justify the interest of the public.[34]

That closing sentence is of great significance. It is strange for the president of a large corporation, who sees great profit in a new innovation, to make the comment that others should be "sincere" in entering this lucrative field. McDonald, like others in the radio art, however, was quite aware of the economic situation between AM and FM interests. He was, evidently, hoping others would not enter FM and do to it what they had done to AM radio sets—cheapen them for more profit.

In the ensuing court trials over FM patent infringements, a number of witnesses had testified that FM radio sets had, indeed, been cheapened in a continuous price war; not the least of the companies accused of this practice was RCA. At that time there were still definitely two camps (pro-FM and against), regardless of what had been said for the benefit of the public and the FCC during the 1940 FCC hearings. It became clear that FM was not to get the promotion envisioned by McDonald, the FCC, Armstrong, the Yankee Network, the trade papers, and the newly organized Frequency Modulation Broadcasters, Inc. (FMBI), when very few manufacturers actually did go into FM production (to any extent or to a very small extent).

The bright picture that opened 1941 soon faded. No sooner had the FCC given its official "green light" to FM, than it decided to hold hearings concerning the fact that so many FM applications were coming from newspaper interests. On one hand it seemed the FCC was really concerned that the new service not end up just as AM had done, that is, with exactly the sort of direct and indirect economic control by monopoly groups (such as newspapers) inter-related by stockholdings and wholly-owned or partially-owned sub-sidiaries. In fact, their own earlier public release had indicated their desire not to let this happen.

The investigation into newspaper ownership of radio sta-tions had taken place once before and led nowhere and caused no change in FCC licensing policy. It was about to take place again because of a fear that this monopolistic situation was not exactly a definition of the democratic ideal, of a multiplicity of separately owned communication channels. On the other hand, critics of this investigation felt it was a subtle way to again hold up FM's progress by denying FM licenses during the investigative period (always from a few months to a year or more). Indeed, this is just what happened. Critics were quick to point out that the FCC grants the original license to begin with and that they know far in advance (since all applications must give the true owners and their backgrounds and other interests) whether or not the newly applied-for sta-tion will be basically independent, or basically part of some other business venture. At this time, many newspaper interests did control AM radio.

From March, 1941, and through the rest of the year, FM licenses were snarled in red tape. The press barrage on this investigation poured out, while the FCC defended its position by saying the public hearings did not imply it was opposed to newspaper ownership of radio stations in general. The FCC said their records showed that one-fourth of all commercial FM applications were filed on behalf of newspaper interests and that in AM broadcasting more than one-third of the exist-ing stations were identified with newspapers; further, that in more than 90 percent of all localities with only one AM station, the station was in the hands of the only local news-paper. A more monopolistic view of communications is hard to conceive. Yet this same FCC granted these licenses with full knowledge of what they were doing.

Since the entire communication art was aware that the FCC was itself solely responsible for who gets a license, their sudden interest in the welfare of the democratic process was viewed with great skepticism. As would have been expected, the FM proponents viewed such interest as a subtle way to hold up FM expansion. Whether or not this was actually the case, of course, cannot be known. Whether the FCC was sincere in its desire to protect the public or not, the fact remains that FM was held up yet again. However, something much more serious held up FM, AM, TV, and possibly the entire planet: World War II had already broken out in Europe. The United States joined that conflagration in December. Before FM could get anywhere commercially, its economic progress came to an abrupt halt less than a year after it had begun.

Between December, 1941, and April, 1941, the newly formed Defense Communications Board (later to be called the Board of War Communications) banned the use of critical materials in construction and put a "freeze" on any further radio/TV development. The board did allow those stations on the air to continue either their commercial or experimental operations. It also allowed some stations, almost completed, to go ahead and broadcast. At the war's beginning, five of the newly authorized FM stations had got their commercial licenses and were operating; twenty-three were allowed to operate with temporary permits; and seven continued experimentally. It was hoped these stations would keep alive the interest in FM until the war was over.

In 1943, the FCC permitted AM stations which also owned FM stations to duplicate programming on both stations. Since this aspect, of how duplicated programming affected the FM economic picture negatively, is taken up in detail later, it is sufficient to point out here that this one rule was almost as serious in preventing FM from creating its own "art" as was the FM spectrum shift in 1945. Briefly, allowing the AM stations to duplicate their AM programming over FM gave the listener no incentive to own an FM set, gave the manufacturer no incentive to make FM radios, and did not foster programming uniquely suited to show off the benefits of FM listening. Further, the sales departments of stations with both AM and FM licenses came to use the FM service as a give-away or bonus buy to advertisers. The merchandising talk went along lines like this: if the advertiser would buy AM advertising at AM rates, he would get as a bonus any FM listeners the station had, since the programming was duplicated anyway.

Any independently owned FM station in that same geographical area found it was competing against an AM/FM operation that gave away free the same FM airtime it was trying to sell. Since there were so few FM sets and programs available at this time, this made competition between the two groups (AM/FM and FM only) lopsided and bitter. Again, FM proponents criticized the FCC for allowing this, as the results for FM broadcasting were only negative. The FCC countered with the argument that since FM was struggling along so badly economically, their action at least insured the continued programming of the FM art, since AM stations could well afford operating their FM service at a loss: Without allowing the duplication, FM might never get off the ground, since there were so few independent FM-only stations for the public to hear. Also in 1943, the FCC adopted the plan to substitute call letters for FM stations, in place of the letter/number system.

Technically, FM made great strides during the war, as do so many things under pressure of war. The army, especially, found it more useful than AM, since it could be heard so clearly and used so well in local situations and used with less expense than AM. In 1944 the FCC decided to put up its own 50-watt FM experimental station to obtain more technical data. At the same time, it announced hearings to be held in the autumn of 1944 to discuss the postwar frequency allocation problem. In January, 1945, it proposed reallocating frequencies between 25,000 and 30,000 kilocycles to various broadcast services. In their report, the FCC suggested FM's future would be better served if it were moved from its ten-year home at 42-50 kilocycles to a higher position at 88-108 megacycles. The FM industry as a whole was against this. The announcements made by the FM industry in public, and in FCC hearings, were highly unfavorable to any move.

If the FCC did move FM to this much higher position in the broadcasting band, it would mean obsolescence of all existing equipment and inventories. This would have been an economic disaster, since, by war's end, there existed some fifty FM stations on the air, many more under construction, about a half-million receivers in the hands of the public, and a potentially lucrative market for the pent-up demand for new sets. There had to be an unusually good reason for the FCC to take such a drastic step. They had refused to do exactly this same thing with AM, that is, abandon AM in favor of FM due to the economic chaos which might be suffered by private companies. They were quite willing to do it with FM, however, since it was for the "good of the service."

They did have a good reason, they said. They found it in an event that takes place every eleven years some 93,000,000 miles away: Sunspot turbulence that in decade-long cycles affects the behavior of radio waves. These ionospheric problems, it was predicted, would seriously interrupt FM broadcasting in its, then, home of 42 to 50 megacycles. To prevent the electrical interference from hurting FM reception every eleven years, the FCC felt the higher frequencies would be safer since they are relatively free from such disturbances.

In the broadcast spectrum, FM and TV were next-door neighbors. Things that could affect certain parts of this band would not be cut off sharply at a certain point but would tend to fade away gradually. Therefore, if FM were in the heart of this serious interference, channels 1, 2, 3, 4, and 5 of the television broadcast band would also be affected. TV channel 2 was probably the best commercial channel for a businessman to receive, for it had the longest distance built into it by nature. Its "home" was next to FM, and therefore would have suffered most from sun-spot difficulties. That it never has is an important point.

In August, 1944, the FCC announced it would hold hearings on just what to do with the newly developed higher frequencies at the close of the war. These hearings were scheduled for November and all testimony for these hearings is covered in the FCC Docket No. 6651, now a rather famous docket in radio/TV circles. After all testimony had been heard, the commission announced it would go ahead with its plans to move FM "upstairs," in spite of the opposition of FM's inventor, the Radio Technical Planning Board, at least thirty-one radio/TV manufacturers,[35] the FM Broadcasters Association (FMBI), and a report of radio engineering experts which indicated the FCC technical findings on the sun-spot activity were in error. The Radio Technical Planning Board (RTPB) was set up at the suggestion of the FCC and organized to include all segments of the broadcasting art. It was to function as a legitimate and "expert" voice, to represent the industry view in hearings before the FCC. The commission had asked for help in allocating the various classes of services at the end of the war and hoped to gain valuable time by having the RTPB use its ability to round up experts and prepare various technical exhibits for them. It was one of the RTPB's recommendations *not* to move FM, based on expert testimony.

The RTPB organized certain groups of industry experts into "Panels"(similar to sub-committees), each with its chairman and each pursuing a special subject. Panel 5, concerning FM broadcasting, and Panel 2, concerning frequency allocations, both turned in reports that concluded that FM should stay where it then was:

> The issue with respect to the best position which FM broadcasting should have in the radio spectrum is the most important one before the Commission in this entire proceeding. The recommendation of the organized body established at the instigation of the Commission, namely the Radio Technical Planning Board, and the finding of the Commission with respect to this issue, are in direct conflict. Panel 5, FM Broadcasting, and Panel 2, Frequency Allocations, both recommend that FM be kept substantially in that portion of the spectrum it now occupies. The recommendation of no RTPB panel is contrary to this. In contrast, it is the proposal of the Federal Communications Commission to place FM broadcasting at frequencies approximately double those now utilized.[36]

Later in this same RTPB report, written in answer to the

FCC decision to move FM in spite of all evidence not to, the RTPB pointed out that the final FCC report quotes a Panel 5 member as saying that FM service would be washed out for as many as four or five hours during the course of an evening during those periods of sun-spot activity. The brief filed by the RTPB points out that the FCC *purposely* included this statement *out of context* and made no reference to the fact that the man who made this statement made it early in the discussion and later voted in favor of keeping FM where it was.

> The Commission disposes of Panel 5's treatment of this issue . . . It makes no mention of the discussion on this subject in panel meetings, the treatment accorded it, or the final vote of 27 to 1 in favor of retaining the present position in the spectrum. The quotation lifted from the panel report to the effect that "FM service would be washed out for as many as 4 or 5 hours of an evening—" was made by Mr. Lodge *at the beginning* of Panel 5's discussion. *At the conclusion* of the panel's treatment of the subject, *Mr. Lodge voted with the majority* in support of the recommendation that FM broadcasting be kept substantially at its present place in the spectrum.[37]

The lone dissenting vote came from Mr. T. T. Goldsmith of the Allen B. Du Mont Laboratories. Whether there is a relation between the scientific facts amassed by the RTPB panel during this investigation and scientific facts amassed by the Du Mont Laboratories is a matter for argument. However, Lessing points out that the particular group of AM-oriented companies and manufacturers who were all in favor of moving FM included Du Mont: "But a long string of witnesses, including representatives of CBS, ABC, Cowles Broadcasting, Crosley, Philco, Motorola, and DuMont, urged that FM be moved 'upstairs'." And there was no doubt that a heavy portion of the industry that had opposed FM from the start was making a concentrated attempt, before as well as behind the scenes, to get FM moved.[38]

The RTPB then asked Dr. J. H. Dellinger, Chief of the Radio Section Of the United States Bureau of Standards and Chief of the Interservice Radio Propagation Laboratories of the U.S. Government, to investigate the whole business of high atmosphere interference and give them a report. Dellinger's answer is quoted in the brief sent to the FCC:

> The point in question is that the frequencies concerned are sometimes affected by long-distance interference, contrary to an expectation that was widely held at one time, and there is a fear that this intereference may be so great as to seriously impair the usefulness of those frequencies for broadcasting. Essentially the Panel appears to request that I inform it whether that fear is well founded. I believe I may with propriety respond to this request, and the answer is that the fear is not well founded.
>
> During certain years of the sunspot cycles F2-layer transmission at those frequencies occurs over long distances for short parts of the day, and Sporadic-E transmission occurs at irregular times in all years. The phenomenon of very short bursts of long distance interference appears to be closely associated with, and possibly a manifestation of, Sporadic-E transmission. The extent of these effects, however, is not such as to seriously impair the value of these frequencies. It may also be stated that no radio frequencies are free from transmission vagaries.[39]

After the presentation of Dellinger's entire report, the RTPB Panel 5, with the exception of the Du Mont executive, who refused to be swayed by the expert report, voted twenty-seven to one to leave FM where it was. In addition, of course, Armstrong and all the FM broadcasters, who had been pioneering the field since 1936, showed evidence that the interference predictions made by the FCC witness, Mr. K. A. Norton, were in actual error.

Since material involved in this area was "classified" due to the war, the final hearings were held in secret. Therefore, the only report of the hearings to be published was the FCC version. This report, it was found, had been purposefully tampered with so as to cover up the error by Norton. Because the war was still on, no one could do anything about it and, when the material was publicly released after the war, it was too late. In the Senate investigation of this incident in 1948 the testimony describes what happened:

> *Mr. De Mars:* ... Matters were brought to a head in a hearing in 1944; in the last days of those hearings the Commission's chief

technical witness, Mr. K. A. Norton, introduced a bombshell in testifying as to the fact that FM was going to be subject to intolerable interference due to ionosphere transmission—that is, in the band 42 to 50 megacycles—long-distance transmission would result in limiting service to a ruinous extent.

Senator Tobey: Is it a fact that Mr. Norton's conclusions were on one side and over and against his were the opinions of 8 or 9 or 10 most eminent authorities who took just the opposite view, but the Commission made this radical and rather tragic change, solely on the justification of one Norton? Is that correct, so far?

Mr. De Mars: That is correct.

Senator Tobey: Is it also correct, and are you familiar with the fact that there is evidence, as a result of hearings before the FCC and conferences in my office where the records of the FCC and reports on this matter were considered, that a part of a report was deliberately changed in the handwriting of an employee of FCC, so that the verbiage which pointed out the fact that Norton had made a mistake was covered up. A mistake by Norton was discovered, a mistake which made his testimony entirely null and void. This substantiated the testimony and results of other authorities. But the record was changed so that the statement proving Norton had been in error was deleted, and innocuous words supplanted it; all this written in by an employee of FCC and wittingly or not made the error appear innocuous and that a mistake had not been made? Are you familiar with those facts?

Mr. De Mars: Yes.

. . . .

Senator Capehart: . . . . You say that this is true, and of course, if it is true, it is an indictment of one Mr. Norton.

Senator Tobey: Not only Norton, but . . . of the FCC at that time.

Senator Capehart: And I say, the entire Commission. I believe that under the circumstances the document that you refer to, which was changed, should be made part of the record.

. . . .

Senator Tobey: . . . The record to which I refer will be made part of the record. . . . In that record an employee of the FCC, a present employee, admitted that he made the change and that it was his handwriting, and he said the trouble is he is unable to tell who told him to do it. Some mental aberration operates to conceal the author of the instructions but nevertheless, the gentleman admits that, and that will be made a part of the record.[40]

As part of the appendix to this Senate investigation, the entire section of the changing of the wording is reproduced (pages 338 to 378)—both the original "classified" version, and the "public" version. The public version deletes classified testimony and shows the changed paragraph which ends with the wording, "A satisfactory explanation regarding the appropriate method to be employed in the analysis of this problem was furnished by Mr. Norton during the closed hearing. This analysis indicated that no error had been made in this report."[41]

Armstrong charged that the above quote, plus what went before it, indicated that Norton made no mistakes in his methodology—whereas the secret session showed just the opposite. Of course, after the war, all of this became apparent. However, surprisingly, no corrective action was ever taken, as by then FM had been moved to what was hoped might be its final burial ground. *FM and Television* magazine followed this whole period very closely and dealt with it in at least one or more articles a month. The "death" of FM was not just a vague fear, as indicated by an opening headline on the FCC decision: "We Don't Want a Successful Operation and a Dead Patient on Our Hands."

> What is wrong with the lower frequencies for FM? Listeners have not complained about bursts or reflections, or any such interference. The broadcasters and set manufacturers are satisfied to have the widened FM band start below 50 mc.
>
> Former FCC chairman Fly, speaking at the Television Press Club ... said of the FM frequencies: "Around the 40's we were worried about certain conditions, and it may well be that if we knew more about the 90's we would have greater worries up there."
>
> Dr. Dellinger, propagation expert of the Bureau of Standards, found no fault with the lower frequencies and no assurance that anything would be gained by an upward shift.
>
> Mr. Norton did not claim to have heard interference with FM reception on the present band. He is only apprehensive about the interference which ... listeners should hear, even if they don't.
>
> With all ... [FCC] enthusiasm for shifting the FM band, it is not prepared to promise that serious propagation troubles will not be encountered ... But even if that is not the case, we might still have a situation where the operation was successful, but the patient died.[42]

There is a suggestion in Lessing's book on Armstrong that

further pressure to get the FCC to do what the AM industry wanted was accomplished by reversing the process described earlier—the hiring of FCC officials by industry at high salaries. The reverse was to put into the FCC high officials who, while in power, carry out industry's wishes. It is a fact that a former CBS legal counsel, Paul A. Porter, was an FCC chairman during part of this time. Early in the hearings held by the FCC, representatives of CBS had appeared to argue in favor of moving FM for its own good.

The pro-FM group asked carefully how, if the so-called "ionospheric" interference was as bad as claimed, TV could remain in the same part of the spectrum? It was answered that the lower TV VHF channels were also "experimental" and no doubt, would also be moved "upstairs." That RCA fought so hard to keep these "temporary" and "experimental" TV channels seemed evidence enough to the FM camp that TV would never be moved—and of course, it never was. Nor has low-band television (channels 2–13) ever experienced any such "intolerable" sun-spot interference washing it out.

> In June, 1945, the FCC ordered all FM radio to be transferred from its old 50 megacycle band, where it had been giving unexampled service since 1940, to a new band of frequencies between 88 and 108 megacycles, where it had neither transmitters nor receivers developed to meet the postwar market. The plain dishonesty of this order was promptly demonstrated when the FCC turned about and assigned the band it had just ordered FM to vacate to television, a service about twenty-five times more sensitive to any kind of interference than FM and which, moreover, was still required to use FM on its sound channel. Later the same band of frequencies was assigned to government safety and emergency radio services, in which interference of any kind could be tolerated even less than in commercial broadcasting or television. The fact is that none of the "ionospheric interference" predicted for this band ever materialized.[43]

Let us repeat in order to save one of Lessing's more pungent remarks that when FM was "kicked upstairs" for its own good, to avoid serious aural broadcasting troubles, television remained in the same "interference" belt with an FCC order to use FM sound broadcasting (while the picture portion was transmitted by AM methods). Television's channel 2 through 6 are definitely in this "intolerable" part of the spectrum during sun-spot activity, yet TV's FM sound remains in good shape.

The FCC was evidently aware of what it had done, or had been led to do. In their own publications of this approximate two-year period of investigation and hearings, they reduce the whole matter to one or two sentences, which have been altered to obscure the real facts. In no less than three separate "historical" accounts of FM, the FCC said the move was due to skywave interference actually hurting FM broadcasting. In these three cases the past tense of the verb is carefully used to indicate that FM was experiencing, and had been experiencing, serious trouble affecting its transmission. This was never part of the truth. Even Norton's own testimony was based on *predictions* of what *might* happen, and, then, only during the sun-spot cycle. The FCC wording was deliberately chosen so that the reader, who may not have followed this two-year battle, would be left with the impression that the FCC made this spectrum move to help FM and that the entire industry agreed. The first published FCC version is in the 1946 annual report:

> During frequency allocation hearings in the previous fiscal year, FM received important consideration. This service had started on the 42–50 megacycle band, *but troublesome sky wave interference developed.*[44]
>
> The Commission's decision was made because sporadic skywave interference *had plagued FM operation* in the lower frequency band.[45]
>
> *Because of skywave interference experienced* on the then FM band of 42–50 megacycles, the Commission in 1945, after public hearing, moved FM to its present higher and less vulnerable position in the radio spectrum.[46]

The above wording, to the unsophisticated, not only means FM was being "plagued" with interference, but that the FCC had made the move only after "public hearings" which seemed to indicate the hearings agreed with the FCC move. Obviously, this is contrary to all the evidence that has been presented here. In fact, the FCC goes so far in this attempt to cover its own questionable part in this particular decision that they imply, in their 1945 annual report, it was the *witnesses* at the hearings which convinced them to move FM and not the opposite:

> .... There was divergence of opinion as to the expected amount and effect of skywave interference that would be expected.... In order to obtain additional data relating to radio wave propagation, a closed hearing was held on March 12 and 13, 1945, since much of this material was classified. This hearing was attended by the Commission, members of its staff, and industry and broadcasting personnel who had been cleared by the military for the purpose.
>
> .... Based on the testimony and data before it, the Commission was convinced that a superior FM broadcast service would be furnished by operation in the vicinity of 100 megacycles and, accordingly, on June 27, 1945, it allocated the band 88 to 92 megacycles....[47]

Nothing could be more misleading or further from the truth than the wording above, which suggests that the testimony, during open and closed meetings, was aimed at convincing the FCC to move FM. The thrust of the majority of witnesses and written briefs filed during this period was to keep FM where it was, and to show that Norton's findings were, in fact, in error. The fact that the "authorized" publications of the FCC contain these deliberate alterations in history is presented to help the reader understand and evaluate the criticisms of that particular body, which are so prevalent in the total history of FM broadcasting.

In November, 1947, the FCC held its hearings on the reallocation of the old home of FM (which had been given to television, sky-wave interference and all). This period also happened to be the height of sun-spot activity, the period Norton of the FCC had predicted would be ruinous to radio transmissions in this band. Yet the same FCC was about to reallocate this band to government and emergency services!

The FM broadcasters were present at the hearings to plead their case again for the return of at least a portion of this band so they could have some powerful clear-channel FM stations, as AM had, to serve rural areas. Armstrong was, for the first time publicly, able to question Norton on the stand. He reiterated in some detail the events of the 1945 hearing, reminded the commission of Norton's dire predictions, and then said:

Mr. Armstrong: . . . . We are now in the peak of the highest sun spot cycle that we know of, and I would like to ask you if that prediction had been borne out.

Mr. Norton: Well, I haven't heard whether signals have been heard from Australia, but it is my understanding, although I do not have direct knowledge of it, that signals have been received from South America.

Mr. Armstrong: On 80 mc?

Mr. Norton: No. Not on 80 mc, no. . . .

Mr. Armstrong: Now, some of us questioned that, Dr. Beverage, Dr. Burroughs, Dr. Pickard, Dr. Stetson, and we filed a memorandum. At the oral argument in the early part of 1945, you declined cross examination on the ground that it was a classified matter, and suggested that a secret hearing be held. . . .

It had been suggested in the course of these hearings when you presented your Exhibit 380 that the curves contained in that exhibit . . . indicated . . . certain fundamental errors in the computation of those exhibits. . . .

Now, did you substantiate them, Mr. Norton?

Mr. Norton: Yes, sir. I did substantiate them.

Mr. Armstrong: On 80 megacycles?

Mr. Norton: The conclusions I had reference to were the conclusions as to the presence of long-distance high signal-intensity F-layer transmissions in the band up to 50 megacycles. . . .

Mr. Armstrong: But, you said 80 megacycles, Mr. Norton.

Mr. Norton: I said 80 megacycles relative to what I would have expected, yes, that is right, at that time, based on the available information I had at that time.

Mr. Armstrong: But you were wrong?

Mr. Norton: Oh, certainly. I think that can happen frequently to people who make predictions on the basis of partial information. It happens every day.

Mr. Armstrong: That is the point I would like to make, Mr. Chairman, the type of engineering advice this Commission had been given, and that has resulted in chaos to those of us who have been trying to do an engineering job.[48]

And with his "Oh, certainly" (I was wrong) Norton ended the episode of the spectrum change. That the FCC in 1945 made the disastrous move on the basis of this man's assumed predictions and against the advice of almost the whole industry was one of the reasons for a sweeping investigation of the FCC. However, even more startling, the 1947 FCC, which heard the evidence of the Norton error and was shown the altered FCC version of the secret hearings, did nothing to change the situation and, further, denied FM broadcasters the rural coverage they wanted, and left television with two bands (while denying FM two bands).

As soon as FM had been moved and all FM equipment made obsolete, the FCC gave its blessing to a plan presented to them by CBS in yet another effort to *help* FM: the "Single Market Plan."

> Nor was this the end of the operations performed on FM in 1945. The Columbia Broadcasting System came forward with a plan for FM called "The Single Market Plan," presented in a handsome booklet and brief by its Executive Vice President Paul Kesten, who had been a caustic prewar opponent of FM. And the FCC adopted this plan, too, in its new postwar regulations. Under the plan, ostensibly put forward to increase the number of FM stations, each FM station was to be limited to a single city or market by having its transmitter power cut back to cover only that area. The plan was as slick as it was transparent, plainly aimed at cutting down the power of the growing FM networks. Under the plan the power of Armstrong's station at Alpine was eventually cut from 50 kilowatts to 1.2 kilowatts, the Yankee Network's main FM station was cut to a third of its former power, and the ability of high-powered mountaintop FM stations to bounce programs from one to the other by relay was severed.[49]

In an editorial on this new plan, *FM and Television* states, "An examination of the Single Market FM Plan . . . , as proposed, would make FM stations play the pauper role to princely multi-market, clear channel AM stations."[50]

In an article, "What's Behind the AM vs. FM Battle?," the editor begins by setting the historical scene and giving the magazine's basic attitude toward the FCC:

> To those who have had an active part in the progress of

Frequency Modulation since the inception of FM broadcasting and communications, the misstatements and the misrepresentations of fact contained in the records of... FCC hearings are, to say the least, appalling.

... And if it seems shocking that radio engineers and executives should be so unethical as to plan and present testimony intended to mislead the Commissioners just because the best interests of their companies would be served by wrecking the expansion of FM broadcasting, it must be remembered that history is just repeating itself.

... On October 11, 1944, Plausible Paul Kesten testified before the FCC concerning the CBS single market plan for FM broadcasting. This plan... has certain admirable features in that it would put all FM in any given area on an equal and competitive basis as to coverage. However, the CBS plan, as it has been presented, is a vicious device which leaves high-power AM stations free to sell multiple-market coverage, while limiting FM stations to the sale of single market coverage only. This is what Mr. Kesten said: "We want FM broadcasting to wholly be democratic... that what we have called the prince-and-pauper status of big and little (AM) stations be avoided as the end result of [FM] licensing" and "That FM licenses be limited, by Commission policy, to coverage of the single market area within which they are broadcasting rather than covering several separate markets by placing a high, and high-powered transmitter somewhere between them." Mr. Kesten further testified: "There are no jokers in this, there are no aces up this sleeve."

Mr. Kesten must have said that with his tongue in his cheek, for the one hope of protecting the 50-Kw AM stations owned by CBS and its 50-Kw AM affiliates, who are the chief CBS customers, is to assure those stations of multi-market coverage on clear channels....[51]

And so FM was saddled with economic burdens never given to AM radio broadcasting. Many people, even today, have the impression that frequency modulation is somehow inferior to amplitude modulation as far as coverage is concerned. The limitation on power and miles is a man-made limitation; one that was given to FM as one of the many "gifts" that were "for its own good" and to "help" it along. The fact that this gift, like the others, managed to hurt it economically, in competition with AM, is as usual a "coincidence."

The FCC had forbidden manufacturers to make FM radios

capable of tuning in both the old and new bands (so that the listener could hear programs on either). The conversion period was estimated to take about a year, but equipment for the new band had to be devised, manufactured, and marketed. The FM broadcasters and manufacturers found great fault with the FCC order preventing them from making sets with both bands. In a most tedious repeat of the same wording (for FM's own good), the FCC said the new radios would accept only the new service and this would help FM. The people who made their living from FM insisted it would hurt FM.

It was now apparent that FM broadcasting would have to start all over again. As though just invented, equipment had to be put on the drawing board and experimented with to develop sophistication in these very high frequencies; stations had to be reconverted before they could program; and most drastic, the public had to be convinced all over again that FM was worth the purchase of another radio. In this great postwar market, then, AM broadcasting was able to step in and fill part of the great demand for new entertainment, with television coming up a fast second.

> Thus, not only was FM pulled up by the roots and forced to establish itself in an entirely new region of the spectrum—making obsolete its fifty-odd prewar transmitters and 500,000 FM sets in the hands of the public—but in this new region it was to find its new stations so limited in power as to be kept on a starvation diet. In addition, with its relay powers severed, FM was now made dependent on AT&T's wire services for any network operations it might still find the strength to engage in.[52]

So ends the first part of FM's economic, or, perhaps more correctly, "uneconomic," history.

NOTES

[1]"The Facilities of AM-FM Radio," *Broadcasting: 1968 Yearbook*, pp. B108–B115.

[2]Lessing, *Armstrong*, p. 208.

³Paul A. Porter, chairman from December, 1944 to February, 1946, had been a newspaper editor and a lawyer for CBS for five years. Wayne Coy, Jr., chairman from December, 1947 to February, 1952, had been in newspaper work and director of an AM/FM radio station, plus a member of the early FM Broadcasters Association. Ewell K. Jett, had broadcasting technical experience, but served as chairman for only five weeks (November 16, 1944, to December 20, 1944). The information on commissioners was collected from FCC biographical sketches of each man.

⁴A notable exception is Robert T. Bartley, a member of the FCC, who worked for the FM pioneering firm, the Yankee Network in New England. He also was an officer of the FM Broadcasters Association and a member of the NAB. Eight out of every ten commissioners has had a law degree and usually practiced as a lawyer. Because of the commission's role as a sort of quasi-law court, it is assumed the Congress believes the law background to be some sort of asset in helping to decide the issues that are brought before the FCC in the form of hearings. It is the opinion of the author that the use of lawyers, to such a great degree, on the commission does not constitute an asset in any sense. On the contrary, the evidence presented in this book suggests the cleverness of the legal mind has been used, not to serve the public, but the very industry the FCC is supposed to regulate in the public's interest.

⁵The "purchase" of FCC members began much earlier, under the older Federal Radio Commission. In 1930, Henry Bellow (former FRC member) left the FRC to become a CBS vice president. There were a number of such cases during the life of the FRC as reported in Barnouw's *A Tower in Babel*.

⁶U.S., Congress, Senate, Committee on Interstate and Foreign Commerce, *On Certain Charges Involving Development of FM Radio and RCA Patent Policies, Hearings*, 80th Cong., 2d Sess., 1948, p. 111.

⁷*First Annual Report of the Federal Communications Commission to the Congress of the United States for the Fiscal Year (1935)*, Wash., D.C.: U.S. Government Printing Office, 1936 (subsequent references are shortened to: FCC—Annual Report, 19—).

⁸The FCC annual report covers the fiscal year from July 1 to June 30 each year. The FCC also releases statistics based on the calendar year from January through December. This book uses

both for sources and accounts for the seemingly occasional differences in statistics. The point made here is that since the annual report of the FCC comes out in June, there was plenty time to include such a revolutionary discovery as a workable FM broadcasting method. Further, this method was capable of reaching far greater distances than the two to ten miles reported in the FCC report for that year. Jolliffe, then FCC Chief Engineer, was totally aware of FM's existence at this time. In this same year (1936) Jolliffe left the FCC to take charge of RCA research and in June, 1936 he appeared before the FCC to testify in some rather important hearings on proposed changes in the use of the radio spectrum. At this time RCA was deep in its television research and wanted no shake-up in the radio spectrum. For a number of years the FCC annual report continued to ignore FM and its true ability to extend its broadcast range over long distances. The following is an excerpt taken from the 1948 Senate Hearings on FM development that will help the reader understand a little more clearly the rather serious suggestion of bribery of an FCC official by offering him a lucrative job in the broadcast industry: "Dr. Armstrong: 'The report of the FCC to Congress for the year 1935—that is, the engineering part of the report—was written by Dr. Jolliffe, who was then chief engineer of the FCC, and he advised the Congress that ultra-high frequencies were useful only for strictly local service, 2 to 10 miles range. Now, Dr. Jolliffe states at that time that he was not aware of . . . the tests I had been making between the Empire State Building and Haddonfield, N.J., 85 miles away. When, a few months later as an employee of RCA, he came on the stand in June 1936 before the Commission for whom he had written that report, he knew that report to Congress was incorrect. He knew that the range was certainly well over 60, 70, 80 miles . . . but he made no effort to say to the members of the Commission, 'Gentlemen, I am sorry about the last report I made. It was the best information I had, but now we know the situation is different, and it will have a great bearing on the future of radio. . . .' He did not say the picture had changed. . . (Senate Hearings on FM Development, p. 184)." So the reader may keep the historical events of this time clear, 1935 was the year the FCC announced a 1936 hearing on what changes may be needed in the broadcasting industry as far as using the newly developed higher frequencies. This was the time when both FM and TV had only a few experimental channels in these frequencies and both services were looking forward to expand to a nation-wide service. Both services wanted to get scores of more channels in the same area of the spectrum. Clearly both could not have them. At this time, FM was perfected, TV was not. There had to be something done to prevent FM from getting these valuable channels. This may explain why an FCC annual report ignores FM, why an important FCC engineer leaves the FCC to join RCA, and why a public relations campaign began at this time to indicate FM was a "limited" service as far as distance goes.

[9]*Christian Science Monitor*, November 18, 1935, p. 6, col. 2.

[10]*Boston Sunday Globe*, November 17, 1935, p. 8, col. 1.

[11]*Armstrong v. Emerson*, p. 440.

[12]Lessing, *Armstrong*, p. 225.

[13]"Top 100 Markets," *SRDS Spot Radio: Rates and Data*, March 1, 1968, inside front cover.

[14]A channel is that portion of the radio part of the electromagnetic spectrum where a station (or any broadcasting service such as police radio) is assigned by the FCC to operate. It is defined by its width—so many kilocycles wide. A station at "710" on a dial uses a channel, the center of which is at 710 kilocycles. It has, in AM broadcasting, an area that includes five kilocycles of space in each direction from the center point (ten in total), to carry its signal. This is called "narrow band" broadcasting. In FM broadcasting, 200 kilocycles are used to separate one channel from another. The reader may think of these channels as broad or narrow highways in space on which the traffic of sound is carried.

[15]U.S., Congress, Senate, Committee on Interstate and Foreign Commerce, *On a Bill to Amend the Communications Act of 1934, and for Other Purposes, Hearings*, on H.R. 814, 78th Cong., 1st Sess., 1943 (from a reprint in the Armstrong Memorial Research Foundation files).

[16]Lessing, *Armstrong*, p. 236.

[17]The figure was supplied by the Institute of High Fidelity in New York City. However, the fifty-one million dollars represents factory sales. The consumer retail value would be considerably higher. Since 1965, the component business statistics have been difficult to obtain since strictly component parts and completely packaged consoles have had less distinct lines. Firms who once made only separate components are now combining some (tuners and amplifiers in one cabinet) and formerly complete-unit firms are now

selling individual equipment (such as enclosed loudspeakers). The Institute (which uses figures supplied by the Electronic Industries Association) estimates the 1968 component factory sales at $100,000,000.

[18]These articles were supplied to Major Armstrong by the Luce Clipping Service in 1939. They are reproduced on a single photostatic page and do not give pages or column numbers and one article is not identified as to which newspaper printed it. Armstrong had hired the clipping service to cut out of the general press all articles that had to do with FM. The service was not as complete as today's standards might wish them to be. Respectively, the articles are identified as follows: *Buffalo* (NY) *News*, February 4, 1939; *Tulsa Tribune*, January 30, 1939; (no identification for "noble experiment" article except the author, Rod Reed); Youngstown (Ohio) *Vindicator and Telegram*, January 18, 1939.

[19]"FCC Deplores Hint It Collaborated In Retarding Technical Advance," *Variety*, October 11, 1939, p. 44.

[20]"Revolution in Radio," p. 116.

[21]FCC News Release, Mimeo. No. 38130, December 19, 1939.

[22]Senate Hearings on FM Development, p. 9.

[23]*Ibid.*, p. 11.

[24]*Ibid.*, p. 161.

[25]John Shepard, "The Broadcaster Speaks,"*FM*, November, 1940, p. 2.

[26]Senate Hearings on FM Development, p. 163.

[27]*Ibid.*, p. 164.

[28]FCC News Release, Mimeo. No. 41117, May 20, 1940.

[29]FCC News Release, Mimeo. No. 41119, May 20, 1940.

[30]FCC News Release, Mimeo. No. 41739, June 22, 1940.

[31]"Revolution for Profit," *FM*, November, 1940, p. 6.

[32]*Ibid.*, p. 8.

[33]*Ibid.*, p. 33.

[34]*Ibid.*, p. 43.

[35]*New York Times*, February 25, 1945, Sec. 1, p. 36, Co. 1.

[36]FCC Docket 6651, *Brief on Behalf of Panel 5 "FM Broadcasting" of the Radio Technical Planning Board*, p. 5 (the brief was printed by the Byron S. Adams Press in Washington, D.C.).

[37]*Ibid.*, p. 7 (underlining is in the original).

[38]Lessing, *Armstrong*, p. 258.

[39]From a reprint of a few pages of FCC Docket 6651 in the Armstrong Memorial Research Foundation files.

[40]Senate Hearings on FM Development, p. 169.

[41]*Ibid.*, p. 342.

[42]*FM & Television*, February, 1945, p. 19.

[43]Lessing, *Armstrong*, p. 258.

[44]*FCC Eleventh Annual Report*, 1945, p. 16 (italics supplied).

[45]FCC, Address of E. William Henry, Commissioner, Federal Communications Commission, before the Georgia Radio and Television Institute, Athens, Georgia, January 24, 1963 (italics supplied).

[46]*FCC Information Bulletin No. 2-B*, February, 1964, p. 13 (italics supplied).

[47]*FCC Tenth Annual Report*, 1944, p. 20.

[48]From a reprint of a few pages of the FCC 1947 hearing in the Armstrong Memorial Research Foundation files.

[49]Lessing, *Armstrong*, p. 259.

[50]*FM & Television*, August, 1945, p. 27.

[51]*Ibid.*

[52]Lessing, *Armstrong*, p. 260.

4

THE SECOND BEGINNING:

1946–1954

For FM, 1946 began—like all previous years—full of hope, but empty of profits for anyone. The battle over the spectrum move was still raging. Zenith Radio had applied to the FCC for revision of the new law so as to reopen the lower band and let both the 42–50 megacycles area and the newer 88–108 megacycles area be used for FM growth. Both bands would insure an adequate number of stations and quality of service for the entire nation. FM broadcasting would then have the added advantage of stations operating in these lower bands which were capable of getting more mileage out of that part of the spectrum. In this area, high-powered FM stations with 50 megacycles or more could cover vast territories, especially if they were fortunate enough to have a mountain or high terrain on which they could put their tower.

General Electric and Major Armstrong, along with Zenith, encouraged the return of the lower band and these interested parties appeared before the FCC in January 1946. Upon hearing all the evidence in favor of the two-band FM service, the FCC denied it, saying that it would not work, that it would be a compromise with quality, and the American public would have to buy more expensive sets. In their public release concerning these hearings, the FCC again does with words what is evidently standard practice; that is, FCC wording indicates that all parties agreed with the FCC decision and that there was great unanimity among all. Since these parties (Zenith, GE, Armstrong, and the FM Broadcasters, Inc.) were appearing before the FCC to argue against the FCC spectrum move, it seems illogical that the FCC should publish that these same parties were in agreement with them. Yet, the public releases (some 300) viewed by the author, on FM matters only, always end up with such wording. Whether this is done by policy or by accident or by normal use of government language, is something that can only be guessed at; but there is no doubt that if one reads only the FCC version of broadcasting, there is no indication that deep and often bitter fighting was going on.

Here is the FCC statement issued at the end of the meeting in which they refused the Armstrong/GE/Zenith petition to reopen the lower bands for FM:

> Perhaps the most significant feature of the January 18–19 hearings was the unanimity with which all parties agreed that FM broadcasting in the region permanently assigned, from 88 to 108 megacycles, will provide an excellent... service.[1]

This assumes, by the wording, that the witnesses involved in this hearing agreed with the FCC decision. Here is what Commander E. F. McDonald, Jr., President, Zenith Radio Corporation, had said a few months earlier, of the FCC decision to move FM:

> The FCC's decision to move FM upstairs to the unproven and undesirable 100-mc area was made against the recommendation of the entire radio manufacturing industry, against a... vote by the Radio Technical Planning Board, and against the overwhelming preponderance of technical testimony gathered by the FCC at the hearings it held on the subject.
>
> This decision will delay FM and thereby contribute to unemployment in the reconversion period. It will obsolete FM receivers now owned by the public.... I do not know the Commission's reasons for the decision because in my own opinion nobody should be happy about it except possibly the radio chains who, by the delays in FM, will for a larger period retain their owner-monopoly of broadcasting.[2]

That the FCC should have indicated that Zenith was now in full agreement with them on this very issue was folly.

The arguments given by the FCC against a two-band FM service are presented below. As he follows them the reader should keep in mind the FCC ruling which allows television to exist in these same two bands (VHF and UHF):

> Testimony in recent proceedings before the Commission indicates that a two-band receiver will cost the public more than a single band receiver. The Commission feels there is no valid reason for requiring the public to bear this extra expense.
>
> .... The only reason that has been advanced for the manufacture of receivers covering the old FM band as well as the new is that by building such receivers demonstrations of FM reception to prospective customers will be possible. This does not appear to be a valid reason.
>
> .... Our purpose in permitting an FM station which had moved to the higher band temporarily to continue simultaneous operation in the lower band was simply to prevent the loss of FM service to persons in the community who possess the old style receivers and who had not yet had an opportunity to convert them or replace them with a new receiver.... However, if new receivers are manufactured to cover the old band, the Commission might very well take the position that it was necessary to put an end immediately to all FM transmissions and to insure that the change-over to FM's new and permanent home should not be delayed.[3]

The above was in the form of a letter from FCC Chairman, Paul A. Porter, to Mr. R. C. Cosgrove, President of the Radio Manufacturers Association. *Broadcasting* magazine reported that a "Furore [was] Caused by Porter Letter to Cosgrove." The article further stated that:

> Set manufacturers, transmitter makers, and broadcasters alike literally "hit the ceiling" last week when the Commission released a letter... threatening to terminate FM in the old band immediately if manufacturers turn out new sets with two FM bands.... That sentence caused a furore among manufacturers. Several already had two-band sets in the making. Their decision to cover both bands was taken, it was understood, because the FCC in earlier releases failed to estimate a date for termination of interim operation for the changeover.[4]

In a later article, *Broadcasting* reported that a member of the FCC "denied that the small added cost was the prime factor in the FCC's decision to take FM off the air."[5] However, the article fails to name the FCC employee or to suggest the real reason for the ban against the two-band sets. Regardless of the reason, the changeover to the higher frequencies could not be accomplished without new equipment. A survey by the FCC showed that manufacturers of various types of broadcast equipment could deliver most of what was needed by the end of 1946.[6] However, these were estimates and not actual events. And in a separate report issued by the FCC earlier, in 1945, time given for the changeover was up to three years to develop transmitters for the higher powers and at least two years to develop tubes.

Another objection of the FCC to a two-band FM receiver set was that "a two-band FM system will have an unpredictable effect upon the listening habits of the public in that it would require that the listener switch to select one band or the other.... Habits of listening on one band to the exclusion of the other might well develop."[7]

Television sets today have two bands. Each set with the VHF and UHF channels has a switch the listener must use in order to watch the two bands. No one seriously regards switching from UHF to VHF any more of a hardship than switching to change channels. Nor does the FCC seem bothered by the fact that television has the two bands to begin with. There was a controversy over this from 1948 to 1951, known as the television "freeze" period. At this time it was argued that TV should be moved entirely to the upper spectrum (where FM had gone). Engineering data presented indicated that if TV were moved up here completely (abandoning the channels 2–13) it would be best for the service. All the problems that were supposed to have "plagued" FM were presented again, plus others that were more serious for television broadcast.

RCA was against this move, as were any network or station owners who happened to own one of the lucrative lower channel stations. Testifying before the Senate in 1948, Dr. Jolliffe, the RCA vice president (and former FCC Chief Engineer) claimed that "someone" was holding up the progress of televi-

sion by suggesting it move out of the lower frequencies—
frequencies which RCA had previously gone on record as
saying were subject to skywave interferences:

> But there appear to be some who would block the progress
> of television with charges which misrepresent the purpose and
> leadership of RCA and NBC in bringing television to the American
> people. One of these misrepresentations is the assertion that
> all television should be moved into the higher frequencies. Let
> us make no mistake about this. If such a move were made at
> this time, it would not mean more television. It would mean no
> television at all.[8]

That there was more than sufficient economic and engineering data presented in favor of moving all of television is evidenced by the fact that the "freeze" took place at all, and
then took three years to solve. The FCC hearings are long
and detailed and have little bearing here, except to show that
the FCC's view on television was exactly opposite to its view
on FM. FM was moved in spite of all economic and engineering
data, to support the status quo. Television was allowed to
stay with two bands even through the reasons given to move
TV and to move FM were almost identical.[9]

With all the tedious turmoil over FM, with it in its fourteenth
patented year, still hardly anybody was listening to it. By
autumn of 1946, there were only sixty-five FM stations on
the air. However, the FCC had 864 applications for FM stations
in various stages of processing. In one year, the FCC managed
to process only seventy-one applications. There were charges
that applications were being held up by almost any means
and excuse.

At the same time, the FCC was granting fully three-quarters
of all FM applications to owners of AM stations; almost all
of the remainder were going to newspaper interests. This was
the same FCC that had recently questioned newspaper ownership of radio as monopolistic in the field of communications.
And the same FCC that had said they did not want FM to
end up as AM had—in too few hands. In their 1947 annual
report, the FCC states, "As of March 1, 1947, three-fourths

of all FM applications were from standard broadcast interests, and one-third were from newspapers, 23 percent of which were in the standard broadcast (AM) field."[10]

In 1946, the Senate Small Business Committee issued a report entitled "Small Business Opportunities in FM Broadcasting." The report states that there should be no cartelization in the media of public information and discussion. The committee felt that monopolistic tendencies in FM broadcasting should be avoided and that the FCC should adopt a licensing policy to foster wide diversity of ownership of FM stations. The FCC completely agreed with the goals and objectives of the Senate Committee and publicly stated so in their news release of April 10, 1946, "The Commission agrees wholeheartedly with the objectives of the Senate Small Business Committee's report."[11]

On January 10, 1947, the FCC issued the following statistics on FM ownership among the "diversified" groups with FM stations actually on the air; 74 percent of licenses were issued to persons in the AM field and 36.3 percent to persons with newspaper interests (the figures are over 100 percent due to the fact that some licensees owned both AM and newspapers and are included in both categories). 12.6 percent were issued to persons with neither AM or newspaper interests. Over 87 percent of all FM stations on the air in 1947 were in the hands of an AM operator or a newspaper, or both.[12]

Only 181,000 FM receivers (1.4 percent of all sets made) were manufactured in 1947. In a speech before the National Association of Broadcasters, in October, 1946, the acting chairman of the FCC, Charles R. Denny, commented on these very few receivers:

Today there is one loud discordant note in FM—receivers. While the manufacturers have turned out an unprecedented quantity of low-priced AM sets, the FM sets have been coming very slowly except from the production lines of several manufacturers who are solidly behind FM. Some say that the other manufacturers are sabotaging FM. I do not go this far. I am convinced that some manufacturers who believe in FM have been handicapped by pro-

duction difficulties and inability to get materials. Others have
been lethargic and said "FM can wait—right now there is a lush
market for cheap AM receivers and I'm going to get my share."[13]

Coming from an FCC chairman, the speech is most unusual.
It publicly draws attention to the AM/FM struggle. It admits
that most manufacturers may not be sabotaging FM but are
doing something close to sabotage. It substantiates Armstrong's charge that the lush postwar market would be given
over to AM by involving FM in engineering problems that
would prevent much broadcasting and discourage manufacturers and listeners alike. The fact that his prediction was
made almost two years before war's end indicates the ability
of the FM camp to see behind the various reasons given for
FCC and industry moves. In other words, regardless of the
reasons given for the actions which affected FM technically
and economically, the result was that FM did miss the postwar
market, as AM manufacturers turned out an "unprecedented
quantity of low-priced AM sets."

Further speeches during this period by the FCC commissioners foresee a glowing future for FM. Two in particular
are noteworthy: they envision 1000 stations on the air within
twelve months. Since there were at least this many applications
in the hands of the FCC, it is a mystery why they did not
get on the air. By 1947, Denny had become FCC Chairman,
and he stated at a meeting of the FM Association in January
of that year, "Today, there are 136 FM stations on the air. . . .
By the end of 1947, I expect that there will be more than
700 FM stations on the air."[14]

His predictions were based, he explained, on the number
of applications pending with the commission and the fact that
they would be processed by Christmas (some eleven months
later). Since he was the Chairman of the FCC, it was assumed
he knew what he was talking about. However, at the end
of the twelve-month period, by January 1948, there were only
278 FM stations operating. Denny's prediction had been wrong
by over 400 stations. In September, 1947, Paul A. Walker,
FCC Commissioner, gave another speech to the FM Associa-

tion in New York. The rosy prediction came again, almost in the same words, "... we have 278 FM stations on the air.... One year from today the number of FM stations on the air should be upwards of 1000."[15] In this same speech, vice-chairman Walker discussed the state of the equipment changeover process that was so badly delaying FM actually broadcasting in its new higher frequencies. Of the fact that the 1945 predictions of up to three years of delay, due to equipment problems, was coming true, Walker said:

> First, the trickle of transmitting equipment is changing to a highly encouraging volume.
> Second, another problem has been the scarcity of FM receiving sets. Manufacturers delayed tooling up for FM while they concentrated on AM sets. That market is now becoming glutted.... Dealers and broadcasters all over the nation are crying for these FM sets. Only about 600,000 FM sets have been produced so far this year... while the industry expects to produce 15,000,000 AM sets.[16]

Again we must assume that Commissioner Walker used statistics gathered within the FCC for his prediction of 1000 stations on the air by the end of 1948. There were 587 FM stations on the air at the close of the year and 1020 authorizations (of which 800 were held by AM licensees).[17] FM receivers in use at this time were estimated at about two million.

Meanwhile, Major Armstrong was busy setting up new demonstrations to show that FM not only worked well in the lower band from which it had been taken but also was capable of long distance communications. Marconi, just before his death in 1937, had made a major discovery in radio-wave propagation—that microwaves could be bent so that the signal would be heard far beyond the transmitting point. It had been believed that the shorter waves were limited to a line-of-sight to the horizon. Armstrong knew of Marconi's theory but was not aware that it had been published. Armstrong decided to try an experiment that would be at once dramatic and lay to rest the idea that FM was a limited service.

Certain layers of the atmosphere act like mirrors and radio waves which strike them are bounced back to the earth. Today this method is known as "scatter" transmission and has been highly developed. FM transmissions in this area were built into this country's early warning system known as the DEWline, which spans the Arctic defenses. The army found it could use FM for distances up to 800 miles by using FM shortwaves.

So, in 1947, Armstrong sent a mobile crew into the South while he beamed, in a great arc, FM signals from his Alpine, New Jersey station:

> . . . . And some 1000 miles away in Alabama, as his hunch had led him to suspect, the crew plucked out of the air, somewhat attenuated but still clear, the signal from Alpine. Later in 1947 he put on a demonstration with Jansky and Bailey, Inc., consulting engineers, from Alpine to the International Telecommunications and Radio Conference at Atlantic City that year.
>
> . . . . But in 1947 the dictum was that for all practical purposes the ultra-shortwaves were limited to the horizon, and neither the FCC nor the big radio industry wanted to hear any scientific facts to the contrary. Both were preoccupied with television and with an internal struggle for power in which business expediency joined with technical half-truths to create one of the major engineering botches of the century. The FM petition to retain some high-power stations in its old band was denied, and all Armstrong's careful work went for nothing. Almost at the same time the FCC rendered a last fateful decision on television. In a bitter squabble, the argument had been reopened that television should be moved before it was too late out of its inadequate twelve channels into the higher frequencies. And again RCA took the position that anyone arguing these unpalatable truths was anti-RCA, anti-television, and probably un-American.
>
> . . . . In a final brief . . . before the FCC in October 1947, Armstrong made a sweeping attack . . . on the whole manner in which the FCC engineering department was allocating frequencies to both FM and TV. He charged that the whole engineering basis of their placement was unsound. He warned that TV stations in particular were being placed too closely together. . . . He pointed out again that beyond-the-horizon transmissions in these frequencies, which he had demonstrated, would cause serious interference between stations. . . .

.... Early in June, 1947, a sizzling letter of complaint had been written to the FCC's new chairman, Charles R. Denny, by Zenith Radio's President, E. F. McDonald.... "The interference now plaguing television on this band... is trivial compared to what will happen when new stations now authorized take the air.... Two injustices have been done, and both television and FM have been seriously injured as a result of engineering errors of 1945. Why not face the facts and correct the situation now, before further damage is done? You can do so by moving television immediately to its ultimate permanent home you have provided in frequencies above 500 megacycles." This letter was buried in the FCC's files, along with an engineering report of the same date by one of its own engineers, turned up later in a Congressional investigation, which warned that television's interference troubles were likely to grow unless allocations were shifted to a sound basis.[18]

What was being argued was the by now old question of the best place to put a national broadcasting service that would serve the entire nation and do it with good quality. FM had been moved out of the so-called terrible interference band for its own good. However, the television group, RCA being the most interested party, did not feel this band, full of skywave and ionospheric problems, was bad for television at all. In FCC hearings in 1947, the commission decided that the lower channels would stay as they were. They took away channel 1 (former home of FM) from television and reassigned it to emergency services without the slightest worry about sunspot troubles. The chairman of the FCC during these decisions was Charles R. Denny:

Three months after rendering this bracing series of decisions, FCC Chairman Denny was hired to be a vice president and general counsel of the National Broadcasting Company, RCA's subsidiary, at a salary of some $30,000 a year. As a result of this and similar cases, Congress belatedly passed a law designed to restrain federal employees of regulatory bodies from resigning to accept positions in the industry being regulated.[19]

This same instance was discussed in the 1948 Senate investigation of FM, and RCA was asked about the hiring of a number

of federal employees, including a former executive of the U.S.
patent office:

Senator Tobey: When did you first learn that Charles R. Denny,
former Chairman of the Commission, was to become one of your
associates in NBC?

. . . .

Dr. Jolliffe: When he announced his resignation and acceptance
at the time that I got official notice of it. However, I had partici-
pated in the negotiations bringing him into the corporation.

Senator Tobey: When did you first talk to him about his new
post as vice president and general counsel?

Dr. Jolliffe: The nearest I can place the time, sometime in September, 1947.

. . . .

Senator Tobey: Did you know at the time you attended the Atlantic
City Telecommunications Conference, over which Mr. Denny
presided, that he was to become your associate in NBC?

Dr. Jolliffe: Not until I proposed the matter to him late in the
conference.

. . . .

Senator Tobey: When did Mr. Henry—C. C. Henry—Assistant
Commissioner of Patents, become an employee of the RCA, if
you know?

Dr. Jolliffe: I don't remember the dates. Maybe you can give it.

Mr. Coe: I think it was . . . in 1946.

. . . .

Senator Tobey: What were the attractive and valuable qualities
that Mr. Denny possessed that caused you to take him out of
his chairmanship into this lucrative job of 30 to 35 thousand dollars
with RCA or NBC. . . .

Dr. Jolliffe: He is a very capable, very excellent administrator,
very good grasp of communications law, which we wanted.[20]

When, in 1947, the commission refused to move TV to
the upper frequencies which it had set aside for this expansion
in 1945, it still continued to approve the applications of TV
stations to go on the air. As more and more stations crowded
into the twelve channels known as VHF, the interference
grew to impossible proportions. Since radio waves travel so
well at night, these shorter waves of both the AM picture
portion of TV, and the shorter waves of the FM sound portion

of TV were doing exactly as Armstrong had demonstrated with his transmissions to Alabama and to Atlantic City. Both he and Zenith Radio, plus one of their own engineers, had warned the FCC of this. By 1948, the crowded TV spectrum had so much interference, and there were so many TV applications pending, that the FCC decided to "freeze" everything while it studied the situation.

In June 1947 Zenith's president had sent the letter to the FCC pleading with it to "correct the situation" before it got worse. Their answer was to leave things as they were, to not move TV, and to authorize more TV stations. In the FCC history of broadcasting, they describe this period as follows:

> In 1945 the Commission allocated 13 VHF (Very High Frequency) channels between 44 and 216 megacycles for commercial television. In doing so, it pointed out that there was insufficient spectrum space below megacycles for an adequate nationwide and competitive TV broadcasting system. Twelve of these channels were to be shared with certain non-broadcast (fixed and mobile) services. At the same time, that portion of the UHF (Ultra High Frequency) spectrum between 480 and 920 megacycles was made available for experimental TV operation looking to future TV expansion, and between 1245 and 1325 megacycles for TV relay.
>
> In 1948, because of interference to commercial TV operation, the Commission stopped the sharing of television VHF channels with other services, and deleted TV channel No. 1 (44–55 mc) by assigning it to the non-broadcast services affected.
>
> As predicted by the Commission . . . it became increasingly evident that the few available VHF channels were inadequate to provide a truly nationwide competitive TV service. Also, operating stations developed interference which had not been anticipated when TV broadcasting began. As a result the Commission on September 30, 1948 stopped granting new TV stations pending a study of the situation. This was the so-called TV "Freeze" order.[21]

Again, it is evident from the wording that the FCC was stepping in to help a situation that had grown like Topsy. Though there was little reason for their inclusion, the 1947 hearings are not discussed or even alluded to. It is not suggested that the FCC did, in fact, have warnings fourteen months earlier that interference had developed and would get worse. Nor does this authorized history discuss the fact that the FCC, one year earlier, went through this same investigation and, under the leadership of their chairman, Denny, created the situation that had indeed grown worse in the ensuing fourteen months.

Early UHF TV had the same economic problems as FM. All the best VHF channels (2 through 13) were already assigned to the major mass consumer markets. The TV networks, notably CBS and NBC, had important key-market affiliates by this time. When a new UHF station went on the air in these lush advertising markets, it found no network with which it could affiliate and, therefore, lost the competitive advantage of the highly professional network shows that attracted so many advertisers. It was this situation and various charges against RCA monopoly practices which led Senator Tobey to instigate the Senate investigation on FM and RCA patent policies. And it was Senator Tobey who suggested that Chairman Denny's influence in gaining decisions favorable to the Radio Corporation of America, and his subsequent employment by them, was more than a coincidence.

The open and unabashed warfare between the FM group and those whom they considered their mortal enemies, namely, the AM radio industry and the FCC, was hardly disguised by this time. A Washington newsletter, the *Capitol Radio Reporter*, made the following remarks concerning the Denny move from the FCC to RCA in October, 1947:

> A sad case of jitters has settled over the FCC. It was caused by the fact of the Denny resignation which will become effective on October 31. Many or most of the prominent and important positions in the FCC are there by reason of Denny backing even some of the Commissioners. Any change in FCC policies would necessarily require a substantial shakeup among those in top FCC jobs....
>
> ....
>
> Now there is a very real and compelling need for a truly good man on the FCC. He should be a man thoroughly adherent to

our system who would be just as determined to protect constitutional rights as to administer the law. A man of the type of Judge
Justin Miller would be ideal. Such a man would provide the needed
balance of power to get the FCC back on the track.

.... As Chairman Denny leaves the FCC he leaves a Commission
over which he has sat as "Boss-Man." Substantially the FCC is
staffed in important positions by those he selected and who are
beholden to him for their jobs. The FCC is following policies
largely formulated by Mr. Denny and his appointees. Now he
goes to NBC as a Vice-President and General Counsel under the
duty to advance the interests of NBC. An extremely delicate situation is presented by reason of these facts. The doors are wide
open for a situation that could be scandalous. The utmost care
on the part of the FCC and NBC will be required or the whole
will burst open with a scandal of major proportions.[22]

And a scandal of major proportions is exactly what followed
as the 80th Congress, in its closing session, voted two separate
investigations of the FCC: one by the Senate and one by
the House.

In the Armstrong vs. Emerson trial of 1958, Dr. Edward
L. Bowles, a communications consultant with the Raytheon
Company, testified about this period of FM/television confusion and the role of the FCC. Bowles had been with MIT
from 1920 until 1947 when he went with Raytheon. In 1956
the Senate Foreign Commerce Committee asked him to make
a study of the overall problems of television:

> ... and I have spent an inordinate amount of time on that
> problem, because it not only became engrossing but it turned
> out to be vital in my opinion as a problem of public interest
> and importance.... That report was published I believe on the
> 25th of this last September, and comprises some almost 300
> pages but it actually amounts to a critical survey of 16 years of
> television regulation, and deals not simply with the technical
> aspects but with the economic, social and political aspects of
> the problems facing the nation today.
> ....
> Q. Is it not true that the FCC has made special effort to increase
>   the use of FM because FM frequencies were going begging?
> A. I wish I could agree with you on that statement, but my own

feeling—and this is based on the study I have just made for the Senate—is that the FCC handled the UHF problems as I am bound to believe that it mishandled FM after the war. I don't believe it gave it a chance, a reasonable chance.

Q. What did it do wrong in that respect?

A. Comparable to UHF, and I would draw a comparison in the instance of UHF, it dedicated itself, or at least declared it was in the public interest to have 70 UHF channels to encourage TV at UHF; and at the same time, granting it was its decision, and it was a public declaration and it was the law once it was issued, it proceeded to permit VHF stations to go on the air though it was clear from the record that the UHF could not live in the climate of VHF.

Some 70 stations went off the air, costing something like $300,000 apiece, and 1952 to 1958 precious little has been done to meet this problem.

After the war, with respect to FM, they again accepted and encouraged this ratio of applications for AM stations, and had they really wanted to make FM work they could very well have held back and encouraged the FM licenses. You will find this discussed even in the Commission's sixth report and order, by some of the Commissioners themselves, who resented it strongly because of the treatment of FM.

Q. Are you saying that the Commission favored AM over FM after the war?

A. I am raising a question of their judgment of how to promote an interest when they declare it to be a public interest.

Q. There were a lot of applications by FM broadcast stations after the war, were there not?

A. There were many for all three services.

Q. Were they more slowly applied for with respect to AM than FM?

A. It is a question of the Commission really endorsing FM and trying to ensure its success, and my feeling is that it did not.

Q. Didn't it grant the applications for FM stations just as fast as the applications for AM?

A. My opinion is that it could have proceeded less rapidly with the AM stations with the idea of encouraging the growth of FM.

Q. You think they would have been better advised to grant the FM applications more speedily and hold back on the AM applications?

A. If they meant to have it succeed. The same thing happened with UHF. We are in the same situation today, and it is almost inextricable.

Q. What are they doing wrong up there?

A. As you may be aware, they established in their own laws and public acts, by law, that it was in the public interest to have 70 television channels in addition to the 12 VHF channels, and that they would put these in the UHF segment of the spectrum. Now this came out as a public document or declaration in the sixth report and order of April 1952. . . . They began to implement that in the summer. The Commission even though declaring these stations in the public interest, went contrary to the advice, predominately the advice, from the industry not to mix VHF and UHF channels. They were unwilling to take any steps with regard to the VHF channels or stations already on the air, and elected therefore to intermix stations, and hurdling some of the details, there has been a series of hearings since then to try to get to the bottom of the problem.

There have been many, many contests, going up to the courts. The courts by law as I understand it pass on the Commission's decisions only in so far as those decisions are in violation of the statutes or the constitutional provisions; they cannot pass on the Commission's expertise or knowledge or ability. In other words, they cannot pass on the wisdom of its judgment.

The end result is that the Commission has been relatively free to do pretty much as it sees fit. The Commission has been strongly divided on these matters, and the end result is that although they have had this intermixture problem under consideration ever since the power hearings back in 1954, practically nothing has been done about it, because there are these strong differences of opinion within the Commission, and it is simply my judgment that the Commission did not have the courage at the time to follow the recommendations of the industry—and I am talking about our large industry as well as small industry—not to intermix. The burden of what I say here is simply that the Commission's actions can have a great deal to do with the success or failure of a communications facility.

. . . .

Q. Has the FCC made many mistakes in its career, in your judgment?

. . . .

A. I made an examination for the Senate Committee on this matter and I feel competent to discuss that because I have gone into great detail, and granted, it is a matter of judgment, and in my judgment and those of the majority of my committee, they have taken some real action that should have been taken and others that should have not been taken.[23]

The following table substantiates Dr. Bowles' charge that the FCC did, in fact, show preference for AM authorizations after the war while it processed FM applications slowly (even though over 1000 applications were pending).

COMPARISON OF AM AND FM STATIONS AUTHORIZED BY FCC

YEAR	AM GRANTED	FM GRANTED
1949	200	57
1950	194	35
1951	116	15
1952	60	24
1953	187	29
1954	148	27
1955	161	27
1956	197	31

Source: FCC Thirty-third Annual Report, p. 162.

With all this, yet another FM battle was brewing, only this one was to go into the courts. Though some companies were paying Armstrong royalties on the manufacture of FM sets, RCA and its associated groups of companies were not. But they were making FM sets. RCA had developed its own set of FM patents beginning with 1936, the year after Armstrong moved his equipment out of their Empire State labs. Until then, no one in the radio industry had ever challenged Armstrong's position as the inventor of FM. Part of the patents Armstrong held on FM included specifications on just how the system was to be accomplished; that is, for FM to work as Armstrong patented it (and the FCC had set the same legal standards as Armstrong's), the equipment must be built a certain way with certain circuits and other engineering criteria met. Anything less or different than this was not Armstrong's wide swing frequency modulation.

One of the things RCA did to get around this was to develop FM systems which did the same things as Armstrong's, but by different methods. One of these methods, was to telescope into one tube what two tubes did. Then RCA patented the result as their own FM system. Armstrong published a paper on this in 1948, analyzing the RCA development and showing that it embodied no new principle at all.[24] He charged RCA and those companies licensed by them (including Philco, Admiral, Motorola, Emerson, and other giants of the industry) were producing FM sets and TV sets (with FM sound systems) of an inferior nature. And so, in July of 1948, he instituted a suit against RCA and NBC in the Federal Court of Delaware charging them with willfully infringing and inducing others to infringe five of the basic FM patents.

The legal aspects of this suit began in February of 1949 in the offices of Armstrong's law firm. This was not a litigation trial before a judge, but a procedure known as pre-trial discovery. It is used in federal cases, and patent problems fall into that category. The "discovery" procedure is one in which the two parties in conflict are allowed to discuss in detail the evidence and exhibits that they hope to use in the trial itself. They are allowed to requisition from each other all the various papers, documents, witnesses, and the like, to see of what use these materials may be, and to decide, further, which of these materials will be used in the trial itself. The reasoning is that this rather unusual procedure will save time, and therefore money, in the trial itself. The procedure allows the parties to forestall any in-trial surprises for which they may not be prepared with proper answers and evidence. It saves money, since the two parties do all this with only a notary public present and a record is kept of the pre-trial meetings. The vast amounts of money and time used up during a trial by the lawyers' fees, court costs, and judge's hours are thus spared the two parties—and the taxpayers. If, in a few weeks or months, the parties in conflict can gather what evidence they need and agree what is to be presented, the length of court trial may be reduced by weeks, or even months. The duration of this particular pre-trial procedure from 1949 until December 1954 (almost six years) indicates that something very unusual was taking place, since the whole idea was to reduce the court trial time to a few weeks at the most. Evidence of the more normal time involved in the Armstrong infringement suits may be seen from the trial time of the Armstrong vs. Emerson suit (involving the identical charges and arguments)—not quite five weeks.

The amount of money spent by both RCA and Armstrong over the six years ran to approximately $1,000,000. Since money and time are the essence of the discovery procedure, obviously there were other reasons for the unusual length of time involved. An explanation put forth by Armstrong's lawyer is that if RCA could possibly stall for a great period of time they would accomplish two very important goals. First, Armstrong would have to pay all the expenses for the pre-trial out of his own pocket, using his personal fortune. RCA, on the other hand, would be able to pay for the time out of corporate funds, which were not only easily available, but continually replenished (and tax deductible). Thus this "wearing down" period would remove one of the major means of fighting a court battle of this scope—without money it simply could not be done. With money gone, the pre-trial period would have to end for Armstrong. The personal deterioration caused by such costly delays would also aid the opposing side.

Second, if the pre-trial discovery did what it was supposed to do (that is, get the court trial over quickly), and if RCA lost, RCA would not only have to pay damages on FM sets produced; they would also have an injunction put on them to stop manufacturing FM sets under their present set-up. However, if the litigation could be delayed and delayed until the FM patents ran out, and RCA lost, even though RCA would still have to pay damages, during the delaying period (in this case, six years), there could be no injunction to stop them from manufacturing FM sets as long as the pre-trial questioning was going on. Only with a decision in favor of Armstrong, during the actual patented period, could a "stop manufacturing" injunction be applied. Though most of Armstrong's FM patents were to run out in 1950, one later and important patent was not due to expire until 1957.[25] Since there was the chance that RCA would lose the trial, they stood to gain at least more money by paying out the smaller court costs of the pre-trial than by allowing an injunction to prevent them from manufacturing any FM radio sets. (And RCA television sets all embodied FM sound systems too.) But how does one stretch over six years what the federal government assumes takes but a few weeks, or, at the most, months? There are in the Armstrong Memorial Research Foundation offices in New York City, twelve normal office storage cabinets, each containing four drawers filled with the testimony and exhibits of this period. The testimony alone fills fifty-six volumes. Lessing summarizes the period as an endurance contest that was to drag on through the next few years and terminate only with the life of Armstrong:

> Under the rules of the procedure, Edwin Howard Armstrong as plaintiff was the first witness to be put in the chair to be examined by RCA's legal forces. And in that chair he was to be kept for an entire year, like an aging lion set upon by midges, to be pricked and chevvied, ragged and goaded.
>
> .... It must be remembered that the gentlemen of law were here addressing the man whose basic electronic-circuit inventions had created the industry on which they lived, otherwise the full acrid flavor of the proceedings cannot be savored. It may be said that the gentlemen were only following legal forms, but if these forms nowhere touch life and reality they become mere grisly charades. Counsel then proceeded to take the witness through the minutiae of the FM patents on which he based his claims of invention, particularly the four key patents that issued simultaneously on the singular day in 1933 and the reissue patent of 1940, in all of which, particularly in the coincidence of issue, the defense seemed to see something of a dark portentous nature.

"Of course, you understand, counsel," said Armstrong at one point, in his dry, ironic drawl, "that I am only claiming to have invented something which is a matter of record in the Patent Office some fifteen years ago." And an invention which in the first five years of its existence was ignored or depreciated by that same industry which was now challenging the right of the inventor to his rewards.[26]

Later, in 1949, while the RCA forces were presenting evidence to show that they had invented FM and that Major Armstrong had not, *Broadcasting Magazine* was referring to Armstrong as the inventor of FM, simply in passing, in articles they were publishing on the state of FM:

Belief that FCC would abandon its proposal to boost FM's minimum operating hours—or use it as a vehicle for a far-reaching hearing—developed last week in the wake of a flood of protests from FM broadcasters, including FM inventor Edwin H. Armstrong.[27]

Jack Gould, writing in the *New York Times*, also in 1949, refers to Armstrong casually as the inventor in an article on FM's growing financial crisis. Though Gould's opinion hardly represents legal proof of an invention, his comments do indicate the general acceptance of Armstrong as inventor.

But why FM was "too late" goes to the heart of the controversy surrounding the medium even today. Actually, Major Edwin H. Armstrong first announced his invention of modern FM as far back as 1935. Although his development of the regenerative and superheterodyne circuits obviously entitled him to the highest professional respect, many engineers, both in government and industry, belittled the Major's latest invention. This was the start of a continuous series of delays for FM.[28]

Gould, in this short quote, touches on two other interesting points. First, the *New York Times* critic publicly acknowledges, fifteen years after the Supreme Court decision gave Lee De Forest the right to claim regeneration as his invention, that the communications industry still regards Armstrong as the inventor. Second, he acknowledges that the industry is quite aware of the "delays" that were "continuous" and that the FCC and the AM industry did "belittle" FM every chance they got.

In spite of this non-legal acceptance of Armstrong as the inventor of FM, RCA and the twenty other companies sued for infringement, still contended he was not the inventor. In the pre-trial discovery proceedings, RCA asked Armstrong detailed questions on why he did his own bookkeeping, what banks he dealt with and just how did he make out his deposit slips. They wanted to know in what way he had promoted FM across the country, before what groups, the size of the groups, and the type of auditorium he had spoke in:

> . . . . Still another preposterous session was spent inquiring into an oval insignia bearing the words "Armstrong FM," which some FM licensees carried on their FM sets. Why was it oval, and who had thought of it and why, the defense wanted to know. Of what relevancy all this was to the issues, except as a time-killer and harrassment, was never apparent to the rational eye, but behind it was the steady, goading implication that the inventor was somehow up to some wrong in promoting and attempting to make a profit from his own invention.
>
> . . . . The record became so burdened with outrageous and vindictive irrelevancies that it was finally appealed by Armstrong's attorney. . . to the ruling court in Delaware, which summarily cut it off at the end of a year. It then became the turn of Armstong's legal forces to dig into the RCA record. And in this pursuit [they] secured from the District Court one of the broadest rulings ever made in a suit of this kind: that the defendants be required to produce from their files every record, letter, report, memorandum, and paper having any reference to FM. The interrogation arising from this monumental flood of paper consumed most of the next two years, for plainly developed from the files were all the shiftings, backings and fillings of RCA policy on FM over the years.[29]

In February, 1953, RCA president David Sarnoff took the stand and was asked to give, in his own words, some of the history of FM and radio broadcasting in general. However, under some rather pointed probing of matters about which he evidently did not wish to be too specific, Sarnoff became irritated:

As the questioning probed on to find out what exactly was RCA's role in the discovery and development of FM, Sarnoff exploded, "I will go further," he stated, "and I will say that the RCA and the NBC have done more to develop FM than anybody in this country, including Armstrong."

At this unparalleled assertion, according to one of the lawyers present, Armstrong's eyes flashed a low flame of pure hatred....[30]

While these proceedings dragged on, the FM industry was itself having a bad time. The thousand applications for FM stations that had come into the FCC offices just after the war had all but ceased by 1949. The optimism of the FM broadcasters and would-be FM broadcasters had faded. Not only were requests for new FM stations practically non-existent, but FM stations on the air were starting to go off the air. The reason was simply that there was no money from advertisers. Financial data on FM for this period are both sketchy and erroneous. Most dollar figures are all "educated guesses," both from the FCC and the industry. The only factual figures available are on the number of stations on the air, under construction, applying for a permit, or going off the air. No really useful economic data on FM appear from the FCC until 1953. At this time industry-wide figures were released on revenues and losses. However, FM financial data is always broken down into two groups: the independent FM station(s) and the AM/FM station(s). This is because only independent FM stations are required to give a complete breakdown of cost of operation, revenues, incomes, and losses. It is assumed that an AM/FM operation cannot make detailed cost accounting analyses of their dual operations since it is too difficult to assign costs (direct and indirect) to shared office space, personnel, equipment, and such things as rent, light, heat, etc., between their AM and FM operations.

Only the independent FM station financial reports reflect a true FM operation. And these stations, a minority of the total FM stations, have shown a consistent industry-wide loss from the beginning to the present day. In a footnote included in the yearly broadcasting data release, the FCC states that:

In view of the difficulty in a joint AM-FM operation in allocating FM operation expense separately from AM station operation expense, licensees of such stations were not required to report FM station expense separately. As a result, FM industry totals for expense and income are not available. AM-FM licensees, however, were requested to report separately the revenues, if any, attributable to FM station operation.[31]

In 1957 the FCC began to release much more detailed information on radio broadcasting data. At this time they separated the television financial data from the radio financial data and published separate reports on them. However, most of the tables of information are devoted to AM radio figures or to broadcasting totals that include AM and FM and also some tables including TV/AM/FM. As an example of the lack of FM broadcasting statistics, of the thirteen pages that make up the 1965 Radio Broadcast Service data, only a page and a half of information is devoted to FM only. The rest is combined AM and FM figures and/or radio network figures.[32]

Critics have found, even in the reporting of FM financial data, yet another "devil" created to hurt the FM art, and to help the AM camp. It harks back to earlier criticism of the fact that an AM operator was allowed to own an FM station in the first place. The argument goes as follows: An FCC declaration, supposed to serve the public interest, is that no one man or firm should have a monopoly on the "idea" market of a community. This is because a community having a newspaper, a TV station, an AM station, and an FM station all owned by the same man or firm cannot be regarded as a community served by a variety of interests. The fact that many smaller communities have exactly that situation, or one close to it, is one of the reasons for the Congressional investigations over the years on newspaper ownership of broadcast facilities. This fact also has resulted in investigations of ownership of broadcast facilities by Congressmen themselves. Earlier it was pointed out that an FCC investigation revealed that, in 90 percent of the communities with only one radio station, that station was owned by the local newspaper. Since newspapers and radio stations both rely on the same advertising dollar for their income, it is not too hard to understand why a newspaper wants to own its advertising competition. Further, a newspaper/radio operation would take the same financial interest in owning any local TV station that might be assigned to its area. Not only does this arrangement restrict the "freedom of speech" concept held to be so essential to the democratic process, it has a further fault. It takes "fair play" completely out of the picture as far as the so-called free enterprise system is concerned. That is, we do not have two or three or four independent businessmen competing for the advertising dollar in a community. The competition engendered by a newspaper, a television station, an AM station, and an FM station all separately owned would, according to theory at least, make all of them perform better in order to gain the advertising dollar needed to run them.

When the above four facilities, or three, or two, are owned by one person or group, the advertising dollars all flow to that one source. Thus, incentive for improvement and innovation can hardly be high, and, the public can hardly be served by this communication monopoly. Law forbids single ownership of two TV stations in the same community, as it forbids single ownership of two AM stations, or two FM stations, in the same community. But, and most strangely, the law allows the same person to own an AM and an FM station in the same community. It has been this way so long that the public has forgotten the inconsistency—that is, if the public ever realized the inconsistency in the first place. AM and FM are not the same thing. They also are in competition with each other. They are both broadcasting facilities requiring separate equipment to send them and receive them (though the receiver may be built to encompass them both). By 1967, most AM/FM operations were required by the FCC to broadcast at least 50 percent of their programming as non-duplicated programs. That means that an AM/FM station must have separate programming going out over the air half the time. This rule is one of the few the FCC has been able to pass that will eventually make FM the service it was intended to be back in the 1930's. It is a slow step to what is called the "100 percent non-duplication" of programming. It is slow because there are so many opponents to it, and with good reason.

When an AM/FM operation must finally program the two stations completely separately, a paradox will follow. A broadcaster may not own, in the same community, two similar broadcasting facilities. At least that is the rule now. If he does, it will be the same as if he owned two radio stations in the same town. He would own his AM station, broadcasting on the lower frequencies, and his FM station, broadcasting on the higher frequencies. Rules forbid his owning a television VHF and television UHF station in the same community, and, therefore, something will have to be done when AM and FM are, indeed, separately programmed.

If the rule still holds, the station owner will have to sell one of his licenses. By this time, perhaps sometime in the 1970's or 1980's, FM, and especially stereo FM, will probably be the predominant radio broadcast service. If it is, it will also be the predominant money maker. Then the AM owners, who for years gave FM radio time away free as a bonus to advertisers, will probably turn their backs on AM and sell that license. Another possibility is that a well organized lobby in Washington will get the law changed so that AM/FM operators can keep both stations. Actually, all that need be done is to convince the FCC such a change is in the public interest. A third possibility is that FM will finally supplant all AM broadcasting and turn this band over to other services. A fourth, and perhaps the most realistic possibility is that AM/FM ownership will be separated and that AM and FM will both continue as *the* total radio service for the nation. The NAFMB believes that AM and FM should both continue to serve the nation, since, by itself, neither service has enough space in the spectrum to give a really national and universal radio service. The NAFMB would rather see the FCC treat AM and FM as one radio service and create whatever rules necessary to make AM and FM more equal in competition. They would even have the letters "F" and "M" dropped from the call letters of FM stations so that the advertiser would choose his stations by the market and coverage patterns, by the merits of a station, and not by whether it was an FM station or an AM station.

The fact that the FCC did give so many licenses to the AM people has been a source of bitter criticism over the years. It was felt that the AM people wanted the FM license just to keep someone else from getting it. Once an AM owner had the FM permit, he could do as he pleased with the station. And if the FM industry was made up primarily of AM interests, there was going to be no healthy FM industry. The argument goes even further, explaining the many ways an AM owner can keep FM from becoming a really competitive service. The duplicated programming is a way of doing exactly this, since it gives the listener no incentive to buy an FM receiver (since the listener may hear the same program "free" over AM—minus the high fidelity, of course). With few FM receivers in a market, the advertiser sticks to AM which can guarantee saturation of the radio market.

The low economic state of FM in 1949 is summarized in the FCC annual report:

> During the year the number of FM stations on the air increased by 150, bringing the total on June 30, 1949, to 737. . . . While construction planned by many FM broadcast stations was completed during the year, many of them decided not to install high powered equipment because of economic problems; in addition many found that the coverage provided by their lower powered installations exceeded expectations and was adequate for their area.
>
> Although FM service was expanded by previously authorized stations commencing operation and by existing stations improving their facilities, the rate of filing of new FM applications fell off sharply during the year . . . only 43 applications for new FM stations were filed during the twelve-month period.
>
> Also, the total number of FM stations authorized decreased from 1,020 to 865. This reduction was largely due to economic problems and uncertainties; the relatively small number of FM receivers owned by the public and the resulting limited audience

to attract substantial broadcast advertising revenue; competition from standard AM broadcast and TV stations (as well as other FM stations); and high costs of station construction. . . . Although most FM stations are at present operating at a deficit, only a few stations ceased operation during the year. Approximately 80 percent of FM stations are operated in conjunction with standard broadcast (AM) stations and operating expenses are thus minimized.

At the end of the fiscal year, approximately 3,500,000 FM receivers were in use.[33]

With this historical and economic setting in mind, it will be easier to see how the AM station may benefit by the particular information which it is required *not* to turn in to the FCC on its financial statements. Because the AM/FM operators do not have to include expenses or income, they can, if they choose, bury in their bookkeeping whatever they choose to, as far as the costs are concerned. That is, FM may be assigned greater expenses than it actually incurred. Thus, the FM operation may show a great loss which can then be used in tax figuring to cut the total tax figure paid to the government. In this way, since the FM tax loss is deductible, the profits of the AM stations are increased.

In the earlier quote from the FCC annual report on the state of FM in 1949 and 1950, it was pointed out several times that the major reason for this depressing market picture was the economic plight of the struggling FM stations. In spite of the decline in FM applications, and in spite of the decline in the number of FM stations on the air, the FCC in November, 1949, proposed the increase of minimum operating hours during which an FM station must be on the air. At first, of course, it would seem that the FM broadcasters would be delighted to give more of the highly praised service to the public. In fact, it would seem that an effort by the FCC to help FM grow prompted them to announce the compulsory increase in FM airtime.

However, the industry did not regard the increase as a blessing. Almost to a man, the industry revolted. With the dreary economic picture just painted for this period, and with the FCC annual report to back up the fact that the industry was, indeed, in serious economic trouble, it was impossible to believe the FCC would now turn around and put into law a requirement that would increase expenses even more. It seemed, to some, that a devil had gotten into the FCC and had been able to dictate the doom of FM. Among this group was *Broadcasting* magazine which, in one of its most sarcastic and damning editorials, said:

> The FCC, which has loved FM wildly, if not well, is now in danger of cherishing it to death. For the proposal to increase FM's minimum operating hours . . . far from spurring development of the new medium, could easily bring its downfall.
>
> It is not the first time FCC's passions have got out of hand. To begin with, it should be no concern of the Commission if a station operates six hours or 16. The individual broadcaster is in a position to judge whether there are sets enough to justify longer or shorter broadcast days. The Commission, in all its wisdom, can make no such seat-of-the-pants determination.
>
> . . . . In FM's present unprofitable state such a requirement not only would doom many an FM station, but would raise a serious threat to their AM partners. The danger to FM-only stations, with no AM revenues to fall back on, would be as great or worse.
>
> . . . . The wonder is that FCC hasn't read the handwriting of some 175 licensees and permittees who have turned in their FM authorizations already this year . . .
>
> . . . . The first big job NAB could do for FM is to come out strongly against the disastrous plan. Otherwise the medium . . . which the Commission has long hailed as "the best system of aural broadcasting extant," is apt to become the best one extinct.[34]

Major Armstrong was moved to comment that the FCC might hold a hearing "if only to determine whether the medicine which the Commission is proposing to administer to FM broadcasting will not kill rather than cure the patient."[35]

The year 1949 was not a good one for the reputation of the FCC. Earlier, a headline in the *New York Times* ran: "FCC FAILS PUBLIC, SENATOR CHARGES." The story reported that the:

> Senate was told by the chairman of its Commerce Regulating

Committee ... that the Federal Communications Commission was playing into the hands of radio and television. ...

Senator Edwin C. Johnson, Democrat of Colorado, broke unexpectedly into Senate consideration of the National Housing Bill to charge that the FCC had "failed utterly" to protect the public interest.

... he made these accusations:

1. That the FCC, while practicing an "alarming degree of absenteeism" (attending international conferences and addressing industry gatherings) was being run by its legal and engineering staff. "This commission was hired to make tough decisions ... not flattering speeches to the industry it regulates."
2. That the FCC staff, in turn, was "the captive" of the "high and mighty in the very industry the commission was created to regulate." Mr. Johnson added: "The plow horse has usurped the plow handles and seized the whip, and the commission is now pulling the plow."
3. That commission decisions were written, not by the commission itself, but by "the identical legal staff which prosecuted the case."
4. That those in the industry—broadcasting companies or their attorneys—caught criticizing the commission's operations "suddenly began to run into mysterious and exasperating delays" (in action on their applications and petitions).
5. That there was going on, with elements of the industry helping, a "surprisingly effective" realization in the transaction of the FCC of its power to "give or take away, to help or to hinder, to grant favors or deny them, to make or break a licensee, to build or destroy," some 2,000 small broadcasting stations throughout the country, Senator Johnson held, lived in "genuine fear" of obliteration and consequent lost investment.
6. That proposed investigations of the FCC had been weakened by a situation in which "the commission's staff is too adroit and cunning to permit a real investigation to take place."

.... As a group ... Senator Johnson contended they had "failed utterly in protecting the people against monopolistic exploitation by not blocking the plans of the conniving Clear Channel Lobby bent on radio domination, by not moving promptly to correct (an) earlier error in adopting a narrow television system which insured the control by a few patent-holding corporations, and by not formulating a television plan which would guarantee the widest and freest competition."[36]

Much of the history of FM was written in the East, mostly New York and Washington. However, the day-to-day struggle to keep the advertising dollar in the AM till, and to keep the AM interests in their role as "King of the Hill" was nation-wide. Typical of this widespread effort to belittle FM as a superior service is the effort of a Bloomington, Indiana station operator named Sarkes Tarzian. Tarzian was one of the witnesses against the Armstrong Estate in the Armstrong vs. Emerson patent infringement trial in 1958.

Mr. Tarzian was, and is, in the communications business. He owns both radio and TV stations and has manufactured electronic components. He worked for RCA from 1936 until 1944 in an engineering capacity. He left RCA to start his own radio and television broadcasting business in Bloomington. During his time with RCA he worked with FM and eventually published a paper entitled "Unpublicized Facts about FM." As the title suggests, the paper was unfavorable to FM.

Q. Did you prepare that paper before you left RCA?
A. Well, I had done quite a bit of preliminary work on it, and I had presented it to some of the key people in the management of RCA, and they felt they didn't want it publicized because of their relationship with the FCC, and they didn't want to do anything in any way to jeopardize that relationship because the FCC at that time was interested in pushing FM.
Q. Did the fact that you could not publish that paper have anything to do with your leaving RCA?
A. Well, that was one of the reasons. Also my wife egged me on for a number of years to do something on my own.
. . . .
Q. Did you operate any radio station shortly after you started in your new business?
A. Yes, my conviction was that you could do about the same thing from a practical standpoint with high-frequency AM broadcasting as you could do with FM. I felt, and I think it is the general consensus of opinion of those people who know, that as you go to the higher frequencies there is less of the man-made interferences that we experience on the broadcast band, and also the static that we have on the broadcast band is not as intensive at, say around 100 megacycles.

So in order to prove that, and since I was on my own, we requested the FCC for a permit to put up an experimental station....

....

Q. And how long did W9XHZ go on?

A. ... it operated until about 1949.

Q. Then you went off the air?

A. Yes.

Q. How did that happen?

A. We were assigned by the FCC to the closest frequency to the FM band that they could give us, and they picked the sound channel of channel 6, which was 87.75 megacycles, and at that time there were no TV stations in that area and there was very little interest on the part of any of the broadcasters to put up a TV station in the Indianapolis area, so they gave us the sound channel of channel 6, on which to operate, and that is where we operated until we went off the air.

Q. And did somebody get a TV allocation for that channel?

A. Yes...

....

Q. What audio frequency band did you transmit?

A. We transmitted as I recall from 30 to 10,000 cycles.

....

Q. This was amplitude modulation?

A. This was amplitude modulation.

Q. Did you actually operate that transmitter?

A. Yes, we operated, as I said, from about 1946 until 1949, and during that period, most of that period, Bloomington, Indiana, did not have a local radio station, so most people in the community were very much interested in our experiment; they bought converters and they bought low price receivers that we built for that purpose.

Q. Tell me about these converters and those low cost receivers.[37]

Mr. Tarzian then explained that his company manufactured both the receivers (for about $13.95) and the converters needed to hear the high frequency, and high fidelity, programs (for about $5.95). He called his AM high frequency system "HI-FAM" and claimed for it characteristics similar to those of FM. Though he admitted he had never made any direct comparisons of FM and HI-FAM, he maintained that his system was ultimately better since it was so cheap to build and less wasteful than FM of the frequency spectrum. He held some demonstrations for a group of FCC engineers who came to Bloomington; however, the FCC never became seriously interested in HI-FAM. As a result, Tarzian was not able to plan a future based on HI-FAM equipment built by him or a national high frequency broadcast service created with the use of his patents. The foregoing may help to explain a full-page ad he ran in the Bloomington *World-Telephone*, on June 1, 1949, discussing AM, FM, and TV:

The Radio and Television Center, WTTS-WTTV, Presents a Radio and Television Report.

"I think television is going to affect practically everything we now have....

"Bloomington will be the smallest city in the world to have a television station. We secured a permit many months ago because we believed then, and believe even stronger now, that television IS the medium of the future....

. . . .

FM radio sets have been on the market for three years but according to a recent local survey less than 3% of Monroe County residents have FM sets.

FM radio has been used as a supplement to AM radio. (Used by daytime-only AM stations to give night-time service).

FM radio sets cost more than AM sets and they require more service.

FM radio sets are subject to interference by automobile ignitions.

PEOPLE HAVE ASKED WHY WE DO NOT INVEST IN FM BROADCASTING. HERE ARE OUR REASONS:

1. Only a small percent of the public is able to receive FM.
2. In 1949 a total of 130 FM broadcasting outlets were withdrawn.
3. In 1949 (5 months) 96 additional FM broadcasting outlets have been withdrawn.
4. These withdrawals are largely due to television.
5. We feel that TV will eventually become dominant in the broadcast field.
6. Outstanding radio station owners are investing in television instead of FM....
7. The rapid month-to-month growth of television does not make FM economically feasible.
8. We want to give Bloomington the best, and we think that television is the best."

Sarkes Tarzian[38]

If one ignores the errors of grammar and construction, plus the errors of fact, it is easy to see how such publicity was not building, what is called today, the best "image" for FM. Tarzian's "months old" interest in TV indicates he no longer cared about HI-FAM. Such was FM's "press" at the beginning of the decade of the 1950's.[39]

By 1950, the number of FM receivers in use had grown to only 5,500,000. FM stations authorized to broadcast had decreased from 856 to 732, and only sixteen applications were filed for new FM stations during the year. By June of 1950 only 691 FM stations were actually broadcasting.[40] The FCC annual report for 1959 stated that "in most cases" FM stations operated in conjunction with AM stations employed the duplicated programming 100 percent of the time. Under this arrangement FM programs designed with high fidelity as a prime consideration of their make-up were almost non-existent. The normal AM programming was merely shunted electronically to the FM transmitter and sent out to the small group of listeners who had FM receivers. Live music was rare on radio at this time. So the FM listener heard music that was recorded by either electrical transcription (just for radio broadcasting) or commercial phonograph records. By 1950 the long playing record was well established, but many small stations still played the older, and definitely inferior, 78RPM records. Daytime radio "soap operas" were still prevalent, along with audience interview and participation shows. This bill-of-fare, recorded music in the popular vein and talk shows, hardly constituted incentive for a listener to spend the additional money needed to purchase FM receiving equipment. Those few FM independent stations which attempted to develop an "FM art-form" based on the unique qualities of frequency modulation broadcasting found that, with no advertising money for experimentation, promotion, and production, they had to resort to long playing records. Since AM radio was already playing popular music continuously, at least the FM operator was able to supply classical and light classical music in great quantity. This not only filled a need for this type of music, but allowed a station to operate for as low a cost as possible, since the records played up to thirty minutes per side. No professional announcer was needed, except for station breaks and for naming the selections.

So FM broadcasting became, by accident and economic need, a classical jukebox. Every community with an FM station was not entirely pleased by this continuous diet of Bach, Beethoven, and Brahms. Early FM programming, by its very nature, tended to drive away even more advertisers, since it offered no variety and since few listeners were apt to enjoy classical music at all or enjoy it in great quantity. Many people will no doubt remember FM stations in small rural communities or in small towns over which the local announcer often mispronounced both the name of the classical selection and the composer's name.

The great optimism that greeted FM at the close of World War II, and the glowing predictions made by FCC commissioners in speeches to FM broadcasters mainly, dwindled rapidly. In 1948, the FCC authorized 1,020 FM station applications. The authorization meant that an FM owner could build his station and go on the air. But getting the station on the air was quite another matter. Therefore, there were always fewer stations actually transmitting than the number of stations authorized. The twelve years following World War II indicate the serious economic plight of FM operators.

	FM STATIONS ON THE AIR	FM STATIONS AUTHORIZED	INDEPENDENT FM STATION INDUSTRY YEARLY LOSSES
1946	55	456	*
1947	238	918	*
1948	587	1,020	*
1949	737	865	*
1950	691	732	*
1951	626	699	*
1952	629	648	*
1953	594	601	$800,000
1954	528	569	600,000
1955	493	552	400,000
1956	472	546	400,000
1957	530	561	500,000

Source: FCC Annual Reports and FCC Selected Statistics of the FM Industry 1953–1962.
*No figures

Beginning with 1957, FM industry statistics begin to show their first upward trend in number of stations. However, the past record shows that industry losses grew from one-half million dollars in 1957 to over three million dollars in 1966. This increase was due, in part, to the greater number of stations on the air. As the FM station saturation point is reached, a levelling off of losses should occur (indeed, for the last three years, a levelling has occurred). Then hopefully, a decline in losses should continue. (The reader should keep in mind that the published industry loss figures represent only the FM independents and, therefore, a most conservative figure.) If AM/FM outlets were required to furnish income and loss figures on their FM operations, loss figures would probably be much higher (since AM/FM operations represent some 75 percent of all FM stations).

In a speech before the Radio Manufacturers Association, in 1950, FCC Chairman Wayne Coy discussed the FM situation and the role of the radio manufacturers in building a broadcasting industry:

> Can we continue to justify our tolerance of these defects in AM when we have at hand another system of sound broadcasting—FM—that has none of these defects and has, moreover, some other highly desirable advantages?
>
> FM's superiority over AM is as unchallenged as ever—freedom from static, noise and fading; with day and night operation and high fidelity and with many more high power stations of uniform range so that competition must be on the basis not of power but of programming.
>
> With FM we can give American communities more local stations to serve their local needs; and stations that will reach far, far beyond their present AM stations with a clear loud signal and with stations that aren't blacked out at sunset.
>
> It is a startling but true fact that a Class B FM station can cover from 300 to 500 times the area now served by many local channel AM stations at night.
>
> FM has had a rough time.
>
> Only a handful of broadcasters are showing a profit or are near a profit status. They complain that networks treat FM as a stepchild; they refuse to affiliate with FM stations even though FM stations provide additional coverage, particularly at night; that

networks have never provided proper, high fidelity inter-city network lines. And they complain that manufacturers are so preoc-
cupied with television that there is a substantial unmet demand
for FM receivers in many communities.

. . . .

And there is another significant fact: FM, despite its many growing pains as an infant service, has in these five postwar years
grown to more than 700 stations that give the nation more total
nightime coverage than is given by all the regional and local AM
stations after AM's quarter of a century existence. The area covered
by these stations holds 100,000,000 people.

A survey just completed in New York City shows that there
are now three times as many sets with FM as there were two
years ago and furthermore that the number of families actually
using their FM sets has also tripled. It also found that more than
10 percent of all the homes are using their FM sets in preference
to AM.

The future of our aural broadcasting system is a matter of concern to the broadcasters of this country and to the Federal Communications Commission. And when it is viewed in the light of
future marketing opportunities for your products, I am sure you
will agree that it is a matter of urgent importance to the radio
manufacturer.

I believe that the points I have discussed here tonight point
to the inevitable conclusion: that radio—all types of radio—is
living in a shrinking spectrum and that the radio manufacturer,
if he is to build soundly for the future, must take the implications
of that into account.

. . . .

Your responsibility for instituting research programs to help
chart a sound course for radio's future cannot be negated by
the claim of the stresses of business competition. In fact the interest of the radio art, the interest of your industry and the interest
of the public would be best served by a healthy competition that
would extend not only to products and prices but to fundamental
research that will pave the way for consistent expansion.[41]

A charge that the radio manufacturers were continuing in
their reluctance to manufacture FM receivers, while they concentrated on AM equipment, was made to the FCC in 1951.
The FM broadcast operators stated that FM receivers were
in short supply in their areas and, consequently, a buildup
of their FM audiences could not be achieved:

.... It has been claimed that the set makers will not supply a pent-up demand for FM receivers. Groups representing the broadcasters and the manufacturers met in June 1951 in an attempt to cooperatively solve their problems. Figures presented by the two groups apparently were at variance, with the broadcasters showing shortage whereas the manufacturers countered with a survey showing large distributor and factory inventories. Both groups agreed that the problem should be attacked on a market-by-market basis.[42]

The FCC again commented, in July, 1951, on this refusal of the predominantly AM industry to manufacture the sets needed. Wayne Coy, FCC Chairman, said in a letter to an FM operator in North Carolina:

As I have told you repeatedly, the FCC is not considering the deletion of the FM band or any part of it. The FCC is not considering allocating the FM band or any part of it to any other service. The approximately seven hundred stations now operating in the FM band is real testimony to the strength of the service, particularly when one considers that many manufacturers do not make sets and none of them have carried on continously aggressive sales campaigns. In almost every area in the country there is an unfilled demand for FM receivers.[43]

Some FM stations, in an effort to supplement their revenues, resorted to what is called "functional music operations"—programs designed for stores, offices, factories, or restaurants. However, the FCC banned this practice on the grounds that it made use of the public airways for too specialized an audience:

It may be remarked at the outset that the Commission has devoted considerable effort to analysis of FM's problems, and is fully cognizant of the character of the financial difficulties which such licensees have encountered in the past several years; it accordingly views with sympathy attempts on the part of pioneers in this meritorious, and as yet, in the main unprofitable field of broadcasting, to ensure the solvency of their operations. However, we are constrained to conclude... that the "beep" services... are inconsistent with basic statutory and administrative duties incumbent upon licensees of broadcast facilities.

... to provide this specific type of programming during such

a substantial portion of the broadcast day to subscribers . . . these
arrangements must be considered to constitute an invalid abdica-
tion of your duty as a licensee to retain discretion, responsibility
and control, and to remain free to alter your service as the changing needs of the public in your area may require.[44]

During 1952 the National Association of Radio and Television Broadcasters did some heavy FM promotional work in
a few eastern seaboard states. Mostly, however, FM's poor
economic picture continued across the nation. Even the FM
receivers manufactured were not of particularly high quality
as far as performance was concerned. Manufacturers were
not making the sets to include one of the basic advantages
built into FM, and one of the reasons people wanted to own
FM—the ability to broadcast the full FM audio range of from
50 to 15,000 cycles.

. . . . The ordinary FM receivers available to the public cannot
receive transmissions covering this frequency range. A considerable number of FM listeners have had custom high-fidelity installation made in their homes to realize the full frequency range
capabilities of FM broadcasting.[45]

The desire of people to own equipment capable of these
ranges can be seen today by the fact that many department
stores and audio specialty shops carry a large variety of brands
of components (and fully housed units) which do give this
frequency response. This equipment often costs more, since
receiving components capable of the full range cost more to
make as the frequency response desired is increased. Whether
the listener can actually hear the difference between 10,000
cycles or 14,000 cycles is a matter of argument. Most people
can hear the difference between 3,000 cycles (an average inexpensive AM radio) and 10,000 cycles (an average FM radio).
However, since the full audio range was one of the advantages
of FM over AM and since it was an advantage which a dealer
could demonstrate in his store, it became a good selling feature
for FM sets. Since the difference in audio range between AM
and FM can be pointed up most dramatically when handled
by a promotion-minded dealer, there came to be a "talk down"

of FM, in general, by some facets of the AM industry—with NBC one of the biggest talkers:

> .... Radio reporters and others got almost the same stock responses from RCA's Chief Engineer E. W. Engstrom and NBC's O. B. Hanson as from CBS's Paul W. Kesten and official spokesman.... Yes, they said, FM was an interesting technical development, but not practical, not economically sound and not anything to get excited about.
>
> Perhaps the most interesting argument put forth mainly by RCA spokesmen, was that the public was not interested in high fidelity and would not pay the extra price for it. They pointed out that the big market was in cheap, low-quality table-model radios. Moreover, they said, high fidelity had been tried in a special AM radio and it had failed. The public invariably turned down the treble control and turned up the bass, indicating that it preferred booming juke box tones.... The public, they said, had a "tin ear." The only fault with this argument was that it was talking about high fidelity through the inherent distortion of the established AM broadcasting system, which was indeed painful to the ear. It was not talking about FM; which eliminated these distortions to make high fidelity palatable.
>
> The myth that "the public does not want high fidelity" was to be promulgated for years, mainly to blunt FM's chief selling point and to discourage the manufacture of FM sets.[46]

One of the men mentioned in that quote, Mr. O. B. Hanson, in association with two others who worked for NBC, wrote one of these talk-down articles in 1944. At that time RCA was not manufacturing FM sets, nor did it own the patents of FM. It was manufacturing AM sets and was, at that time, looking forward (as were all businesses) to the end of the war and the beginning of the lucrative postwar market. Some of the quotes from Hanson's article explain more clearly how this talk-down was done. The article is entitled "Down to Earth on High Fidelity." It was originally published at a time when the FCC was setting up rules and standards for FM broadcasting to go into effect at war's end. It was republished July, 1951, by *FM-TV Radio Communication*, with an editor's note stating that it was being republished to show, among other things, that "it discloses some thinking that is slanted

more towards network policy than optimum public service."[47]
At the time of the writing, Mr. Hanson was Vice-President
and Chief Engineer of the National Broadcasting Company.
Discussing the capability of an FM system to embody the
full 30 to 15,000 cycle, the article states:

> A system as described ... is not too difficult of realization from
> a transmitting standpoint. It might be approached closely in a
> receiver reproducing system, but the cost would probably be
> beyond the value which would be placed upon it by the purchasing
> public, particularly if the receiver were required to reproduce
> frequencies from 30 to 15,000 cycles.
>
> . . . .
>
> In an appeal to common sense and practicality in the matter
> of fixing an audio band width for receivers, it is suggested that
> the range from 60 to 8,000 ... cycles be considered for all types
> of broadcasting, including frequency modulation. There is very
> little question in the opinion of those who have devoted their
> lives to the problems of sound reproduction, that good reproduc-
> tion over a practical band will provide a better service to the
> listener than one of controversial and indefinite quality over a
> theoretically complete audio spectrum.
>
> How can publicizing and creating a demand for 15,000 cycle
> receivers or systems be possibly justified, when a good 10,000
> cycle receiver than can be made available to the greater part of
> the public, has not yet been designed? For the sake of technical
> integrity and the future of the radio industry, let's get down to
> earth in the matter of high fidelity. We are faced with the prospect
> of a post war era in which it is very likely that many claims for
> new materials, techniques and overall improvements will face
> the spotlight of public test—and fail. Let us not, therefore, in
> our enthusiasm, make claims that are too difficult, if not impossi-
> ble to realize.[48]

It must be remembered that an article appearing under the
name of the premier radio corporation in the country (if not
the world) would have a tremendous impact on readers. Most
of the article is too technical for this book, but it is equally
damning to FM and to the standards Armstrong wanted the
FCC to set up for nationwide FM transmission. RCA had
sold many small table model radios with a frequency response
of from 200 to 3000 cycles for about $35. Even console models

at higher prices had a top limit of 4000 cycles.[49] As stated earlier, Hanson's article appeared when the FCC was setting up the standards of the number of cycles and the extent of the frequency swing (that is, whether it would be the very wide "door" that Armstrong insisted gave the best performance for the public, or some compromise) to be used. When NBC states "it is suggested," it means NBC is suggesting these things to the FCC. It has already been established through sworn testimony and several investigations just how much attention the FCC did pay to RCA and NBC. Such suggestions therefore were hardly to go unnoticed in Washington. Further, the suggestion that the range of from "60 to 8,000 . . . cycles be considered for all types of broadcasting, including frequency modulation" reduces frequency modulation to the same lower level the best AM broadcasting could ever hope to achieve. If this had been done, one of FM's chief advantages and competitive selling points would have been lost. It does cost more to produce an FM than an AM receiving set (it cost substantially more fifteen years ago), and the consumer would be unlikely to pay more for something that delivered the same quality sound as the lower-cost AM set.

It might be argued that it would be unjustified, as the article says, to create a demand for a receiver capable of such high cycle response when none had yet been designed. However, there are two things wrong with that argument. First, such receivers had been designed, but again not by RCA or NBC, who did not own the patents and, therefore, were not that interested in designing them, nor in pushing the designs of some competing company. Second, "on the drawing boards" and marketing the product can often occur at vastly different dates. At a later period, when stereo is discussed, we will show that stereo broadcasting could have been achieved, promoted, and probably accepted by the public, ten years earlier than it was. Stereo broadcasting is partly an off-shoot of the original FM patents, the last of which expired in 1957. Stereo is part of a technical process called "multiplexing." Multiplexing as we have seen, was achieved by Armstrong back in

1934 when he sent out the four different transmissions from the Empire State Building (two programs from NBC, a facsimile of a newspaper page, a telegraph message). The fact that manufacturers and marketers did not produce and promote stereo until after the last FM patent had expired and no royalties had to be paid to the inventor cannot be considered just one more "coincidence" in the line of FM "coincidences."

There are no laws governing the performance standards in the manufacture of receiving sets. The rules and regulations and standards all apply to the transmitting end of broadcasting. Thus, when the FCC annual report pointed out that in 1952 the public had to get "custom high fidelity" FM receivers made, as the "ordinary FM receivers available to the public" could not receive the full audio range, their statement was a measure of the success of the campaign to convince manufacturers, dealers, and the general public that high-fidelity just was not worth the price. That today the general public seems vastly interested in high fidelity and is paying the price may be what led the editor of *FM-TV* to make his comment about corporate policy hardly being in the optimum public interest.

In April, 1952, *FM-TV* devoted its audio section to a report of hi-fi business, saying that estimates for the year indicated that one-half billion dollars would be spent on sales of hi-fi equipment and classical LP records. The article explained the financial boom as a series of things "which may seem unrelated at first thought, although they tie together to make a picture of important changes under way."[50]

First, the article stated that a revival of interest in all kinds of music seemed to be under way, limited only by a person's financial ability to enjoy it; further, that an appreciation of high fidelity was spreading beyond the small group of engineers whose interest was mainly in developing the art of more faithful reproduction:

> But today, the rapidly increasing hi-fi sales are being made to people who are discovering that, through the medium of fine audio equipment, FM radio, LP records, and 15-in. tape, they

can have musical entertainment in the home that is virtually equivalent to the original performance.

. . . . The mechanical phonograph flourished because it had great appeal as a novelty, but it faded out because it had no permanent status as a means of realistic reproduction.

AM radio rose to popularity as a scientific marvel of universal appeal, but it settled down to the status of an essential home appliance, important mostly because it furnishes listen-while-you-work soap operas, makes it possible to hear crime stories instead of reading them, and provides communication in the form of news and weather reports.

. . . . As the number [of people] continues to grow, the demand will increase for FM programs using live talent or 15,000 cycle tape, for LP records of uniformly higher fidelity. . . .

. . .public interest is already at such a level that any city of 100,000 population can support a store specializing in hi-fi equipment sales and installment work.[51]

In June, 1952, *FM-TV* reported that high fidelity was the highlight of the national electronic parts show: something had been added to the parts show at Chicago that sent manufacturers back home with more new ideas about stepping up sales and profits than they had picked up at this annual event for many a year. "This refers, of course, to equipment for high-fidelity reproduction from records, tape, and FM broadcasting."[52]

The article contained some further criticism of the AM manufacturers in the production of their equipment:

The high fidelity idea represents a simple yet revolutionary departure from the old concept of putting a radio receiver, record player, and loudspeaker in a single cabinet. Cabinets, whether of console or table model size, have always put a limitation on the size, cost, and performance of the units mounted in them. Eye-appeal, not ear-appeal, became the manufacturers' primary consideration.

Thus, from year to year, the quality of reproduction deteriorated until the performance of current AM table models is about on a par with the mechanical phonograph circa 1910.[53]

In 1952, the British Broadcasting Corporation gave a report on its proposal to make FM broadcasting the national radio service using the high frequencies. They had made experiments comparing conventional AM and something called AML (amplitude modulation with a noise limiter built into the receiver) with FM. The results indicated that FM gave a greater service area of noise-free operation. One of the things the BBC pointed out specifically was that manufacturers of FM home receivers had to make very careful (but not necessarily costly) designs in order to achieve the full advantages of FM.[54] In the United States, FM transmission is regulated by the FCC to embody these advantages, while it is left to the discretion of the receiver manufacturer to build his receiver as he sees fit. With no laws governing their manufacture, early American FM receivers were criticized specifically for not embodying the full advantages of FM transmission.

In the same year that Britain was planning its nationwide FM service, FM in the United States was in one of its very bleakest economic periods. And to aggravate the financial situation even more, especially because of the advertising dollars lost to FM, was a report that "Most manufacturers are still entirely indifferent about FM."[55] In the following year, the FCC authorized only two new FM stations; forty-seven had quit operating over the previous year and most of these deletions were because the stations were losing money:

> As a means of obtaining additional revenue, various commercial FM stations are engaging in supplemental services known as "functional music," "Storecasting," and "transit radio." In the functional music operation, an FM licensee undertakes to supply background music programs to commercial establishments having special receiving apparatus which, when activated by a supersonic signal, eliminates the spoken material. In storecasting and transit radio, the programming is designed to reach store customers and transit passengers in public vehicles, respectively, with the supersonic signal employed to increase the sound level of the spoken word.
>
> These specialized operations are under Commission study in connection with the overall FM situation. Determination is required as to several legal and policy questions—whether such operations are "Broadcasting" within the meaning of the Com-

munications Act, whether they meet the Commission's rules, and whether they are in the public interest.[56]

The FCC, on July 1, 1955, allowed FM stations to engage in this functional music business to increase revenues. The station could do it one of two ways; by the simplex system or by the multiplex system. In simplex operations, a station transmits the special programming on the same radio carrier wave it uses for normal FM broadcasting and the programs may be received on an ordinary FM receiver. Subscribers to this service, however, have special FM receivers. These receivers are activated by an inaudible supersonic or "beep" signal, transmitted by the station, which cuts out or amplifies mainly commercial announcements received by the home receivers. If, for instance, a doctor's office is a subscriber, the simplex operation allows the waiting room to have the same musical program being heard by the general FM population, but without the commercials.

In the multiplex operation, a station transmits programs by a special means of the same FM carrier wave (this is the piggyback method described in Chapter 2) used for FM broadcasting, but the programs cannot be received on ordinary FM receivers. These subscribers are furnished with special multiplex receiving equipment and the programming can be entirely different from that of the regular FM station. There are no restrictions as to amount of time the station engages in multiplexing programs, since multiplexing and regular FM transmissions can be carried on simultaneously. In simplex operations, there are restrictions holding such operations to certain hours of the day since the FCC does not want the stations to be held to a rigid menu of the same type of background music. This would be boring to the general audience whose FM receivers could tune in to the entire day's broadcasting. Simplex operations were permitted for only a short period of time and were to have ceased by July 1, 1957, at which time all such functional music programming was to be conducted by the multiplex system of broadcasting.[57] However, due to delays, simplexing did not end until 1964.[58]

At the end of 1953, the FCC amended its ownership rules of commercial broadcast stations. The new rules forbade any party, or any of its stockholders, officers, or directors, to have an interest in more than seven AM stations, or seven commercial FM stations, or five commercial TV stations. Noncommercial educational FM and TV stations are not subject to the multiple ownership rules. Prior to this time the limit to any one party involved in FM broadcasting was six stations.[59]

In January of 1954, the Armstrong vs. RCA pre-trial procedures were still going on. The "discovery" process instituted to save time and money had now run on for five full years! When Armstrong had not been busy with this legal behemoth, he had kept to his electronic experiments. The FCC had been pondering just what to do about the "functional music" problem for a number of years. Major Armstrong, meanwhile, had with his assistant, John Bose, been working on a type of multiplexing that would be of a higher quality. Multiplexing in radio signalling had dated back to the year 1900 and to some work done by Marconi with spark transmitters. In 1919, R. A. Heising had done some work with AM multiplexing; however, too much noise and fading were involved to make it useful to general radio broadcasting:

> The practical art of multiplexing in radio signaling, we believe, begins with the advent of the wide band system of frequency modulation in 1934. In November of that year, four different sets of signals were successfully transmitted from Station W2XDG located in the Empire State Building, New York City, to Haddonfield, New Jersey, a distance of 85 miles.... The signals transmitted on that occasion were a musical program on the main channel, a facsimile program on a superaudio subcarrier on a second channel, a synchronizing signal for the facsimile on a third, and a telegraph "order" channel on a fourth subcarrier frequency.... Subsequently, two musical programs... were simultaneously transmitted, using the same system....
>
> These transmissions, while successful according to the standards of the times, would hardly measure up, either to the signal-to-noise ratio, or the quality of reproduction that are now the accepted standard of FM broadcasting. Nor would the receiving equipment designed to operate in that ideally untrammeled wil-

derness of the wide open spectrum of 1934, when there was in existence one wide band transmitter and one receiver only, perform too satisfactorily in the presently well-settled FM territories where in many locations, signals on a score or more different channels may be picked up in a sweep across the dial of an appropriately sensitive and selective receiver.[60]

To bring the piggyback subcarrier waves up-to-date, Armstrong and Bose developed a new multiplex system—a vast improvement over the previous method. This resulted in Armstrong's last patented invention. The invention is patented in the names of both Armstrong and Bose (who had done nearly all the work on the new development).[61] This was in October, 1953:

> .... Later in the month, Armstrong presented the usual technical paper and demonstration on the new development before the Radio Club. He was not in his usual good form .... his speech was halting and all ease gone. It was destined to be the last technical paper he would ever present.
>
> Early in November [1953] Armstrong saw another item settled in his affairs.... In 1948 he had made a grant of $50,000 to the Columbia University Law School to finance a study of court decisions involving complex scientific matters to discover how well law courts were deciding such issues and to think about all the mishaps and misrepresentations of scientific fact that had occurred in the now classic regenerative-circuit litigation. In 1953 the committee in charge of the grant finally found the man to direct the study—John C. Palfrey of Columbia Law School—and the project was moving forward at last.[62]

In making the grant, Major Armstrong explained that it was for making a study or studies of problems affecting the public interest which were of mutual concern to the engineering and legal professions:

> It has been my observation over a long period of years ... that public bodies, in order to discharge their functions, are frequently required to make findings of fact on technical and scientific matters that are beyond the comprehension of laymen, and that the techniques involved in the ascertainment of such facts have not been adequately developed, with the result that important deci-

sions are sometimes made, and important action taken, upon erroneous findings of fact in technical and scientific fields.[63]

Not only must the De Forest litigation have been in his mind but also the FCC decisions affecting FM over the years, the patent interference suits brought against every one of his major inventions, and the then-current RCA legal marathon over FM. The money used for this pre-trial period had finally taken its toll of his personal fortune:

> His finances were running out. Few except his wife had more than an inkling of the crisis closing in on him, and even she had no knowledge of his financial situation. From the start he had directed his life with the pride, secrecy and shrewdness of a lone wolf. Now, however, unless he could soon begin to collect his due on the wide uses to which FM had been put in radio, television and communications, his old mode of operation was at an end, his laboratories and his research wiped out.
>
> .... It did not seem, after five years of pre-trial proceedings that the main action could be much longer delayed.... What if this suit, too, were carried to the Supreme Court? He could not last so long.
>
> Zenith Radio, after having paid him over $1 million in royalties... announced that it would pay no more. Of all Armstrong's licensees, Zenith had been among the most aggressive and technically forward-looking promoters of FM receivers... but all royalties from other licensees were now greatly reduced and most of the industry had never paid anything. The sharp cutting off of Armstrong's income in 1953, coupled with his heavy running expenses, left him with barely enough to see himself through another year.[64]

The "most of the industry" who had never paid anything were primarily those companies tied to the RCA patent pool. These firms had decided not to pay Armstrong royalties basically because they knew RCA had not paid them. The assumption was that if the leader of the industry did not pay, the leader certainly must know what it was doing. There is a time limit involved in which an inventor may bring suit against companies which he feels have infringed on his patent. This time limit was about to run out at the end of 1953, but Armstrong had hoped the RCA case would have long since been settled in his favor and then the other companies, rather than go into court, would make out-of-court settlements with him. However, the RCA pre-trial proceedings were obviously going to run over this deadline, so Armstrong's lawyers filed suit against all remaining companies that were infringing the FM patents.[65]

At the close of 1953, RCA made an attempt to settle out-of-court:

> ... seeming to sense that Armstrong was at the end of his rope, [RCA] came through with a last offer of settlement that to him was more outrageous than anything that had gone before. This time the terms were put in the form of a one-year option. At the end of that time, if the suit were called off, RCA would or would not make a total cash settlement of $1 million for itself, and $1 million for the rest of the industry, against any liability for infringement by its licensees—leaving Armstrong dangling in the air for a year while his subsidiary claims were wiped out by statute of limitations. This Armstrong rejected, as he had rejected the 1940 proposal of settlement for a flat $1 million, for it presented an abasement that he would never submit to or endure.
>
> Thus, as Armstrong's life darkened in these closing months, the sense of rejection that had started innocently many years before with his father's refusal of patent money for his first invention, and that had mounted on his way up through the Supreme Court and the corridors of government offices and corporations, now swelled... in the empty and echoing rooms in River House. How many times did they want him to prove that he was an inventor? What was a man to do to insure his honor, reputation and fortune in this country?[66]

To add to this sad state of affairs, Marion and Edwin Armstrong had had a personal clash over the whole matter of the RCA case, the disastrous state of finances, and Armstrong's refusal to make any sort of compromise. Marion Armstrong had wanted her husband to tell his brilliant lawyer and personal friend, Alfred McCormack, all the details of his problems in an effort to solve them. She had hoped, above all, that Armstrong might settle the RCA case and retire to their farm in Connecticut to set up his own laboratory and enjoy their remaining years in some semblance of normality. However,

Armstrong was a headstrong man, and the idea of compromise was alien to him.

> The climax came after a traditional Thanksgiving party.... After a heavy argument and irrevocable clash of wills late that night, Marion Armstrong, sick and heartsore, went to Connecticut with her sister ... to wait out the struggle that had taken on the dimensions of an ancient tragic dilemma. Ill and attended closely by doctors, she was advised not to return to River House until the Major had made a full disclosure of his situation to McCormack.
>
> ···
>
> .... The Christmas holidays came and went and he was still alone in River House. Toward the end of January, 1954, he finally brought himself to have a thorough talk with McCormack, who was shocked at his frame of mind and tried to assure him that a swift settlement with RCA could be reached.
>
> ···
>
> Of that fateful weekend no account can be put together except a few telephone calls: with McCormack, to whom he talked every morning... , and who called Sunday morning from Washington... to reassure him that he would be back early in the week to devote full time to negotiating a settlement....
>
> Sometime on that Sunday night of January 31, 1954, he wrote a two-page letter to Marion Armstrong.... Its gist ... was that he found it impossible to understand how he could have hurt "the dearest thing in the world to me. How deep and bitterly I regret... what has happened to us." His solvency was assured, he wrote, especially if the Telephone Company and RCA "come through anywhere near making good... for they know they have been using my invention."
>
> He was completely and neatly dressed, in hat, overcoat, scarf and gloves. He did not walk out of the door, however, but out of the window, thirteen stories above the street, falling from the last high place to which he would ever climb.[67]

Later in 1954, the FM infringement suit against RCA was settled by agreement, with RCA and NBC paying the Armstrong estate just over one million dollars. Ahead, lay seven and a half more years of patent litigation over the FM patents. Behind, lay the dead inventor, 209 FM stations that had gone off the air since the end of World War II, and an FM industry which had lost an estimated three to six million dollars since war's end.

Armstrong's funeral was held in Merrimac, Massachusetts, where he and his wife had been married thirty years before. "Heading the list of attendants at the funeral, as reported by the newspapers, was Brigadier General David Sarnoff and other top figures of RCA."[68]

NOTES

[1]FCC News Release, Mimeo. No. 90423, March 5, 1946.

[2]"FCC Allocates 88–106 mc Band to FM," *Broadcasting*, July 2, 1945, p. 74.

[3]FCC News Release, Mimeo. No. 84329, August 21, 1945.

[4]*Broadcasting*, August 27, 1945, p. 18.

[5]"RMA Asks FCC Action on FM Band,"*Broadcasting*, September 3, 1945, p. 20.

[6]FCC News Release, Mimeo. No. 87220, December 14, 1945.

[7]FCC News Release, Mimeo. No. 90423, March 5, 1946.

[8]Senate Hearings on FM Development, p. 42.

[9]Comments in support of leaving television in the very high frequencies (channels 2-13) were filed by ABC, RCA, and NBC. Against the two-band (UHF and VHF) system were many small broadcasters who argued that all television be shifted to UHF. The FCC dismissed their arguments by saying not enough testimony existed to justify all television in the ultra high frequencies. It should be noted that, in the case of FM, the FCC acted in a completely opposite manner. Overwhelming evidence and expert opinion was presented to show FM should not be moved. In this case (that of FM) the FCC chose to ignore the evidence. In the case of television, the FCC claimed not enough evidence was present. It would seem, to this author, they adjust their arguments to fit their needs.... or to be more accurate, to fit the needs of the companies they are truly serving. In answer to those who wanted all television moved to the UHF area, the FCC said: "Statements were filed... that all commercial television stations should be assigned to the UHF band. The statements allege that many of the economic and competitive problems which would arise because television broadcasting will be expanded in the UHF portion of the spectrum would be obviated if no commercial television broadcasting were permitted in the VHF. These objections, however, do not point out any specific testimony or evidence to support the large scale reallocations and

reassignments which would thereby be required nor do they make any concrete proposal. We are not, moreover, convinced that an adequate showing has been made that sufficient spectrum space would be provided for an adequate nation-wide television service if only the UHF portion of the spectrum is allocated for commercial television. Accordingly, we have decided that commercial television operation should be provided for in both bands of the spectrum allocated for television broadcasting." (Quoted from the *Federal Register*, Vol. XVII, No. 87, Part II, May 2, 1952, Title 47—Telecommunications, Chapter 1—Federal Communications Commission, Sixth Report and Order, p. 3905).

[10]*FCC Thirteenth Annual Report*, 1947, p. 20.

[11]FCC News Release, Mimeo. No. 92927, April 10, 1946.

[12]FCC News Release, Mimeo. No. 2468, January 10, 1947.

[13]FCC News Release, Mimeo. No. 99555, October 23, 1946.

[14]FCC News Release, Mimeo. No. 2467, January 10, 1947.

[15]FCC, Address of Paul A. Walker, Vice Chairman, Federal Communications Commission, at the first Convention of the FM Association, New York City, September 12, 1947.

[16]*Ibid.*

[17]*FCC Fourteenth Annual Report*, 1948, p. 36.

[18]Lessing, *Armstrong*, p. 264.

[19]Lessing, *Armstrong*, p. 267. The law, as applied to the Communications Act of 1934 was amended to read: "No Commissioner, if he resigns before his term of office has expired, may for 1 year thereafter, represent before the Commission any person or corporation who comes within the jurisdiction of the Communications Act. This provision [is] intended to halt the practice by persons and corporations, who have business before the Commission, of employing Commissioners with the obvious purpose of benefiting themselves, perhaps unfairly, through the influence that such a Commissioner might have with employees in the agency. It is also intended to restrict a growing practice of using appointments to high government posts as stepping stones to important positions in private industries which have business before the Commission." The quote is from the *Pike and Fischer Radio Regulation Service*, a compilation of broadcasting regulations and laws which are quoted and explained.

[20]Senate Hearings on FM Development, p. 109.

[21]*Broadcast Primer*, FCC Information Bulletin No. 2-B, February, 1964, p. 16.

[22]*Capitol Radio Reporter* (newsletter), Vol. 1, No. 46, October 18, 1947.

[23]*Armstrong v. Emerson*, p. 737.

[24]Edwin H. Armstrong, "A Study of the Operating Characteristics of the Radio Detector and Its Place in Radio History," *Proceedings of the Radio Club of America*, November, 1948 (from a reprint in the Armstrong Memorial Research Foundation files).

[25]The patent to expire in 1957 was issued in 1940 and was a major improvement in the quality of the FM sound. The patent concerned *de-emphasis* and *pre-emphasis* which was a method by which certain noise characteristics of FM in the high frequencies were reduced sharply.

[26]Lessing, *Armstrong*, p. 279.

[27]"FM Hours: Protests Mount to Proposal," *Broadcasting*, December 26, 1949, p. 44.

[28]*New York Times*, December 25, 1949, sec. 2, p. 9, col. 1.

[29]Lessing, *Armstrong*, p. 281.

[30]*Ibid*, p. 284.

[31]FCC Public Notice, Mimeo. No. 67238, December 23, 1958.

[32]FCC Public Notice, Mimeo. No. 90562, October 18, 1966.

[33]*FCC Fifteenth Annual Report*, 1949, p. 39.

[34]*Broadcasting*, December 19, 1949, p. 38.

[35]"FM Hours: Protests Mount to Proposal," p. 44.

[36]*New York Times*, April 21, 1949, p. 50, col. 1.

[37]*Armstrong v. Emerson*, p. 1245.

[38]*The World Telegram* (Bloomington, Ind.), June 1, 1949, p. 9.

[39]The pamphlet was published in Bloomington, Indiana, by Sarkes Tarzian and printed in September, 1944, at his own expense. The paper was never given before the IRE. Among the "facts" presented were the following: that " . . . evidently the masses do not care whether the radios they buy have 'high fidelity' or not. Indeed there even seems to be a certain dislike for 'high fidelity'." To show that FM cannot operate in every conceivable location in the United States, Mr. Tarzian uses a sample survey of "one" to indicate poor reception in a remote mountain area. "The sad experience of an F.M. receiver owner is outlined. It shows that there are areas around Asheville, N. C., where it is not possible . . ." to get good reception. Mr. Tarzian asks the question, "Why is F.M. being promoted in view of these facts?" Mr. Tarzian then answers his question. "Because it will be more profitable to broadcast equipment manufacturers

and to radio set manufacturers, distributors, and dealers." He adds
that most of the claims for static-free radio, and the claim that there
will be more stations available with FM, can be done better with
AM and done "more economically" with AM at the higher frequencies (above 50 Mgc.). Mr. Tarzian carefully neglects to mention
in this pamphlet anything about his own high-fidelity invention,
HI-FAM, developed for these high frequencies. If the public truly
"disliked" high-fidelity, Mr. Tarzian wasted a lot of time and money
creating high-fidelity for AM broadcasting. Further, his anger at
the equipment manufacturers for promoting FM would have been
sharply cooled, it is assumed, if it had been his patented HI-FAM
that the FCC had accepted for nation-wide use. He made a concerted
effort in this country and abroad to get his invention accepted,
which it never was. Sour grapes seems to be a popular fruit among
some pioneers of broadcasting.

[40]*FCC Sixteenth Annual Report*, 1950, p. 109.

[41]FCC, Address by Wayne Coy, Chairman, Federal Communica-
tons Commission, at the 20th Annual Convention of the Radio
Manufacturers Association, Chicago, Illinois, June 8, 1950.

[42]*FCC, Seventeenth Annual Report*, 1951, p. 124.

[43]FCC Public Notice, Mimeo. No. 66152, July 13, 1951.

[44]FCC Public Notice, Mimeo. No. 62825, April 12, 1951.

[45]FCC Eighteenth Annual Report, 1952, p. 117.

[46]Lessing, *Armstrong*, p. 240.

[47]"Checking Up On Audio Progress," *FM & Television*, July, 1951,
p. 34.

[48]*Ibid*. The reader is referred to footnote number eight in Chapter
IV. It is stated there that RCA did not discuss FM in the 1936
spectrum hearings before the FCC. In other parts of this paper,
sworn testimony to this fact is also presented. Yet in a privately
published booklet by RCA on FM, they make the following statement: "A copy of the report of RCA and NBC engineers upon
the FM tests which they made with these facilities was placed in
the record of the 1940 hearing of the Federal Communications Commission. These tests were also referred to in testimony before the
Commission in June 1936." (*FM Broadcasting*, issued by RCA
Laboratories, undated but probably 1944, p. 30.) In this booklet
and two other RCA histories of their growth and contributions to
broadcasting the following statements are made: "RCA did much
of the fundamental research and development work that made FM

broadcasting possible" *(FM Broadcasting,* p. 30); "RCA had worked on FM since 1924 and had made notable contributions to its development. Its pioneering in this field has never stopped." *(33 Years of Pioneering and Progress,* New York: RCA, 1953, p. 35); "Early tests of frequency modulation which afforded valuable information as to its advantages and potentialities were made by RCA, and its pioneering in this field has never stopped. For many months during 1934–35, the RCA-NBC experimental television transmitter in the Empire State Building was used for extensive field tests of FM broadcasting under practical operating conditions." *(25 Years of Radio Progress with RCA,* New York: RCA, 1944, p. 52) It should be noted that the above booklet entitled *FM Broadcasting,* was issued in 1944, just prior to the FCC hearings on the proposed spectrum move for FM. In the booklet RCA paints a rather pleasant view of FM giving its advantages over AM. However, it points out certain disadvantages of FM which do not agree with the inventor's claims for FM—that FM does not work well in automobiles due to the ignition systems and that FM will not work well near busy highways. More "facts" are presented, including the one that FM will run into the skywave problem of interference. That was another fact, it might be added, which turned out not to be a fact. In its closing remarks, however, the booklet's true reason for existence comes to light. Though the booklet is on FM, there is a section on television, which begins, "While television is not the subject of this booklet . . . still a brief discussion of television is desirable to clarify its relation to FM. . . . RCA's faith in television as a service to the public has been backed by more than 10 million dollars expended by it in research and development. Despite its great promise, television has been allocated a band of frequencies which provides for only 18 channels, of which only 7 are now usable owing to a lack of radio tubes and other apparatus suitable for operation at the very high frequencies of the remaining channels. This compares with 35 usable channels allocated to FM. . . . One channel formerly allocated to television was taken away from it and given to FM by the Federal Communications Commission. It has been suggested that still another channel should be taken from television and allocated to FM; also that television should be operated on higher frequencies for which suitable apparatus has not yet been developed. This would set television back still further. Television should not be further retarded by giving preference to FM. Television and FM are both meritorious services. They should go forward simultaneously." *(FM Broadcasting,* p. 31) With that statement out of the way, RCA and the rest of the AM/TV industry pulled off the FM spectrum move and did move FM to those ultra high frequencies where it was gladly admitted no equipment was developed to make any broadcasting system work. That is "going ahead simultaneously!" Armstrong's name is not mentioned in any of these history booklets on FM.

[49]*Ibid.,* p. 36.

[50]Milton B. Sleeper, "Report on HI-FI Business," *FM & Television,* April, 1952, p. 35.

[51]*Ibid.*

[52]"Chicago: Big News Was HI-FI," *FM & Television,* June, 1952, p. 27.

[53]*Ibid.*

[54]"BBC Scheme for VHF Broadcasting," *FM & Television,* April, 1952, p. 11.

[55]*Ibid.,* p. 4.

[56]*FCC Twentieth Annual Report,* 1954, p. 97.

[57]*FCC Twenty-second Annual Report,* 1956, p. 104, and FCC News Release, Mimeo. No. 17282 (no date).

[58]Richard Lee Beard, "Development and Utilization of the Frequency Modulation Subcarrier as a Commercial Communication Medium" (unpublished Ph.D. dissertation, University of Illinois, 1966).

[59]FCC Public Notice, Mimeo. No. 98434, November 27, 1953.

[60]Edwin H. Armstrong and John H. Bose, "Some Recent Developments in the Multiplexed Transmission of Frequency Modulated Broadcast Signals," *Proceedings of the Radio Club of America,* XXX, 1953, p. 3.

[61]Lessing, *Armstrong,* p. 294.

[62]*Ibid.*

[63]*News Office Release No. 5329,* Columbia University, November 16, 1953.

[64]Lessing, *Armstrong,* p. 293.

[65]Admiral Corporation; Arvin Industries, Incorporated; Avco Manufacturing Corporation (Crosley Divison); Bendix Aviation Corporation (Bendix Radio); Allen B. DuMont Labs., Incorporated; Emerson Radio & Phonograph Corporation; Fada Radio & Electric Company, Incorporated; Gilfillan Bros., Incorporated; Hoffman Radio Corporation; International Telephone and Telegraph Cor-

poration; Motorola, Incorporated; Packard-Bell Company; Philco Corporation, Philharmonic Radio & TV Corporation; Radio Corporation of America; The Radio Craftsmen, Incorporated; Radio & Television, Incorporated (Brunswick Division); Sentinel Radio Corporation; Sylvania Electric Products, Incorporated; and Wells-Gardner & Company.

[66]Lessing, *Armstrong*, p. 296.

[67]*Ibid.*, p. 295.

[68]*Ibid*, p. 300.

5

THE RECOVERY PERIOD:

1955–1972

The change in the FM "atmosphere" began shortly after Major Armstrong's death. After the RCA settlement in 1954, almost all of the companies sued by the Armstrong Estate settled out-of-court. These were the same companies which had not paid for the Armstrong royalties because RCA was not paying. When RCA made the settlement, they followed suit, assuming they could not win in court. However, two companies, Motorola and Emerson, decided to go into court with the fight. Even RCA had not chosen that final legal route; for, had the decision been against them, the amount of money to be paid to Armstrong or his estate would have probably been much greater than the one million dollars they did pay.

In October, 1958, the Armstrong Estate and the Emerson Radio & Phonograph Corporation began their five-week court litigation. Armstrong's lawyers had only recently spent six years collecting evidence in the RCA pre-trial proceedings. Though Armstrong's former lawyer, Alfred McCormack, was now dead, his colleague, Dana M. Raymond, took over the case. Raymond had moved to a new firm but had served during the RCA period and become not only a law expert on the case but a technical expert. In fact, it must be said for the lawyers on both sides that they became very proficient in the technical matters concerning the actual workings of radio and radio equipment. On dozens of occasions during the trial the opposing lawyers were able to catch errors of fact in testimony of the engineers who were called to testify. There can be no doubt that the expertise of Mr. Raymond, in his ability to examine and cross-examine engineering experts, helped to win all these cases for the Armstrong Estate.

Emerson and Motorola used similar tactics in their defense, as RCA had been doing in the tediously long pre-trial proceedings. In such a trial, the defense must prepare to deny that it did, in fact, infringe a patent willfully and wantonly. Since there was no question that the companies had built FM equipment and sold it, the question was whether or not they had built FM equipment by some method different from Major Armstrong's patent. The defense then attempted to show that they had used other patents (all of which were controlled by RCA and its vast patent pool arrangement). Most of these patents had issue dates that came after Armstrong's 1933 patents. Therefore, the prosecution was not overly hampered in dismissing most of these arguments as irrelevant. A few patents had earlier dates than Armstrong's, but, it was shown, they did not disclose any workable frequency modulation system that embodied any significant noise reduction, nor did they embody any transmitting/receiving system at all.

During the trial, most of the witnesses who appeared for both sides were technical ones, engineers in great manufacturing companies and in private engineering consulting firms. Most interesting is the conflicting testimony given by these engineers on points of technical understanding and accepted theory. About the only thing it can be compared to, that would be familiar to the layman, is testimony given by two psychiatrists appearing for each opposing side in, say, a murder trial. One psychiatrist might say that the defendant is, indeed, insane, while the other psychiatrist might insist the defendant is perfectly sane. The jury is left to ponder if schools of psychiatry, perhaps, have alternate courses of study, or if the services of professional men may be purchased by the highest bidder.

Quite often, the arguments were reduced to semantic problems in which one side insisted a word did not mean quite the same thing in 1958 as it meant in 1933. An example of this occurs in the Emerson trial when Mr. Raymond (for the Armstrong Estate) is cross-examining the main technical witness for Emerson. In this particular instance Mr. Raymond was trying to establish just what Armstrong had done in his 1933 patents in terms of improving the radio signal heard by the listener. Part of his legal argument was a buildup of the high quality of the audio range (the frequency cycles the system was capable of reproducing). Mr. Raymond was trying to get the witness to indicate what was an accepted figure of extremely high performance, in cycles, in 1933. The reader may remember that in 1944 the RCA article titled "Down to Earth on High Fidelity" discussed the upper limits of practical cycle reproduction as 7,000 to 9,000 cycles, while the average set of that time was 5,000 or less. These were published, accepted figures in 1944. Yet, in the 1958 trial, the witness insists that figures were "fuzzy." Mr. Raymond had asked the witness, Mr. Leo A. Kelly, if 10,000 cycles was the generally accepted limit for high quality transmission of speech and music in 1933:

> Q. I am asking you if you recall whether that was an accepted figure at the time.
> A. I wouldn't say that any particular figure was an accepted figure. . . .
> Q. . . . . My question is whether this was an accepted figure for the upper limit in the transmission of high quality program material by radio.
> A. No, sir, I wouldn't say so. I don't think it was as definite as that.
> Q. Do you see the item for 7,500 cycles considered as satisfactory upper limit for high quality transmission of speech and music?
> A. Yes.
> Q. Was that figure 7,500 cycles accepted for that purpose as being a satisfactory upper limit?
> A. My problem, Mr. Raymond, is in the universality of these figures. I don't think there was any such thing as that. It could be considered good, and maybe by a large group, but all of this deals with a subjective matter and matter of judgment and opinion, and it varies. I certainly have no objection to saying that the 10,000 cycles per second upper limit would,

all other things being equal, give a more satisfactory reproduction than the 7,500.

Q. If in 1933 you could have transmitted up to 10,000 cycles and had a receiver which would reproduce up to that range, it would have been a good radio service indeed, is that correct?

A. In comparison with broadcast bands which, of course, were narrower.

Q. In comparison with any service in operation at the time?

A. Well, I can't make as general an answer as that because there were systems of sound reproduction which were very good and there were systems of sound reproduction which were not so good.[1]

This is like saying that in any crop of apples some will be good and some will be rotten. And three pages of testimony later, Mr. Raymond was still asking the same question and getting the same answer:

Q. My question is what was considered as the upper limit in 1933. It is perfectly clear that there is a different view today.

A. Well, I think it was variable; it was a matter of opinion.[2]

And after two more pages of getting nowhere, Mr. Raymond, in an attempt to show that the Armstrong patent did increase the audible range from a lower limit of 5,000 cycles to something much higher, asks:

Q. Now, with that in mind isn't it perfectly clear that Major Armstrong was talking here about audible frequency ranges of 5,000 cycles and 7,500 and that the figure of 10,000 cycles and 15,000 cycles refers to the radio frequency band widths required for the transmissions of these ranges in modulating frequencies?

A. I think it is fair to take that interpretation of it, although the statement itself is quite ambiguous. My answer was that these frequencies of 10,000 cycles or 15,000 cycles are in the audible range, which is true.

Q. I don't expect to get too much help from you, Mr. Kelly, in interpreting the wide band patent.[3]

At which, the defending lawyer, hearing his witness abused, objected:

Mr. Crews: Your Honor, I object to that. I think it is completely uncalled for.

The Court: I regard it purely as an oratorical flourish.[4]

That interchange proved only that witnesses, lawyers, and judges are human.

In case the defendants could not prove that Armstrong did not really invent the FM system that had been in use for the previous twenty-five years, the next line of argument to be used was that FM was not a really important invention anyway. This argument subtly admits Armstrong did invent FM but asks "so what?" It is a useful argument because it will help the person infringing the patent if he can convince the judge that the invention is of minor value, or perhaps useless, to society. If convinced, judges are prone to find in favor of the alleged inventor but to give him almost no cash rewards. Thus, his victory is mostly a paper one. It is of historical worth, but he does not receive the damages he had hoped to get.

Both Emerson and Motorola had a third line of approach in case the first two did not work—that FM broadcasting was not an invention at all, but simply a slight improvement over an already invented entity (radio broadcasting) and an already known method (frequency modulation). In this argument the fact that no one, prior to Armstrong, had shown how to use FM to achieve useful radio broadcasting is ignored. The assumption is that something already known to the art and which is only a minor improvement cannot be patented. As precedent, the defense used a case concerning an improvement in light bulbs (The Jewel Incandescent Lamp Case [1945] 326 U.S. Supreme Court 242) in which the court held the inventor's improvement (in a frosted light bulb) was not patentable since the inventor had merely found latent qualities in an old discovery and adapted them to a useful end (a stronger frosted light bulb). The court held that this improvement did not advance the frontiers of science. Armstrong's lawyers maintained that the new wide-band FM system, as disclosed by

Armstrong, did advance the frontiers of science greatly. In finding for Armstrong, the court agreed.

When all three of these approaches failed, a last resort by the defendants was to ask that the case be dismissed on the grounds that Major Armstrong did not comply with the statute of limitations in regard to giving notice to the defendants of his intent to sue.

> Motorola contends that Armstrong's notice of infringement to Motorola as of December 20, 1948 . . . did not comply with the statutory requirement of notice. One of Armstrong's communications to Motorola dated December 20, 1948 . . . , identified the three patents in suit by number and date of issue and was in the form that has been used for generations for giving notice in compliance with the patent statute.
>
> . . . . Motorola's contention that the notice of infringement as of December 20, 1948, was inadequate is totally without merit. . . .[5]

In the case of the Emerson litigation, the Armstrong Estate won the court decision and collected damages. However, Motorola appealed the decision against it and the process dragged out until 1967 when the Supreme Court refused to review the Chicago Federal Court's verdict. Motorola was allowed a further appeal, and it was also turned down, in April, 1968. The amount paid by Motorola to the Armstrong Estate is an undisclosed figure. However, it is estimated to be about five million dollars.

Newsweek magazine, in a short article summarizing Armstrong's career and the Motorola case, comments again on the conscious effort of the AM industry to knowingly infringe on his patents and to consciously ignore FM:

> . . . . Ill and weary of battling manufacturers who had pirated his FM patents, Armstrong died a tragically broken man of 63, who considered himself a failure.
>
> By any other measure other than his own final desolation, however, Armstrong ranked as the U.S.'s greatest inventor since Edison. One of the last of the free-lance attic tinkerers, his inventions provided much of the basis for modern broadcasting.
>
> . . . . For sixteen years he carried on an ugly patent fight with . . .

Lee De Forest, who claimed to have invented the regenerative circuit. While the U.S. Supreme Court twice supported De Forest, engineering societies have given Armstrong the credit. But his fight for his FM patents was the bitterest of all—and the one that pushed him to suicide.

When Armstrong discovered static-free FM . . . in 1933, the radio industry was completely apathetic, partly because it was bewitched by the glowing promise of television. . . . But many others, including Radio Corp. of America, ignored his patents and turned out FM sets anyway, contending that his patents had roots in previous developments and that their systems were different.

Understandably, Armstrong was outraged and threw himself into a nightmarish sequence of complex patent-infringement lawsuits. After five years, he seemed to be making little headway. Physically, emotionally and financially drained, he despaired of ever establishing himself as the undisputed inventor of a revolutionary form of broadcasting. At his death, his major personal legacy was 21 unsettled lawsuits.

But his widow, Mrs. Marion Armstrong, pursued them, and through the years the manufacturing firms began to capitulate. RCA was the first late in 1954 when it settled out of court for $1,040,000. Gradually, the others followed, for total out-of-court settlements of about $5 million. . . . Edwin Howard Armstrong at last had won his full measure of vindication.[6]

And, while the inventor's widow was winning her case, the FM industry, spawned by that invention, was beginning to win its case.

For the first time in 9 years, the number of authorized commercial FM broadcast stations showed an annual increase rather than a decrease. From a peak of 1,020 authorizations in 1948 the commercial FM total had fallen to 546 in 1956. But figures for 1957 show 561, a net gain of 15.

Also, applications for new commercial FM stations doubled from 28 in 1956 to 58 in 1957. . . . Also, for the first time in many years there were competing applications, and 4 of these cases have been designated for hearing—2 in the New York area and 2 in the Los Angeles area. The number of operating commercial FM stations remained the same as for the previous year—530.[7]

Since 1957, the increase in number of FM stations has been

continuous and dramatic. In just the first five years of this upswing, FM stations increased from the low of 533 at the beginning of 1958 to 993 by 1962. In that same five-year period, FM receivers manufactured went from 764,000 in 1958 to 2,241,000 by 1962; and in 1963 almost three million sets were produced.[8]

It was in 1947 that the FCC Annual Report stated that three-fourths of all FM applications were from AM stations —which eventually led to the situation in which 80 percent of all FM stations actually on the air were AM owned. Astonishingly, this same report states that there "is little danger of AM interests monopolizing FM. . . ."[9] In the 1959 FCC Annual Report, the commissioners state that "The majority of the new applicants [for FM stations] are licensees of AM broadcast stations who propose to duplicate their AM programming over their FM facilities."[10] Of what economic value, or of what public service, it is to have AM broadcasting duplicated over FM receivers in the 1960's was even more questionable then, than it was in 1947. Such duplication amounts to the same economic waste that might result if a VHF television station owner were allowed to also own a UHF television channel in the same community, one on which he then broadcast the same program. To have two valuable broadcast facilities in the same community broadcasting identical material is a dubious value, to say the least. However, the FCC continued to give FM licenses to the AM interests, in spite of continued protests from independent FM petitioners and many in the FM industry.

In 1961, two FM highlights occurred. First, the number of authorized FM stations reached and passed the high 1948 mark of 1,020 with 1,092 authorized by the middle of 1961. Secondly, on June 1, the commission amended its rules to permit the transmission of stereophonic programs.

> . . . . Any FM station may transmit these programs without further Commission authorization. A subcarrier is used in conjunction with the main channel operation of stations offering the service.

.... While FM stereo must be regarded as an adjunct to aural FM service, the Commission is hopeful that it will add a new dimension to FM listening.[11]

One of FM stereo's proponents in the FCC was Commissioner Robert T. Bartley. He had joined the FCC in 1952 and prior to that he had been involved in FM broadcasting at various times since its inception. He had worked at the Yankee Network as far back as when Major Armstrong had demonstrated FM for John Shepard, the network's president. Mr. Bartley was the secretary-treasurer of the original FM Broadcasters, Inc., organized in 1939. In 1962, after the FCC rules were passed allowing stereophonic broadcasting, Commissioner Bartley spoke of the new stereo service before the Electronic Industries Association, in New York City.

The world is beginning to beat a path to the door of FM stereo. It was only a year ago last April that the Federal Communications Commission adopted rules for implementation of this service. But already 120 FM stations are broadcasting stereophonically. They are located in 95 markets—34 states. Approximately 90 percent of the population of the entire United States is within their service area. Industry sources estimate that, by the end of the year, more than 300 FM stations will be broadcasting stereophonically. This marvelous medium is fast becoming the "darling" of the industry.

Why is FM stereo better? My answer is it adds a new dimension of realism to a system heretofore capable of rendering a very superior monaural high fidelity service.

It brings to the public a new sense of reproduction which has previously been lacking—it brings into the home a realism which one experiences in the presence of an orchestra or other source of sound—it adds depth and separation....

The development of FM and stereo rests in large measure on Hi-Fi bugs. Some may think of them as over-demanding—striving for something which is unattainable. But, thanks to their demands, much has been done by the audio component manufacturers to improve receivers, amplifiers, speakers, and associated equipment. This improvement has necessarily raised the quality of the service. The connotation with the public is that FM means high fidelity. To me this is most significant. First of all, it implies that "Hi-Fi" is synonymous with quality. Secondly, it demonstrates industry's desire to capitalize on the term.

There is a great temptation to capitalize on the term "hi-fi" without actually giving the public true "hi-fi. I would urge that it is better to build your house on a foundation of solid rock than on shifting sand. We at the Commission have established engineering standards for stereo which provide a solid foundation for the medium. We have no control over the quality of receivers and parts which the industry may manufacture or advertise. But, I caution you, don't kill the goose that's about to lay the golden egg!

The trade press reports that our sister agency, the Federal Trade Commission, is keeping a watchful eye on manufacturers' claim as to the high fidelity equipment. A Federal Trade Commission spokesman is quoted as saying that, when a dealer advertises a high fidelity set for $49.95 it's pretty certain that it isn't high fidelity in any sense of the word. The Federal Trade Commission indicates that it will keep close tabs on spurious claims by corner-cutting dealers; and that present thinking is toward issuance of an industry guide, with some definitive terminology to protect the public. Again, I beseech you not to compromise with quality.[12]

The last two paragraphs are significant because it was not the first time that an important government or industry leader had warned the manufacturers in general not to produce mediocre equipment. It is not the first time that such a warning has been included in this book and there were similar warnings for which the author simply had no room. The point being made to the reader, obviously, is that from the beginnings of mass-produced receiving equipment manufacturing, the leaders of the industry (whose names need no repetition here) were continuously guilty of producing equipment of less than adequate performance. This applied both to AM and FM equipment. In AM manufacturing, the reason for the poor receivers seems to have been to use them as a competitive price weapon. In FM it was more in the way of an attempt to make sure the listener did not hear the quality difference between AM and FM, thus assuring the vested AM interests of a continued market for their products. Commissioner Bartley continued along these same lines:

A word about the market for high quality FM Stereo receivers. Already to date, 90 per cent of the population is within range of an FM station broadcasting stereo.

This is the present FM Stereo market ready made for your sales-manship. Not nearly everyone is yet sold on the value of qual-ity—many are not "sold" on the idea that the enhanced quality is worth the added cost. Many more cannot yet afford the price required for attaining a quality system. The question it seems to me is how can this vast potential market be saturated with a quality product? It occurs to me that more money will be made over the long run if quality is maintained even if the price required postpones the time when a portion of this potential market can afford to purchase. This suggests to me that dealers may find, for this prestige product, something new to the set distribution business—with a quality product with a trade-in value, it may be practical to develop a healthy and profitable re-sale receiver market. Or perhaps here we should adopt the Rolls Royce conten-tion that there is no such thing as a "second hand Rolls Royce but there are some which have been "previously owned." I believe this proposition should appeal to manufacturers of sets, too, because in the long run, more net profit would be made on each unit produced and more units would be manufactured because of the expanded market base.

Whether the world continues to beat a path to the door of FM Stereo depends largely, I believe, on whether its *quality* is maintained. Remember, in FM Stereo, the quality's the thing! It is the very foundation of the medium. But, if quality is sacrificed for economic expediency, it has lost its birthright.[13]

With stereophonic hi-fidelity programming to offer to an audience far more sound-educated than in the 1940's, FM stations increased not only their numbers of listeners, but their advertising clients. And with the increase in stations, receivers, listeners, and advertisers came an increase in pro-gram variety. No longer were communities confined to the classical "jukebox" menu of former years. Areas with only one FM station found, in many cases, that the station varied the programming over the day with several musical varieties, plus local "talk" shows. Communities with more than one station were able to support stations that appealed to diverse language groups, that offered popular music, classical music, and a variety of combinations. The prediction that the FM broadcasting approach would eventually become like a magazine marketing approach was being realized. Like many magazines, which appeal to many unique markets rather than to a homogeneous mass, FM in larger areas was able to develop programming that would appeal to smaller but loyal group interests: the Spanish-speaking people, the teen-age music group, the adult popular music group, the Negro audience, the lesser-known classical music group. It may be that this FM competition in "non-mass" audience programming led to some of the first AM innovations in programming in years. In New York City and elsewhere, a development of the mid-1960's was the all-news and talk programming. WCBS in New York City, for example, is on the air twenty-four hours a day with only news, time signals, and weather reports.

To deal with the upsurge of FM and the technical and other developments which had occurred in FM since 1941, the FCC in 1961 proposed to revise completely the covering rules. As a result, it created three classes of commercial FM stations based on power and divided the United States into three FM zones. It took almost two years to work out all the problems involved; and during this period, which ended in July of 1963, an FM "freeze" was on: no new stations were authorized. It took until 1964 for every state to have an FM station.

Among the new rules pertaining to FM were the following:

1. The country was divided into three zones for FM broadcast operation. Zone 1 (the same as TV Zone 1) includes part or all of 18 Northeastern states plus the District of Columbia. Zone 1-A is confined to the southern portion of California. Zone II includes the rest of the United States.
2. Three classes of commercial FM stations were created (over the previous two). Low-power Class A stations were assigned to all of the above zones; higher power Class B stations were assigned to Zones I and I-A; and higher power Class C stations to Zone II.
3. Power and antenna heights were given new regulations that confined stations to certain areas and protected against certain types of interference:

Class	Power	Antenna
A	3 kw	300 feet
B	50 kw	500 feet
C	100 kw	2,000 feet

4. The three classes of stations were given protected service ranges when they shared the same channel or co-channel with another station. Class A stations have a service range of 15 miles, Class B 40 miles, and Class C 65 miles.

5. In preparing new allocations for the number of FM stations in an area, the FCC set up the following "priority" in considering this matter:

1960 City Population	Number of Commercial Channels
1,000,000 and over	10 to 15
250,000 to 1,000,000	6 to 10
100,000 to 250,000	4 to 6
50,000 to 100,000	2 to 4
under 50,000	1 or 2

Priority considerations in preparing a new table of FM allocations to communities were to consider (1) existing FM stations, (2) giving FM service where none had existed before, (3) providing insofar as possible, each community with at least one FM station, (4) providing at least two FM stations to as much of the population as possible, (5) providing two local FM stations to all communities able to support them, (6) providing a substitute for inadequate AM service by using FM where possible, and (7) assigning channels to communities on the basis of their size, location, and number of outside services available.[14]

The FCC of this period, roughly 1961–1963, was made up of commissioners placed there by President Kennedy. Whether or not there is any correlation between the Kennedy administration and the help given to some really serious FM growth can probably only be a matter of one's political views. However, it was under Kennedy that Newton Minow became chairman of the FCC. And it was Newton Minow who described television programming as a "vast wasteland," which is hardly a remark an FCC chairman in the grip of the broadcasting industry would make publicly. After Kennedy's untimely death, many of his political appointees remained under President Johnson and followed the same plans they would have followed under Kennedy—that is, at least for a while. With Nixon comes Broadcasting's Dark Age!

One of the more far-reaching decisions concerning FM, which began under Minow and was finished under his successor Commissioner Henry, was that of non-duplication of programming in an AM/FM operation. Because of the increased demand for FM stations, the commission finally had to reevaluate the policy of allowing the AM station to duplicate, in most cases a 100 percent duplication, its AM programming. A speech by Commissioner Henry in 1963 indicates some of the new thinking about FM and this problem of programming and FM economics:

> True, the FM stations for which we have separate financial figures are, as a class, losing money, and although they represent about 15% of all aural stations, their gross revenues are only about 2% of the total. During 1961, of the independent FM stations, approximately one station in four made a profit, and they as a group lost $2.6 million. However, there is a growing evidence of advertiser interest in FM's command of a market which has both a high educational level and high income. This interest should be reflected in a more favorable picture in the future. Apparently 150 hardy souls think so, since they presently seek Commission permission to enter this impoverished field.
>
> In addition, the factors presently affecting FM's economic prospects differ greatly from those present through the doldrums of the 50's.
>
> Except from that small but intrepid band of independent FM operators, the public had no opportunity in the 1950's to listen to programs not available on AM, and little opportunity to appreciate the wide range characteristics of FM. Most of the dual programming was network, and characteristically this arrived at each station after being constricted through 5000 cycle telephone lines. If music was originated locally, it too often came from the 78 rpm shellac discs, whose main contribution to wide range reproduction was needle scratch and distortion. Also, many of

the early FM receivers, even those included in fairly expensive FM/AM consoles, were not satisfactory. . . .

It has remained to a large extent to the phonograph industry, once feared by many broadcasters as a competitor, to educate the general public in the virtues of high fidelity. The great breakthrough in this industry was, of course, the development of the vinyl phonograph record which, with greatly lowered surface noise, for the first time convinced the great mass of people that an amplifier tone control does not have to be glued to the full bass position. . . .

And these receivers are being purchased. A study for the QXR FM network in June of 1962, estimated that between 14 and 16 million homes now have FM, with a growth rate of 2 million sets per year. . . .

Now with all these portents for future FM prosperity, I suppose a number of you are wondering why the Commission has imposed a "freeze" on the processing of FM applications. . . . Of course, some sources have a morbid propensity for saying that the Commission always does the wrong thing at the wrong time. Discounting this criticism, why this preoccupation with a table of allocations when a similar table was jettisoned only four years ago? Doesn't the Commission want FM to grow like AM? The short answer is that it doesn't—not like AM. AM grew like a luxuriant jungle, and we who must administer its rules long for a highway instead of swampy paths hacked out with a dull machete.[15]

Commissioner Henry tactfully ignored the fact that since the FCC was the tool responsible for creating the rules that governed AM growth, it therefore contributed the fertilizer for the luxuriant jungle, but he continued:

There are, at the present time, about four thousand AM stations. The AM allocation picture, to a large extent, permits an applicant . . . to select the community he wishes to serve, regardless of the number of AM services already provided. . . . Most assuredly, there have been positive achievements under this system. Practically every community with a population of 10,000 or over . . . has its own local AM outlet. Daytime primary service by one or more signals is provided to almost the entire country. At night, however, the AM picture is dismal. A service map of the United States for the nighttime portion of broadcast hours resembles a teenager with a bad case of acne.

It is estimated that more than half of the land area of the country receives no primary service at night, and over 23,000,000 people are without such primary service.... Although over a thousand full-time stations have been added to the AM band in the last fifteen years, the nighttime coverage situation has remained substantially unchanged on paper....

Now I am not suggesting that any pre-planned system of AM allocations could have resulted in a really satisfactory nighttime primary service picture. The nighttime signal propagation characteristic of AM frequencies would forbid any such result. However, we might all agree that had the growth of standard broadcast stations been better directed and controlled in the past, AM service would have been provided more equitably and efficiently than is presently the case.

.... However, after nearly five years of experience with the application of a first-come, first-serve allocation system to FM, it has found the same undesirable tendencies of the AM system developing—principally the concentration of multiple FM stations in the large communities to such an extent that local FM service is being denied small, but still substantial communities.[16]

This new, liberal viewpoint of the FCC again became apparent in its Public Notice of May 16, 1963. Therein, it discusses why it feels that the AM/FM operator should begin substantial separate programming for his FM outlet. What it says is exactly what had been said for the previous fifteen years by critics of the whole AM/FM broadcasting set-up—critics who were mostly ignored.

It is still true that most independent FM stations do not report profitable operations. We believe, however, that the prospects of profitable FM operation may be improved if these stations are not forced to compete for advertising revenues with AM/FM duplicators giving away FM advertising free with AM time sales. Moreover, we have considerable doubt that AM-FM duplicators are a substantial force acting to put FM sets in the home or automobile. With certain localized exceptions, it does not appear reasonable to assume that significant numbers of people buy FM sets merely to hear what they can receive, quite adequately, on their AM radios. These factors, combined with our great concern over the frequency wastage represented by program duplication in areas where no more vacant FM channels remain, have caused us to reach the... conclusion that total AM-FM duplication is no longer a force to promote FM but is, to the contrary, a practice which, in many areas, will retard the growth of an efficient and viable service.[17]

For the critic, he might have added that total AM/FM duplication is certainly no longer a force to promote FM if, indeed, it ever was. The very reasons against duplication as given in 1940 and 1950 (that such duplication would retard the growth of FM) were still relevant in 1960. And all the reasons given by Armstrong, the Yankee Network, the FM Broadcasters Association, and individual station owners over the years (such as the lack of FM receivers on the market, the financial loss to FM caused by AM's giving FM time away free) were admitted without reservation by the FCC (which had allowed it in the first place). The goal of the present FCC is to separate the two services entirely, which, of course, brings on the headache of what to do with an operator who owns two radio stations serving the same market.

> Our ultimate goal, of course, is to achieve a system in which all... of the programming broadcast by AM and FM stations in the same community is separate. At the present time we propose to make a start toward this ultimate goal in the larger cities where vacant FM channels are no longer available and in which there are the most FM receivers.
>
> The Commission recognizes that considerations pertaining to common ownership, or "duopoly," are closely related to the problem of AM-FM duplication. At such time as FM stations are independently programmed and reach some degree of independent economic viability, the same policy that bars ownership of two AM stations or two FM stations in the same community would apply to AM-FM ownership. The Commission believes that separating ownership of FM and AM stations in the same community is a necessary long range goal. We do not feel, however, that the present state of FM development permits us to initiate a general process of separation at this time....
>
> Although we do not propose any rules regarding AM-FM duopoly, we believe that there is another factor which will work naturally toward our long range goal of independent FM operation. As FM frequencies become more and more scarce, it is to be expected that there will be an inevitable increase in the number of competing applications filed at renewal time against

dual AM-FM operations in the largest markets. In these situations, some dual AM-FM operators may well be vulnerable as against competing renewal applications, particularly if the existing licensee has been presenting the bare minimum of non-duplicated programming and has otherwise indicated that he regards his FM obligation as secondary to those in the AM field.[18]

The new proposal said that, in cities of over 100,000 population, the AM/FM operator shall not devote more than 50 percent of his average broadcast week to duplication of the programs of a commonly-owned AM station in the same local area. As could be expected, there was a revolt among the AM broadcasters—notably, the National Association of Broadcasters, the Columbia Broadcasting System, and the Storer Broadcasting System. The NAB, of course, represented most of the individual AM/FM operators, who, through the NAB, hoped to beat down this new rule and continue to be free to give away their FM air time as a bonus to sell AM. The other petitioners appealing to the FCC to reconsider the rule all had large holdings in AM stations in the big markets. CBS had the legal limit of seven AM/FM stations, all of which were duplicating completely the programming on both services. Storer Broadcasting Company had five AM/FM stations—also completely duplicating programming. The petitioners argued, first, that the FCC had no right to interfere with judgments concerning the programming of a station. With unusual candor, the FCC brief on this matter dismissed this plea with, "This argument is without substance."[19] It said further that the FCC is required to encourage the larger and more effective use of radio in the public interest and that this mandate clearly forced them to make a decision as to what extent they should permit two frequencies to be used to transmit the same signal in the same area.

Then, the petitioners argued that increased cost entailed by separate programming would be prohibitive. They said that programming would be more difficult, since the increased costs involved would have to result in the trimming of program budgets. This, in truth, would result in less desirable programming. Most AM stations in this group were "programming" popular music of the "top ten records" or "hit parade" type. For many, though it is a personal opinion, this is already a type of "less desirable" programming. If the FM outlet of an AM station had to switch to something else, a large number of listeners might consider that somewhat of a blessing. In any case, the FCC commissioners dismissed the argument almost without comment. In fact, all they said was:

> With respect to the ... programming arguments mentioned ...
> that ... we believe—and it is still our view—that there will be
> no net loss of FM service available to the public or substantial
> reduction in its quality.[20]

The FCC brief further stated that the fundamental principle involved was the wasteful and inefficient use of two frequencies to bring a single broadcast program to the same community. This waste and inefficiency is particularly significant when a demand arises for use of the FM frequencies, as it had been during this upsurge of FM building in the early 1960's. It will be remembered that the AM networks, engineers, station owners, and trade associations of the 1930's and 1940's argued against FM because they felt it was a waste of the high frequencies. At that time any broadcasting system that would require a larger use (wider bandwidth) of the limited radio band was considered anathema. Clearly, if FM required the larger "door," it should not be allowed. But in a different year and different situation, it was perfectly all right for the AM industry to use two separate radio frequencies to broadcast the same program to the same prospective audience. The fact that it took the FCC almost twenty years to view the situation as it was (and as it was it was hurting FM growth), is the wonder, and horror, of the communications critic. The new rules for non-duplication in cities over 100,000 went into effect in August of 1965. The broadcasting trade press generally reacted with approval. *Billboard* said:

> This is the first step in what is regarded as a certain move to
> eliminate all AM-FM programming duplication. The current ruling
> affects more than 200 of the most important AM-FM station pairs
> in the U.S.

What will this mean to already-rising FM sales? If history is a pattern, it should accelerate the growth of FM sets quite sharply. It means FM is finally coming into its own as an individual broadcast service. It offers some outstanding promotional opportunities.

The new FCC rule redresses a 20-year-old grievance. When commercial FM got its real start at the end of World War II, the FCC—after a bitter fight—agreed to permit duplication of AM broadcasting on FM channels. Although there were some FM only stations, much of the FM band was a carbon copy of AM. AM stations "gave" their FM affiliates to advertisers as a bonus for buying time.

FM's long, lean years are usually blamed on TV's competition. But program duplication probably was every bit as responsible—if not more.

. . . .

The new ruling means the end of FM's stepchild status as an appendage to AM. Already there is talk of setting up a new network services for FM programming. Already some stations are informing advertisers that they'll no longer get FM time as a bonus with AM commercials.

What does this mean to the dealer? Obviously, it means the FM's biggest growth period is still ahead. In the long run, when all program duplication is eliminated, it will mean at least one FM receiver for every home—and every automobile—in the United States.[21]

And from *Radio-Television Daily:*

ABC-Radio president Robert R. Pauley told *Radio-Television Daily* his network is now notifying AM affiliates that network commercials no longer are to be aired on FM sister stations unless specifically ordered.

Greater variety of programming on FM, whose set saturation is mounting strategically throughout the country, particularly in the top-100 marketing areas, is expected to affect Madison Avenue's demographic approaches to radio advertising buys. Those agency sources willing to offer comment indicated that the past two weeks have seen stepped up activity on FM in their research organizations—particularly along the lines of percentages of FM penetration in the top-100 markets and whatever audience compositions for FM are now available. These, they realize, will change radically as new programming begins to appear. But, they also realize, at least it provides a starting point for future analyses and comparisons in media buying—particularly against TV.[22]

In July of 1965, the FCC released some figures on the growing economic health of the FM industry. Total FM revenues (both independent and separate FM revenues of AM-FM combinations) increased from $13.9 million in 1962 to $16.3 million in 1963 and $19.7 million in 1964. The total losses for independent FM stations also decreased in 1964 as compared to 1963 (3.2 million for 294 stations reporting in 1963, $3.0 million for 306 stations reporting in 1964). For the first time in several years, more than 30 percent of the independent FM stations reported a profit (93 out of 306); this represented a post-1960 trend.[23]

The FCC also reported that FM saturation of large urban areas was beginning to show real progress:

> We also note what appears to be a fairly high degree of set saturation in large cities. According to a survey conducted by the Pulse, Inc., for the National Association of FM Broadcasters in 1963–1964, FM set saturation (percent of radio homes) in ten large cities was as follows: New York, 51.3%; Detroit, 37.7%; Los Angeles, 45.3%; San Francisco, 41.8%; Philadelphia, 35.2%; Boston, 38.2%; Cleveland, 34.8%; Chicago 44.7%; Pittsburgh, 31.1%; Washington, 36.6%. FM set sales have also shown a continuing increase. According to E.I.A. [Electronic Industries Association] data, the number manufactured increased from 905,000 in 1960 to 2,391,000 in 1964, with a projection for 1965 of more than 3,000,000. *Television Digest* estimates that 7,570,000 sets able to receive FM will be sold in the U.S. this year, compared to 6,000,000 in 1964.... In the trade press and by the NAFMB, this FM growth is attributed to our actions looking toward non-duplication.[24]

Whatever did it—non-duplication, stereo, increased appreciation of high fidelity, better public education generally, greater desire to hear fine music, or perhaps even the Beatles—by January 1967, there were 1631 FM stations in operation in the commercial FM band, with 223 stations under construction, for a total of 1854. There are almost 3000 assignments to this FM band, but there still remain great sections of the country where there is no satisfactory FM service. However, if the economic picture continues its upward surge, the remaining unassigned stations will accommodate these sections.

Working toward FM progress, in the industry, with the public, and as a lobby in Washington, is the National Association of FM Broadcasters. Founded in 1958 by a small group of independent FM broadcasters, the NAFMB is the only group exclusively devoted to the welfare of FM broadcasters. The association was created especially because this group felt the AM-owned FM stations were either "ignoring FM or, occasionally, opposing measures necessary for its growth."[25] The 1968 membership was approximately 320 FM stations. With some 2000 FM stations on the air, the reader may wonder why membership was so small. The answer, as the author sees it, is not difficult at all. The great majority of FM stations have as their parent company an AM station (often combined with a TV station). These joint operations have been a major deterrant to FM from its inception and not until 1965 did the owners begin to see the future of radio in FM. Old habits die hard and joining a pro-FM organization such as the NAFMB was hardly in the AM interest.

The NAFMB strongly supported the FCC's separate programming policy in contrast to the National Association of Broadcasters' (AM interests) opposition to it. The NAB, in its comments before the FCC arguing against the non-duplication rule said flatly, "The Association is opposed to this proposal."[26] Their entire argument is presented below. It makes interesting reading since the NAB contends that the previous AM/FM program duplication and ownership is *the* reason for FM's past successful growth. Since it is the opinion of almost all FM proponents (including this author) that this arrangement is responsible for FM's past *un*successful growth, the reader may find the two points of view enlightening.

> The Commission seeks comments on certain proposals to start its conclusion that ultimately there must be established an integrated AM-FM aural service. As is stated in the Notice, the Com-

mission proposes to accomplish this objective gradually and believes that the beginnings should be made in this proceeding.

In this regard, the Commission reaches certain conclusions on the function of FM services; proposes regulations relating to duplication of AM-FM programming; outlines possible future policies concerning separation of AM-FM station ownership. In view of the fact that none of these matters was discussed at the January 7th and 8th conference regarding AM growth problems and allocations, their inclusion in this proceeding is surprising and causes needless confusion.

The Association believes the Commission should separate any consideration of FM questions from AM allocation proceedings. We urge that paragraphs 11 through 22 referring to FM be deleted. The matters proposed, discussed and analyzed therein raise substantial policy questions that deserve and require separate consideration. Furthermore, and perhaps more importantly, resolution of the FM questions raised is in no way required for expeditious treatment of the issue concerning AM assignments. Their inclusion complicates resolution of the matters concerning AM radio and therefore may unnecessarily delay lifting the freeze which has been imposed on AM broadcasting.

Nevertheless in recognition of the possibility that the Commission may not accede to the Association's above-stated request for the separation of FM and AM matters, we believe it imperative to express our position on certain of the FM proposals.

The Commission states that its ultimate goal is to achieve a system in which all, or nearly all, of the programming broadcast by AM and FM stations in the same community be different. To make a start toward this goal, the Commission proposes to require FM stations located in cities of greater than 100,000 population, in which no unassigned FM channels exist, to devote no more than 50% of their average broadcast week to programs duplicated from any AM station in the same local area. The Association is opposed to this proposal.

The public interest, convenience and necessity is best served by the individual licensee, programming in a manner he believes to be best suited to the need of his particular community. There are numerous situations in which AM station reception is severely limited because of interference or power restrictions. Under such circumstances, licensees are justifiably duplicating the AM programs on affiliated FM stations. This enables all of the public in that station's service area to receive the Presidential speeches, baseball games and other fare on whichever receiver is best suited to their particular location.

The Commission appears to recognize this need for duplication, but then fails to grasp its significance in terms of service to the public; preferring to dispose of it on the grounds that it does not provide sufficient impetus to FM set sales.

We believe it evident any rule requiring non-duplication would have an adverse effect upon the continued existence and the further development of national AM network service. If duplication limitations are imposed the ability of national AM networks to provide a national program service for listeners will be diminished to the extent that such programs are not duplicated over FM facilities.

We are deeply concerned with regard to the Commission position that the same policy that bars ownership of two AM stations or two FM stations in the same community should apply to AM-FM common ownership. The long-range goal apparently is separate ownership of AM and FM stations. The Commission does not, however, propose to implement such a plan at this time. The Association desire to express its disagreement with this expressed future policy. AM stations have been the pioneers in the development of FM service.

The technical advantages of FM have permitted the provision of service with less interference and with greater fidelity. Moreover, the reach of the FM signal never coincides with the nighttime pattern of its AM companion. This fact is especially noticeable in the instances of a great many stations with FM facilities, where program duplication on the FM station gives much greater physical coverage than does the AM signal.

For example,

1) Daytime AM stations which duplicate on their FM facilities during the day and continue to provide program service on their FM station at night.

2) AM stations whose power limitation diminishes at night, while their companion FM station continues to render service in a constant area.

3) AM stations which must operate with a directional antenna at night, while their companion FM station continues to render service in a constant area.

4) Class IV stations whose nighttime coverage is minimal while its FM coverage remains constant.

As the Commission almost seems to recognize, if the FM service is to continue to develop and improve, it is essential that AM station licensees be encouraged to apply for and operate FM stations. As we stated in Docket 14185, as economics permit, FM stations may be expected to abandon duplication on a voluntary basis without Commission fiat. Duplication of programming has contributed to the survival of FM and the development of its steady growth pattern. The continuance of this policy will ensure this service's continued growth. While the Commission does not present a specific proposal to require separate AM-FM ownership, it extends a open invitation to the filing of competing applications against such operations at renewal time, especially when the licensee is presenting the proposed minimum amount of non-duplicated programming. The Association submits that such an expression on the part of the Commission is totally unwarranted and serves no purpose but to discriminate against AM licensees who pioneered in the field of FM broadcasting at great financial cost. The adoption of a policy encouraging competing applications in order to bring a station in line with Commission policy is certainly without justification and foundation in the Communications Act.[27]

Some of the misunderstandings that have surrounded FM broadcasting seem hard to dispel, even after years of experience. For instance, the idea that FM radio is naturally limited to very small service areas of only a few miles still persists. High-power FM stations, with service areas of fifty-miles or more, are broadcasting; but so many low-power FM stations, designated so by the FCC, are in existence that this idea tends to be substantiated. Similarly, the 1945 spectrum move occasionally pops up in the popular press and the discussion still tends to justify that move on the basis of "ionospheric" interference. As recently as October, 1966, an article in a New York regional magazine, *FM Guide*, contains such an example. This article is a written transcription of an FM radio program carried on WABC-FM in New York. It was hosted by Harry Maynard, himself a hi-fi stereo fan and admirer of Armstrong, who at that time worked for Time, Inc. The guests on this particular program, titled "Evolution of a Hi-Fi Broadcast," included John Bose, Armstrong's lifelong assistant from Columbia University; Murray Crosby, consulting engineer; and William Halstead, President of Multiplex Development Corp.:

Maynard: ... you told me the other day when we were discussing the content of this program, FM was moved from one band to another—what did you call it? The VHF band?

Crosby: There were two changes. The very early work was on the HF band which was 3–30 mc, and then Armstrong moved up and the FCC allowed him to use 42 mc. But later on, when the FCC changed to the present band of frequencies...

Maynard: But the second change obsoleted—I've seen the figure —7 million FM sets right away. I heard you tell me, Bill, if my memory is correct, that this was perhaps a blessing in disguise. Could you tell us something of that?

Halstead: I think experience has shown that if the lower channels had been used, there would have been a future problem because of long-range propagation effects which cause interference from stations 1,000 or 1,500 miles away.

Maynard: TV took over this band, didn't it?

Halstead: Yes.

....

Maynard: Armstrong didn't agree with that decision, did he?

Crosby: He didn't agree with that decision, I'm sure.

Maynard: What would be his position if he could speak now? John, you worked with him for years, what would he say about it?

Bose: I can't speak very well for him, Harry. I think the problem here is that we made tests at the time... and ... the data at that time—submitted to the Commission—showed that the performance on the lower band was superior. Now, of course, the problem here is that perhaps you'd have to do this over a period of eleven years to cover the sun spot cycle. I don't really know; I've been out of the business for some time, but I think if the Major were here you'd hear an interesting discussion.[28]

Murray Crosby, it should be noted, was working for RCA during the period in the early 1930's when Armstrong was doing his Empire State laboratory experiments. Crosby also delivered an important paper on FM to the Institute of Radio Engineers several months after Armstrong's November, 1935, FM demonstration before that same group.[29] It was one of the several papers to which Armstrong took exception, since he claimed that now he had demonstrated, as a fact, what radio scientists had said was impossible, that they were all now climbing on the bandwagon to show how it was done and could have been done all along. Another paper in this category was published by the same Bell scientist, John Carson, who had earlier stated that static would always be with us, like the poor, and that FM was inherently an inferior method of broadcasting. In October, 1937, he wrote on how well it worked and gave the mathematical data to support it.[30] His earlier articles, predating the Armstrong FM demonstrations, gave similar mathematical data to show why FM did not work. Some years later, Armstrong, bitter over the way FM was progressing and never quite having forgiven the industry and the radio scientists for their disbelief in what he had done, wrote a scathing paper titled, "Mathematical Theory vs. Physical Concept," which criticized sharply the use of pure mathematics as a tool of research:

> In the invention of the FM system and its subsequent development, there is a fundamental lesson that ought to be brought home to the radio art. It is a lesson of much importance to the younger part of the engineering profession who, never in direct contact with the facts, of necessity get them second-hand from text books, technical journals, and writers of tales with axes to grind. Anyone who has had actual contact with the making of the inventions that built the radio art knows that these inventions have been the product of experiment and work based on physical reasoning, rather than on the mathematician's calculations and formulae. Precisely the opposite impression is obtained from many of our present-day text books and publications.
>
> . . . .
>
> These writers, now knowing the result which the FM system produces, have merely set up new equations for it which "proves" that such a system eliminates noise. The effect, of course, is impressive. Yet, if one looks back a few years, one will find articles by some of these same writers, with other formulae, equally impressive, which proved that frequency modulation was quite useless.[31]

Armstrong continued the article quoting a half dozen authors, of between 1907 and 1935, who discussed the inferior qualities and characteristics of frequency modulation. He then quoted some of these same authors, after his 1935 demonstration, as they discussed the mathematical formulas they derived to show how FM does, indeed, suppress noise.

Another group organized to promote FM interests was the Armstrong Memorial Research Foundation. The foundation was formed in 1955 by friends and associates of the inventor to honor his memory and to aid in the continuation of the basic research in the radio art. The foundation also makes grants for research in electronics and related fields and provides scholarships for deserving undergraduates and graduate students. Among its activities is a yearly presentation of awards to FM stations for original and improved FM programming. These are called the "Major" awards and FM stations are invited to submit tapes in the various categories set up by the foundation. Its resources come from the Armstrong Estate, gifts from several other foundations and radio industry firms, and from member dues.

By 1965, the progress of FM broadcasting could be described as spectacular, considering its previous history. At the meeting of the second Armstrong "Major" Awards Banquet in New York City in December, 1965, Mr. Frank A. Gunther was speaker for the evening. Mr. Gunther was president of the Radio Engineering Laboratories, the major company which Armstrong used to build much of his equipment; a past president of the Armed Forces Communications and Electronics Association; past president of the Radio Club of America (the oldest radio society in the world); and a member of the National Industry Advisory Committee of the FCC. He summed up the progress of FM to date:

> Returning to FM broadcasting, everyone knows about the efforts of intrenched interests to shelve or degrade the use of FM, not to mention the intervention of World War II which delayed its development. With some encouragement from governmental sources, FM broadcasting, including commercial and educational, now boasts of some 1700 stations in the United States alone. Correspondingly, to listen to these stations we have estimated more than 30,000,000 receivers equipped with FM. To these figures we could add an immense number of FM broadcasting stations and FM receivers in foreign lands, where, particularly in Europe, the advantages of FM were recognized before they were in the United States, and where, after World War II, the relative development of FM broadcasting far outstripped that in our own country. . . .

Dry statistics have no place in a talk of this nature, but it is interesting to compare what has been done with FM in other areas of our economy and national life. The Safety and Special Radio Services include the following general categories of radio services using FM:

Business and special applications
Forest products and Forestry Conservation
Industrial radiolocation
Manufacturing
Motion picture production
Petroleum
Power generation and distribution
Press relay services
Telephone maintenance
Emergency automobile service
Motor carriers
Railroads
Taxicabs
Fire fighting
Broadcast Studio links and remote pick-ups
Highway maintenance
Police and other local government services
Special emergency and State Guard units

This array of services now has 350,000 FM transmitters in operation, plus at least an equal number of FM receivers....

We should also remember that the audio tracks of TV transmissions utilize FM, and there are approximately 70 million TV receivers in the United States alone. When all these are added to the regular FM broadcast receiving equipment, plus the FM equipment employed in Safety and Special Radio Services, the total use of FM in the U.S. is staggering.

To this Foundation it should be interesting to note that the National Aeronautics and Space Administration is now involved in ... broadcasting radio signals from satellites directly into home receivers using FM....

One important use of FM should not be overlooked ... the Armed Forces of the United States.... FM is now ... used for:

Air-to-Air communications
Air-to-ground communications
Ship-to-shore circuits for amphibious operations
Mobil tactical field radio equipment
Point-to-point microwave circuits
Point-to-point tropospheric scatter systems
Satellite communications

Space communications
Transportable tactical tropospheric scatter circuits
Underwater radio communication circuits
Best estimates I can obtain indicate that there are currently about
150,000 sets of FM equipment in use by the Armed Forces...
in use wherever our forces are deployed, including Viet Nam.[32]

The following "Selected FM Statistics..." table shows the recent economic upward growth of FM stations and the trend to a more favorable financial situation. Even at this writing some of the economic pieces of the FM puzzle are missing and may be missing until all AM/FM operations are extinct. That day may be coming close, since beginning with January, 1967, 50 percent of the programming of 100 FM stations previously exempted from the non-duplication rule had to be separated from that of their AM counterparts.[33]

TABLE 1

SELECTED FM STATISTICS ON NUMBER OF STATIONS,
REVENUES, EXPENSES AND INCOME

Year	Total FM Stations Reporting	Total FM Revenues (AM-FM & FM Only) (Millions)	Total FM Only Stations Reporting[a]	FM Expenses (FM Only) (Millions)	Total FM Only Revenue[b] (Millions)	FM Losses (FM Only) (Millions)
1970	2,105	84.9	464	46.8	40.6	6.2
1969	1,961	67.5	442	38.9	33.4	5.5
1968	1,888	53.2	433	32.2	28.3	3.9
1967	1,706	$39.8	405	$26.8	$22.6	$4.2
1966	1,575	32.3	381	22.7	19.4	3.3
1965	1,381	24.7	338	19.0	15.7	3.3
1964	1,175	19.7	306	15.8	12.8	3.0
1963	1,071	16.3	294	14.6	11.4	3.2
1962	993	13.9	279	12.5	9.3	3.2
1961	983	10.0	249	9.7	7.1	2.6
1960	789	9.4	218	8.2	5.8	2.4
1959	662	5.7	148	5.9	4.3	1.6
1958	533	4.0	93	3.2	2.5	0.7
1957	499	3.1	67	2.5	2.0	0.5
1956	472	2.4	51	1.8	1.4	0.4

[a]The figures in this column represent only those FM stations reporting to the FCC. The actual figure of on-air stations is slightly higher (from a half-dozen to a dozen or so) since there are always a few stations who are late in getting their

reports in. The actual number of FM stations on the air is always lower than the authorized number of FM stations since the authorized figure includes stations under construction.

ᵇFM industry totals show no net income. These figures represent only a small percentage of all FM stations as AM-FM licensees (about 75 percent of all present FM stations) are not required to report FM expenses and income to the FCC. If all FM stations were required to include these figures, the industry loss figure would undoubtedly be much higher.

SOURCE: FCC public notices on annual broadcast data 1956–1970.

"The New York City area magazine," *FM Guide*, said of this extension of non-duplication ruling:

> Up to now if you listened to many a major AM-FM station, you often heard the same programming of FM as you did on AM. With all major AM-FM stations in the New York City area now complying with the FCC ruling, you, the listener, will have at your fingertips the equivalent of at least half a new station.
>
> What do we at *FM Guide* think this FCC regulation adds up to? Many more listening alternatives for the listener. Look what's happened! We now have over 50 FM stations in the New York area. This ought to be a big enough table of listening to serve the most catholic of tastes.
>
> And now with stereo, FM brings a new realism which allows the listener to hear recorded and live broadcasts just the way you normally hear all sound—in stereo. Stereo does to sound what color does to color TV—it gives you a rich new dimension to all of your listening experiences.
>
> We believe radio has now arrived with the full program development of FM-Stereo. Every kind of musical taste is now served by FM Stereo. This means a new renaissance for radio.[34]

During 1968, the FCC investigated two areas significant for the FM industry—the multiple-ownership rules of broadcasting and the freezing of all AM radio applications. The first of these areas, prohibiting multiple station ownership in one market, is a laudatory example of the FCC's concern over the problem of monopoly and concentration. In their memorandum of this action, they stated that objectivity and promotion of diversity of viewpoints and programs were of utmost importance to their decision.[35] Of course, this has been the *stated* view of the FCC since its inception. Waiting until 1968, when, for all practical purposes, no major-market AM allocations remain and fewer than one-third of all FM allocations remain is not going to prevent monopoly. Monopoly occurred in the first thirty-five years of FM's history and can hardly be reversed now. As of July, 1968, total authorized radio stations (AM and FM) numbered 6772. Of that number, 2472 were authorized FM stations.[36] Three-fourths of that number were owned by AM stations in that same market. The present rule-making on preventing one-market monopolies is very much like locking the barn door after the horse has run away. The major AM and newspaper interests long ago monopolized the communications field in their respective communities, and the best radio licenses in the major advertising markets have been sewn up by these interests for many years. The new ruling does not affect these existing stations. The proposal does not require giving up any already held AM/FM operations. It will affect only any future applications for AM, FM, and TV facilities. The remaining AM allocations are few and far between, as the AM band is so crowded now that the FCC fears serious interference problems will jeopardize the entire service. The FM picture is not much brighter, since the remaining allocations are mostly in small communities where only one station is allocated anyway. Under this new rule, prohibiting multiple-station ownership in one market may result in a different kind of communications empire. Up until now, a businessman found it natural and convenient to have his AM, FM, and TV stations (assuming he was granted all three) in the same city or market. And the rule, as we have seen, allows him to have seen AM, seven FM, and seven TV stations—a total of twenty-one under single control. Under the new proposal, he could still own twenty-one stations and it is conceivable they would have to be in twenty-one different markets. Whether this type of ownership pattern is really any improvement over the older method is arguable. He may still own twenty-one licenses! If that's not monopoly . . . !

As of August 1, 1968, there were 4300 authorized AM stations. In July, 1968, the FCC said no new applications for AM radio stations would be accepted.[37] Their reason for the freeze was that there had been no significant changes in their attempt to eradicate "white" areas in broadcasting areas lacking primary radio service. Primary service is that service rendered by an individual local station that serves a community. This station can be a low-power one whose coverage is usually one town, or a high power one—that covers large areas.

> .... At the same time, this tremendous proliferation of stations has occurred without significant reduction of "white" areas. The outlying areas which lacked primary service in 1946 have been reduced only a minute degree by the continual flow of new assignments. More than this, concentration upon the creation of multi-station markets has led to a derogation of engineering standards, so that service rendered by existing stations in the outer most regions of their normally protected service areas has been imparied, future power increases to extend the interference-free contour over growing suburban populations are often rendered impossible, and available channels for... new stations... have been reduced in number.[38]

The FCC, in applying this freeze, wanted time to study the whole radio spectrum problem. Among the areas to be evaluated was whether or not there was any further need for any AM stations, except in areas not already served (the "white" areas) by AM, whether all existing AM spectrum space should be reserved for "white" areas only, and whether any future allocation plan of the remaining spectrum should view AM and FM as a single aural service.[39]

This is what many in the FM industry have always wanted. When treated as part of one aural service, FM cannot help but begin to receive some preferential treatment. Under this concept, a community is seen in the light of its lack of, or need for, a radio outlet(s); not in the light of how many AM stations or FM stations are present or absent. Had this been the philosophy some years ago, the FCC would have granted more FM licenses, since differences in AM and FM power would have had to be put on a competitive basis. Such a move could not be made, however, until the number of FM receivers in any one community was significantly high. Today that number is significant, and the pending legislation on the proposed AM-FM two-band receivers makes it even more significant. A station owner who knows that an advertiser is equally interested in AM and FM may prefer the FM license because of the greater technical superiority of FM and the coming financial importance of FM stereo.

A review of 1966 shows that the broadcasting industry (AM/FM/TV) reported an annual revenue figure of just over three billion dollars ($3,075,100,000). Of this, radio (AM and FM) accounted for 28.3 percent of total broadcast revenue ($872,100,000). FM's share was 9.5 percent ($32,300,000) of the total broadcasting revenues, and 27 percent of just radio's share. [40]

Broadcasters Daily reported that 13,564,000 FM-equipped radios were manufactured in 1966. This was more than all the FM sets made in the previous five-year period. As a percentage of all radio sets sold in 1966, FM-equipped models accounted for 36 percent of the total. The estimate for 1967 was 45 percent and for 1968, 50 percent. [41] At the 1967 annual NAFMB convention, industry leaders attributed the FM upsurge to the non-duplication rule; the public demand for more quality listening, especially stereo; more advertising and promotion; and a 70 percent increase in the number of FM stations over the previous five years. The effects of non-duplication was the subject of an NAFMB survey in January, 1967. It indicated that in that same month, 86 percent to 93 percent of the AM/FM stations in the top fifty markets were already broadcasting separate programs. [42]

The major disappointment in this FM growth picture was in auto radios. Of all car radios made in 1966, only 7 percent were equipped with FM tuning. [43] This is attributed partly to the introduction of car tapes and partly to the resistance of auto manufacturers and dealers to include the more expensive FM equipment. FM auto set prices are way out of line when compared to AM prices. FM sets for new cars are usually priced two to three times higher than similar AM equipment.

Car salesmen are reluctant to push the higher-priced units, fearing the customer may find the total price too high, after adding up all the usual extras (such as power equipment, air conditioning, white wall tires, etc.). An average FM car radio in 1966–1967 was $159.00, while a similar quality AM unit was about $70. Car manufacturers have shown a reluctance to make AM/FM tuners for cars. FM proponents are still fighting to get the Congress to pass legislation requiring all radio sets to have both AM and FM bands (similar to the legislation that now requires all television sets to be capable of receiving both VHF and UHF stations). Two bills were presented to both Houses of Congress in 1968 to amend the Communications Act of 1934 to require the manufacture of the two-band sets. At this writing, action is still pending. Pushing this legislation is the NAFMB. The president of that group wrote that the congressmen who have introduced the bill are:

> .... well aware of the artificial barriers that are holding back FM and denying its superior service to the public.... All-channel AM and FM legislation is just as vital to the full development of an aural broadcast service as the All-channel Television Receiver Act passed in 1964 was to the development of a complete television service.... In view of aural radio's greater mobility and more convenient availability under most circumstances, the AM-FM legislation actually has more to offer the American public when public safety, emergency, and like information are considered.
>
> When it is also considered that practically all educational aural broadcasting is FM and that in many communities... the only available service is FM, this legislation is a realistic must.[44]

The fact that FM had finally arrived as an important and competitive medium was especially evident in the reaction of advertising agencies. This optimistic view has been reflected in the trade press over the past few years, both in their editorial columns and in the various money and equipment statistics they present. It was further evidenced by the FCC figures on the growing number of stations reporting a profit. Likewise, the FCC figures on FM money losses showed a levelling off. The FCC also reported that there was an increase in the number of applicants for a particular FM allocation, thus reflecting the new-found worth of an FM license. The trade press also reported that advertisers were treating FM on an equal footing with AM. Because of increases in listeners, many major markets in 1968–69 had FM audiences which were capturing 65 percent of the total radio audience. The national average of FM's share of this total radio audience was 50 percent, and this was in the prime evening hours.[45] In addition to the more selective audiences that FM delivers, advertisers find FM offers a generally more prestigious audience than does AM. FM often offers the advertiser a degree of commercial isolation in that most good music stations allow six commercial minutes an hour. FM advertising rates also remain the biggest bargains in broadcasting.[46]

Major rating and research services, including Pulse, Inc., the Hooper organization, the American Research Bureau, and the Radio Advertising Bureau, are active in the FM field, bringing the long-needed data on FM receiver ownership, FM listening habits, FM share of audience, and the make-up of that audience to the industry. FM stations are being given lower rates for the use of these services to encourage them to use the research firms. Pulse, Inc., in 1967, cut the normal rate of their services to independent FM stations by 50 percent. This cut was based on the fact that about 50 percent of U.S. homes were then equipped with FM receivers.[47] Further evidence of the growing set penetration of the market and the growing size of FM audiences was revealed by the American Research Bureau in a thirty-market survey conducted in January and February, 1968. Results showed that the top-ranked FM station in four markets was also in the top-ranked five stations, overall, in those markets. In twenty-four markets the top-ranked FM station was among the top ten stations (AM and FM) in those markets.[48]

With the increasing requests for FM stations and growing scarcity of channels available, the FCC on May 12, 1967 announced a more restrictive policy on granting license requests. All new requests for FM stations have to include a convincing show of need for the station and a showing that the new FM assignment would not prevent future needed stations in other nearby communities.[49] FM Class C stations were given permission to increase facilities to provide interference-free reception in a service area of about sixty-five miles.

By 1968, FM stations were using the services of old, established station representative firms. This gave FM greater stature as a competing medium. A spokesman for one such firm in New York City said that his company had "been built on AM... but we must recognize the inevitable.... FM is here as radio.... FM deserves major representation."[50] Another station representative firm pinpointed the turning-point for FM as a non-salable item to a marketable commodity in 1965, when research services began publishing AM and FM figures in the same book.[51]

By mid-1968, the number of authorized FM stations on the air was 2392, with 670 broadcasting in stereo.[52] By the beginning of 1972, there were 2762 operating FM stations with 713 broadcasting in stereo. Further, the FCC had before it in January of 1972 almost 300 applications for new FM stations. The FM growth pattern will greatly slow down now since almost all allocations (licenses) have been assigned. About the only way to get an FM station today is to try to buy one; that is, to get a license transferred and then buy the building and equipment from the former licensee. License transfers need FCC approval. If a present licensee is not trying to sell his station, an FM (or AM or TV) license is still available if a concerned group or individual wants to challenge that licensee at the time of license renewal (every three years). This entails legal expense and proof that the incumbent licensee is not doing a responsible job of broadcasting for and to his community. That ought not to be too hard to prove in some cases!

The Electronics Industries Association felt that 1968 was an unusually good year for FM growth. In its 1968 yearbook the association stated that:

> An upsurge of a consumer interest in frequency modulation (FM) radio has been a pronounced trend of the past several years.

> Last year 34.3% of all table, clock and portable radios in the United States were designed to tune the FM Band, the vast majority of these being combination FM-AM radios. Some 55% of all factory dollar sales in these categories represented radios with FM. In addition FM last year made its first important inroads into the auto radio market where it totalled 10% of unit sales.
>
> The full story of FM isn't told in radio sales figures alone. Last year 95.7% of all TV-radio combinations... and 96.1% of radio-phonographs... contained FM-AM tuners.[53]

The number of FM-equipped cars grew by over two million between 1966 and 1970. In 1970, there were over 3,100,000 cars on the road so equipped. General Motors put FM tuners in 50% of their 1970–1971 models (99% of all Cadillacs and Corvettes have an FM radio). In the 1970–1971 car model year, 30% of all U.S. cars had FM tuners added and Motorola reported over 20% of its auto radio production was FM tuners.[54]

The research firm of Pulse, Inc. surveyed FM set ownership in the top 90 market areas in 1971. The set penetration estimates (households owning an FM set) ranged from 71% to 95%. The New York City metropolitan area had an FM set penetration of 82.4%; Chicago, 87.8%; Los Angeles, 84.2%; Honolulu, 71.8% and Detroit, 95.8%. With such high figures for set ownership, national advertisers still have not flocked to FM. There remains an AM advertising bias that is slowly changing. Much, if not most, of FM advertising remains at the local or regional level.

It seems somewhat unusual that so few commercials have been designed for stereo radio. With stereo broadcasting now ten years old, there are only a few scattered instances in which a radio commercial or campaign, made by a national advertising agency, attempted in any serious way to use the stereophonic art as part of the selling message (not the usual gimmick of two announcers merely speaking from either channel). No doubt a number of reasons have contributed to this situation; there have not been enough FM sets in use to warrant the extra time, talent and money for such commercials (today this is no longer the case with set penetration figures so high); advertising agencies, in general, are seldom innovators, but copiers and followers of sales-proven techniques; and (quite personally) advertising people who create ads and ideas are not often very creative in new fields until someone else comes along and does it. In other words, the creative and persuasive ART of stereo is not presently one of the strengths of the very industry that could use it. Let one really successful stereo-oriented radio sales campaign happen and then there will be, no doubt, a rush to similar commercials.

It should come as no surprise, by this time, that another battle of quality vs. mediocrity is now going on over the latest FM improvement—quadraphonic broadcasting. Two basic systems have evolved; the "not-really" four separate chan-nels—the matrix system, and the "true" four-channel separation—the discrete system. In the former case, the sound received has been compared by its critics to having a double stereo sound effect. In the latter case, one hears four separate signals blending. Proponents on both sides (with patents and profits at stake) bombard the public and the FCC with the virtures of their particular system. One can only hope the FCC will act in the name of quality and public interest this time and not repeat their four-decade history of succumbing to the loudest voice and largest pocketbook.

The discrete system (referred to as a carrier-multiplexing approach) may lose out because of some very old and tired (but profitable) arguments. The matrix (pseudo) system group insists that their equipment is ready to go now, less expensive, compatible with present consumer-owned equipment and gives excellent 4-channel "effect" sound. Further, the matrix system requires no special or changed FCC rules for immediate broadcasting.

On the surface, all good reasons. Let us add one more: it gives this group all the profits if the FCC gives their blessing to the matrix system. On the other hand, if the FCC supports the true four-channel discrete system, that group gets the profits. But the public also gains a better quality sound service. There should not be a serious concern for today's compatibil-ity, when ten years from now most present-owned sets will have been discarded for new receivers anyway. RCA once made a pitch for its color TV system based on the fact that their color could be received on then-owned black and white TV sets. Today RCA is hardly interested in selling black and white TV sets. The manufacturers of color television receivers could care less about compatibility in the 1970's when they would just as soon the public junked them and bought the newer more expensive color sets. But RCA won its argument (over what many consider were far superior color systems) and got its patents approved and its royalties in the bank.

This same kind of short-term philosophy, coupled with fast profits may yet stick the public with a less-than-better radio quadraphonic sound system, when with some patience and quality arguments the public might for once get what it deserves—a superior quadraphonic broadcasting service.

A summary of comments on the fate of the better system from one of the trade magazines (in 1971) indicates how little things have changed at the FCC over the years.

OUTLOOK DIM FOR DISCRETE 4-CHANNEL FM:
... What are prospects for reasonably speedy approval of companion discrete quadraphonic stereo-FM system? ... inquiries at FCC produce this answer: Lousy.

... FCC feels no sense of urgency... the issue is "way down on the list" because of FCC budget problems, lack of personnel for such a large proceeding.

When proceeding does start—and it's by no means certain for 1972—FM broadcasters can't be depended upon to support it. Many may actively oppose it because switch to FM stereo was more expensive than anticipated and resulted in little or no increase in revenues. Four-channel threatens more expense.... Any record companies which cast their lot with matrix 4-channel systems (including CBS) also can be expected to oppose new broadcast standards. Matrixed 4-channel material, live or recorded, can be transmitted over regular stereo-FM outlets without FCC permission and can be played back in 4-channel mode through decoder. About 70 stations are believed to be broadcasting encoded 4-channel music now.

If FCC should eventually start 4-channel stereocast proceedings, it will be lengthy process, with plenty of systems proposed, field-testing, etc. It took 7 years from start of stereo recording to FCC's establishment of FM stereo standards in 1961.[55]

What is implied in the above facts and inferences is that the FCC usually drags out investigative proceedings when great fortunes are at stake. This could be done in order to allow the time for the vested interests to get their products out and marketed in such quantities that those interests can then use the excuse that the public already owns millions of their sets so why should there be changes that will obsolete all those products . . . and their profits.

Another interesting line in the above quote is that the FM broadcasters themselves may oppose the discrete system. If this is true, it will be because three-fourths of all FM stations are still part of an AM parent company whose financial interests are still tied to a TV station and/or newspaper or a network or record manufacturing company. Therefore, these FM stations would find themselves financially hurt while the independent FM station would probably support the better quadraphonic system since it has (usually) no outside interests in AM, TV, or record and equipment manufacturing.

If the matrix system builds in momentum and large manufacturers of transmitting equipment, receiving equipment and the matrix records played over that system are making great fortunes, then there is seldom much chance for any competitor to elicit some change, *even if that change is toward a superior service or product*. That must be the most evident business "fact" to come out of this research!

If FM broadcasting has begun to realize some of the promise predicted for it thirty years ago, it will be a somewhat hollow victory. Some FM pioneers are dead and others have lost great sums of money or perhaps never made any to speak of. In the coming decade, with profits becoming a daily reality, it will not always be the pioneers of FM who will be reaping the financial rewards; it will often be the newcomers, the Johnny-come-latelys, and (most galling of all to old-time FM proponents) many AM license owners who own most of the present FM stations: Those owners and companies who for so many decades did their best to retard FM broadcasting and who now, like a mindless mistress who switches loyalty with each passing stranger, will now embrace FM for its future financial rewards.

NOTES

[1] *Armstrong v. Emerson*, p. 1153.

[2] *Ibid.*, p. 1157.

[3] *Ibid.*, p. 1159.

[4] *Ibid.*

[5] United States District Court, Northern District of Illinois, Eastern Division, Civil Action No. 54-C-19, Esther Marion Armstrong, Executrix, Plaintiff, v. Motorola, Inc., Plaintiffs Reply Brief, p. 5.

[6] "PATENTS: An Inventor's Vindication," *Newsweek*, October 30, 1967, p. 70.

[7] *FCC Twenty-third Annual Report*, 1957, p. 115.

[8] *FCC Thirtieth Annual Report*, 1964, p. 75.

[9] *Ibid.*, p. 21.

[10] *FCC Twenty-fifth Annual Report*, 1959, p. 69.

[11] *FCC Twenty-seventh Annual Report*, 1961, p. 55.

[12] FCC, Address by Federal Communications Commission Robert T. Bartley, before the Electronic Industries Association Symposium, New York City, June 26, 1962.

[13] *Ibid.*

[14] All material in this list was summarized from FCC Public Notice, Mimeo. No. 23315, July 26, 1962.

[15] FCC News Release, Mimeo. No. 30352, An Address of E. William Henry, Commissioner, Federal Communications Commission, before the Georgia Radio and Television Institute, Athens, Georgia, January 24, 1963.

[16] *Ibid.*

[17] FCC Public Notice, Mimeo. No. 35534, May 16, 1963.

[18] *Ibid.*

[19] FCC Public Notice, Mimeo. No. 58052, October 7, 1964.

[20] *Ibid.*

[21] David Lachenbruch, "New FCC Rules Seen as Boosting Sales of FM Sets," *Billboard*, August 8, 1964, p. 1.

[22] Hal Gold, "FCC's Pep Shot for Nets: 50% Separate FM Slate," *Radio Television Daily*, July 27, 1964, p. 1.

[23]FCC Public Notice, Mimeo. No. 80342 (no date).

[24]*Ibid.*

[25]From a short mimeographed history prepared by the National Association of FM Broadcasters entitled "NAFMB: PAST... PRESENT... FUTURE."

[26]From a reprint of the National Association of Broadcasters brief to the FCC "Comments of the National Association of Broadcasters," September 9, 1963. The original is part of the FCC Docket No. 15084.

[27]*Ibid.*

[28]Harry Maynard, "Evolution of a Hi-Fi Broadcast," *FM Guide* (New York City), October, 1966, p. 31.

[29]M. G. Crosby, "Frequency Modulation Propagation Characteristics," *Proceedings of the Institute of Radio Engineers*, XXIV, June, 1935, p. 898.

[30]J. M. Carson and T. C. Fry, "Variable Frequency Electric Circuit Theory with Application to the Theory of Frequency Modulation," *Bell System Technical Journal*, October, 1937, p. 513.

[31]Edwin H. Armstrong, "Mathematical Theory vs. Physical Concept," *FM & Television*, August, 1944, p. 11.

[32]Address made at the Armstrong Memorial Research Foundation's Second Major Armstrong Awards Banquet, The Engineers Club, New York City, December 16, 1965.

[33]FCC Public Notice, Mimeo. No. 81217, March 10, 1966.

[34]"The New Voices of FM," *FM Guide*, January, 1967, p. 25.

[35]FCC, Docket No. 18110, FCC 68–554, Mimeo. No. 15881, May 17, 1968.

[36]FCC, Report and Order, FCC 68-739, Mimeo. No. 1850, July 18, 1968.

[37]*Ibid.*

[38]*Ibid.*

[39]*Ibid.*

[40]"Auto FM Sets Way Out of Line is Claim," *Broadcasters Daily*, April 3, 1967, p. 5.

[41]"FM Set Sales at an All-time Peak; Kinship with AM Formats Also Rises," *Variety*, April 5, 1967, p. 39.

[42]"The Acceleration of FM Radio Down a Road Paved With Gold," *Merchandising Week*, April 10, 1967, p. 10.

[43]Consumer Electronics," *Television Digest*, April 3, 1967, p. 10.

[44]NAFMB News Release, April 26, 1968.

[45]"FM Captures 25% in 7 Markets," *Broadcasters Daily*, April 1, 1967, p. 2, and "FM Reaches New Plateau at NAB-Time," *Sponsor*, April 3, 1967, p. 76.

[46]*Ibid.*

[47]"Survey Costs Down, Audience Up," *Broadcasting*, April 3, 1967, p. 70.

[48]From an undated industry newsletter (1968) called *Radio Audience Measurement*, distributed by the American Research Bureau.

[49]*FCC Thirty-third Annual Report*, 1967, p. 51.

[50]"FM Catching the Bridal Bouquet." *Broadcasting*, April 1, 1967, p. 98.

[51]*Ibid.*

[52]*Consumer Electronics 1968: An Annual Review of Television, Radios, Phonographs, Tape Recorders and Players* (Washington, D.C., Electronic Industries Association, 1968), p. 23.

[53]*Ibid.*, p. 14.

[54]*Ward's Automotive Report*, November 2, 1970, and *Broadcasting*, May 24, 1971, p. 60.

[55]"Consumer Electronics," *Television Digest*, Vol. 11, No. 49, p. 9 (no date, but 1971; a photocopy page used as a handout).

A VERY PERSONAL CLOSING

> Maj. Armstong! Sometime get one of the old men of radio to tell you how the wretch Sarnoff took crazy Maj. Armstrong for a ride, took all his patents.... Sometime see if you can find how the early history of radio is littered with the bodies of the make-a-buck artists screwing the inventors—and those who hoped for some chance to use broadcasting for the beauty of words, and the thousand voices of the poor and scared, and hungry. Ask an old radio man about how that didn't happen![1]

That's from an anti-establishment, quasi-underground magazine titled *The Realist*. The article is called, "Everything You've Ever Wanted to Know About Radio and Television (Which Your Friendly Local Broadcaster Would NEVER Tell You...)". I include it here for a number of reasons. First, I found it interesting that the Armstrong/Sarnoff feud (if it can be called that) is still popping up in print even after all these years. Both men are now dead. Both men will be part of our history but for vastly different reasons. One was a business genius. One was a great man.

The quote is also interesting to me because of the remarks about the littered bodies of inventors. I don't think the author of the above has ever read a speech that will be shortly quoted and was written back in 1936. In that speech I would ask the reader to note the very same kind of remarks concerning how our business society has treated the inventors who have made our nation the technical wonder that it is. I located this particular speech in some ancient files of the FCC library (in an old building that they no longer occupy).

At the beginning of this research in the late Sixties, I was almost totally unaware of the history of frequency modulation and certainly unaware of its inventor (is it a plot that his name is so unknown?). Except for one classroom lecture on FM, for me the agonizing story of FM and its inventor was yet to come. It was not until after I had collected a vast amount of data and read and digested it that I began to fit the pieces of this financial, political, technical, and social puzzle into some thread of a story or pattern. If some of my personal feelings have been obvious in this book, it is because you cannot know the FM story without becoming personally involved. The written evidence that documents this book is overwhelmingly on one side; of that I am quite aware. However, there has been precious little written by the "other" side that has come to my attention. In one of the hearings (the 1948 Senate Hearing on FM and RCA patent policy), an RCA executive gave a historical version of FM history so contrary to all other written versions that I had to view it as suspect (that's a nice way of saying it was a bunch of lies and half-truths). It contained the same kind of "facts" as General David Sarnoff's statement in court that RCA had done more for FM than anybody, including Major Armstrong.

One of the people who heard this story for the first time from me was amazed by it. He asked a rather interesting question: "What possible good or result can come from the publishing of such a book?" His implication, which he explained, was that the people and companies involved were so powerful that, except for scholars, no one could benefit from the information. He felt something should happen, but doubted it would.

That is too pessimistic an attitude. This story is made up of the same kinds of ingredients that a report from Ralph Nader would contain. Mr. Nader attempts to do something about the sad shape of our country by gathering evidence of poor performance and demanding action. There is also a growing number of consumer-movement organizations coupled with the various liberation movements of minority groups (though I hardly consider woman's lib a minority!). This still embryonic power is beginning to make some inroads into changing the Establishment that has done such a poor job in solving our nation's problems (probably because that Establishment helped create them). The release of the Pentagon Papers indicates that, even in the case of men's lives, our government and its major and minor leaders (few of the former, plenty of the latter) make terrible errors and foolish decisions in such an important area as foreign policy and war. The government and the business institution can and do cover up and water down any kind of information that would truly inform. They are able to do this because of the almost unholy marriage they have with the mass media. The media, in the main, must rely on business for its advertising revenue and they must court government officials to keep restrictive legislation away from their door and also get what "doctored" government news releases they can so the media have something to print and air as news content.

Tracing history, we find that the mass media, along with most social and political institutions, change with government, population growth, the move from rural to urban-oriented living, industrialization, and even changes in man's thinking about his role toward his fellow man, the state, and God. Some of these changes are so great that they alter institutions completely. The mass media represent one of the fastest growing and most altered of our social and cultural institutions. What they were, and what we were as a nation in 1800, hardly represent what we are, and what our nation has become in the late twentieth century. Large corporations, and what they stand for and accomplish, cannot be viewed naively as "good" or "evil." Large corporations and conglomerates simply "are" and will continue to be what they are. They are the end-product of the last two hundred years of growth and progress in the business world. Monopoly is another word which no longer can be viewed as "evil" since it is now a basic form of business practice that cannot be easily reversed, even if we had the power. The thought of aggressive competition in a field such as communications is appalling to many economists, who would view with horror many telephone companies or many telegraph companies. The duplication of resources would constitute a staggering economic loss and would lead only to obvious inter-company agreements to allow a customer to use the service of one company to call a friend served by a competing company. One could add, it would be a further horror to have ten telephone companies put up all those extra telephone poles. Ten times the number of such poles would make our ugly city and country viewing intolerable!

In our private thoughts and lives, certainly we can lament something we think is good, but lost. However, we can hardly afford the luxury of having "the good old days" in a world that simply cannot accommodate those days without paying a high price in inefficiency and waste. But if we are to save some of the principles on which this country was founded, and principles for which many thousands have died to protect, we must decide on the ones worth saving and still operable in our present highly industrialized and urbanized world. Free enterprise seems to be one of the principles which we abandoned some time ago but which we like to pretend we still have. It is true that an individual still can open his own gas station or grocery store. If the argument is reduced to that dreary level, we still do have free enterprise. However, if one wishes to open his own newspaper, television station, department store chain, car dealer agency, or satellite communication service, the door is hardly open to free access. Astronomical costs, labor restrictions, government restrictions, licenses, fees, imbedded competition, interest rates, race problems, zoning problems, inflation (the list could go on for pages) all combine to make "free enterprise" something to take the kids to see in a Museum of Business History (provided the museum could dig any up to put on display).

But perhaps the democratic process does not depend too greatly on the economic pillar upon which a particular society is built. If other pillars are strong, such as the freedoms promised by our Constitution and Bill of Rights, surely that society can still function as a passable facsimile of a democracy. Perhaps by the year 2000 that is all we can hope for, considering the crushing force of history and the present trends of automation and de-humanization. If the whole world eventually becomes prey to these forces, what will distinguish one people from another will have to be, finally, their political and social life. That we should retain as much of our revolutionary spirit of free speech, of the search for truth, of the dignity of the individual seems to me to be a worthy goal.

Viewed in this setting, the history of the development of FM is really not so strange. If we erase the names of the individuals and companies concerned with this particular plot, we have a play typical of the twentieth century. They are, in another writer's words, merely players upon a stage, who had little control over what they did. It is History that authored the FM "play," provided a protagonist and an antagonist, spelled out the conflict, added tragedy for a more profound story, and gave it a somewhat happy if anti-climactic ending. But as I learned, this was a real story with real people. And when real people die, they don't get up from the stage and take off the make-up and have a martini.

With Madison Avenue recognition growing, FM broadcasting seems assured of a bright future. A significant portion of the research in this book was conducted as informal interviews with FM broadcasters, educators, public relations people, technical engineers, lawyers, and all levels of FCC employees (from Commissioner to library staff). Most of this information is in the book as background. However, the future of FM inevitably came up in interviews—with interviewees in almost unanimous agreement about its coming importance. FM stereo broadcasting is seen as the quality service of the future, serving an audience of generally higher economic and educational levels than AM. To keep this level, both the FCC and advertising agencies have warned that this audience can be held only if FM keeps its programming selective, does not become as "commercial" (in total time) as AM, and takes advantage of its own special technical attributes. Some FM broadcasters feel AM and FM must continue together as a total aural service. They feel, as do many now, that the population of the United States demands the 8000-plus stations AM and FM allocations can accommodate. They feel the number of stations that can be supported technically by either band alone is not enough for the present and future population; both have to be used. Implicit in the thinking of the present FCC is the ultimate separation of all AM/FM operations. That is, an owner of an AM and FM license in the same market will have to sell one of them. This will, no doubt, be the next major development in radio legislation. Whether it is fought bitterly, mildly, or not at all depends on which license the AM/FM operator judges will bring him most profit. That separation is now inevitable is well recognized in the industry, for the FCC had made it plain. The major question is when it will take place. This author feels it will take place before 1980.

Like most political speeches and Sunday supplement "uplift" stories, this book ends with a prediction of a glowing future. Glowing, in spite of a past that has contained very few incidents to justify the optimism now being voiced for FM. A few last personal comments seem appropriate. The raw data used in this book contain far more than a simple history of FM broadcasting. The data are an explosive history of the entire field of the electronic communications art as practiced by private enterprise and regulated by government. It is not an atypical history but a very typical one. It is a story of U.S. business in transition—transition from the open and unabashed hoodlum tactics of the late nineteenth and early twentieth centuries—the tactics of the land barons, railroad magnates, oil kings, and newspaper chieftains—to the more discreet and covert methods of the present day. I have lived so closely with the material presented here that a seemingly valid criticism might be that I have lost sight of the trees for being myself lost for so long in the forest. However, that is not the case. I see all too clearly! The FM story is not that unique.

What is surprising is that the story has been so well preserved in darkness. It involves so many charges of unethical and dishonest behavior and so many of them seem (or are) backed up by sworn testimony and events that reading it can change the reader's whole outlook on some parts of our system. If all the charges are true, they are shocking and, to some, they are enough to question the very system that spawned such actions. If the charges are only half-true, they remain just as shocking and enough to question the leadership value of many high-ranking business and government leaders of the country.

In 1967, Robert V. Cahill, legal assistant to the Chairman of the FCC, said in a speech that FM's slow growth was due to "... decades of mistakes...." He was including the FCC in this charge. Thirty-one years before this, George Henry Payne, FCC commissioner, made a speech entitled, "Is Radio Living Up to Its Promise?," in which he indicated the role of the radio industry lobby in its attempts to influence the commission. Presented here, at the close of this book, his words will be most relevant to all the charges the reader has read so far. Back in 1936 we get:

> But—and this is the question—when we have allowed private corporations to develop a national resource that elsewhere in the world is government owned and controlled, should not those who are making large fortunes from this resource give us better programs?
>
> To anyone who studies the situation from the inside there is quite evident a contempt for educational and cultural influences that is most unusual in any field of scientific development.
>
> . . . .
>
> A more disagreeable aspect, and a more sinister one, deterring radio from living up to its promise, is the fact that the radio lobby in Washington has filled the radio "industry" with the novel idea that they control the government.
>
> For two and a half years I have watched the operations of this lobby which has endeavored to dictate the actions of the Federal Communications Commission.[2]

Commissioner Payne also commented on the role of the lone inventor in our time, and, like the ghost of Hamlet's father, Edwin Howard Armstrong can, perhaps, be dimly seen and heard too.

> Of the forty-three scientists who, since 1912, have contributed most to radio's scientific development and progress, only two have received compensation in any way commensurate with their achievements.
>
> We have here a complex and serious economic phenomenon. Great discoveries are made and the discoverers profit little. The public which owns the ether... profits little. A third party steps in and, discovering nothing, inventing nothing, and owning nothing, nevertheless makes great fortunes.
>
> Mr. Gifford, President of the American Telephone and Telegraph Company, went so far as to say in a paper, brought out by the Federal Communications Commission telephone investigation: If anyone tries to tell me that he is acting in a business capacity in the public interest, I am inclined to say, "Oh, bunk!" ... those who are organized for selfish and greedy purposes have been stronger than we thought and more arrogant than it is possible to believe.[3]

With statements like that coming, as they do, from the FCC itself, it is hard to disbelieve any of the charges made against any of the groups or individuals or government bodies which had a part in the FM struggle. It is my opinion that most of the charges made against the government and business world about the retarded growth of FM are substantially true. The events of thirty-five years cannot be explained away as coincidence or as "just one of those things." It is not believed that any detailed master plan was used, but that the various interests for and against the success of FM handled each crisis as it came along. The "handling," when large fortunes were at stake, probably did consist of various questionable methods. Such handling is not unique to the FM story. It is the story of the growth of the telegraph industry, the telephone industry, the oil industry, the railroad industry, real estate, and journalism—to name a few. And indeed such handling is not unique to our country. It is men that must be blamed, not systems.

It has been pointed out that the history of FM broadcasting is also the history of Edwin Howard Armstrong. The two cannot be separated. Likewise, the history of FM broadcasting is also the history of the Federal Communications Commission. This government agency's role in any broadcasting service (AM, FM, TV, telephone, telegraph, satellite, CATV) cannot be understated or overemphasized. The blame for the rather difficult time FM broadcasting has had is laid squarely on the doorstep of the FCC. In turn, the FCC's failure to do its job in the public interest is directly the result of its total and complete loyalty, not to the public but to the broadcasting industry. In recent years the Federal Communications Commission has had two outstanding commissioners, in the author's opinion, actually acting in the *public* interest. As a result, they have been severely criticized by the broadcasting trade press, which regards them as some kind of "fuzzy-brained, mulish" beasts.[4] Since "mulish" is an adjective based on the noun "mule," it is assumed *Broadcasting* magazine may actually have wanted to use the word "jackass" but thought "mulish" had more decorum.

The two Commissioners are Kenneth A. Cox and Nicholas Johnson. Cox's term ended in 1970 and he was not reappointed by President Nixon. Johnson's term expired in 1973. Nixon does not reappoint rebels! Commissioner Johnson is especially critical of the role the FCC has played in broadcasting regulation and leadership. In a searing article in *The Atlantic* in the summer of 1968, he condemned the FCC decision to let International Telephone and Telegraph merge with the American Broadcasting Company. He described the way the FCC has authorized licenses, so to create serious monopoly problems, as "dreadful" and explains this as a threat to our traditional ideal of having many voices in the marketplace of ideas. Johnson also related with some horror a remark of the late General Sarnoff of RCA, who envisioned, with relish, the coming era where a company owns all the "idea" vehicles that are possible.

Sarnoff hailed the appearance of "the knowledge industry"—corporate

> casserole dishes blending radio and television stations, networks, and programming; films, movie houses, and record companies; newspaper, magazine and book publishing; advertising agencies; sports or other entertainment companies; and teaching machines and other profitable appurtenances of the $50 billion 'education biz'.[5]

This can be conceived of as nothing less than the uncomfortable world of control as described so well in such books as *Brave New World* and *1984*. Somehow such a conglomerate does not seem to be what our Founding Fathers had in mind concerning free enterprise and diversity of ideas. Johnson's article, with the provocative title, "The Media Barons and the Public Interest," ought to be required reading of every serious communication student or anyone who has an interest in this country's welfare. Anything written by Nicholas Johnson ought to be read!

Commissioner Johnson, who has evidently done some serious research on the matter, made some further pronouncements on the FCC which more than corroborate the charges made in this book by the many critics of the FCC. His remarks are from a speech to a broadcasting group:

> "Witness the disreputable record of the FCC that continues week after week."
>
> Throughout . . . his talks, he stressed the view that broadcasters do not have to worry about the commission. "You've always had a majority at the FCC and you always will . . . The only thing you have to fear from the FCC is it permitting such low standards to this industry."
>
> "You have enough power in our country that you are beyond check, in my judgment, by any institution in our country today—the President, the Congress, the FCC, the academic institutions."
>
> " . . . the FCC is a do-nothing FCC. . . . You've got them captured."[6]

The "you" Mr. Johnson refers to is, of course, the broadcasting industry. No statement this author has read, in the millions of words that made up this research, is quite so candid, so true, and so shocking. Another article, in the magazine *Consumer Reports*, entitled, "The Tuned-out, Turned-off FCC," is equally damning as the previous one, and states, as though it were an everyday accepted matter-of-fact, "The FCC is in trouble today because of its long and implacable neglect of duty."[7] It is this agency, then, that must be given "credit" for FM history, as it has been described in these pages.

A pessimistic view taken, after this reading, could be that, out of this rather "purple past" seemingly so typical of U.S. business history, we have become, even so, a rich and affluent nation. If an individual were actually to defend this notion, it might be useful to find out what that individual may define as "rich" and what share of that affluence he may possess. Rich people seem more optimistic. I was once told that Chicago received most of its parks, lake-front beautification, bridges, and city improvements under one of its most corrupt mayors. The argument speaks for itself, especially if one believes any means justifies any end.

A more optimistic view might be that evil is always present in man's destiny and truth must always battle for survival. Under that philosophy, FM survived, in spite of everything, because it was a superior service and therefore destined to win out. Perhaps the best advice to give the novice communicator is that truth, like love, can always use a little help. To have a communications system in our country serve the triple masters of the public, the economic necessity of the business world, and the changing politics of government is asking almost the impossible—to serve them all well, that is. Surely there are men and women who can solve this problem in a better way than it has been solved.

In March, 1969, Bantam Books published a paperback version of the Lessing biography of Armstrong. For this printing, Lessing wrote a new final chapter bringing the story up-to-date. He paints a continued bleak picture of what the broadcasting industry, in collusion with the government, has managed to do to retard a system of world-wide direct broadcasting. This system would allow the use of satellites and FM to provide for revolutionary changes in world communications. Such a system (which is less expensive than our present one) could

help solve a number of problems of a serious nature such
as reaching areas not served because of severe terrain features.
Developing countries could use such a system to gain a much
needed national program service. But this whole system of
having signals come from a satellite directly to a home receiver,
has run into the usual stumbling blocks built of AM/TV vested
interests who foresee no profit for them (you don't need land-
based transmitting stations if you use a satellite) and from
the telephone company that would be largely by-passed by
such a non-wire, non-cable, non-relay station system. However, as soon as these communication giants are able to use
their financial and political power to their fullest extent, the
government will create the proper laws and rules by which
they will no doubt help the already rich and powerful become
even more rich and powerful (and all in the name of business
expertise and flag waving). Then will there be nationwide
and worldwide satellite systems.

As COMSAT (a communication satellite system created
by the government with private interests involved) has developed and as the newer satellite systems are developing, it
is the same companies that are mentioned over and over again
in this book who are the major shareholders and decision
makers. I'm not sure I'm all that unhappy that a company
which knows something about communications should run
a satellite system. Perhaps what bothers me is that I simply
don't like how these men think. They don't think as human
beings; they think as cash registers, Presidential hopefuls,
social ladder-climbing mistresses. They worry so much about
today, they forget tomorrow is begging for a chance. And
when tomorrow finally arrives (somehow a little bleaker and
with less shine than hoped for) our leaders look back to yester-
day for excuses. I'm tired of buying Cracker Jack futures only
to find the prize is always plastic and breakable.

Lessing, in his up-dated book, seems a bit more optimistic
about the future. Why, I have no idea. He actually suggests
the American people will wake up to what has been done
to them and do something about it. I don't know where he

gets this kind of faith. My own experience is that my fellow Americans only get upset when they see a television documentary on some national crisis. And when television (or any of the mass media, for that matter) gets around to finally reporting the crisis, its always too late to do much about it. (That's how it got to be a crisis!) In any case, Lessing's remarks on FM, Armstrong, and the future in communications make a fitting close to this book.

> The lonely man listening to music in the night, the isolated farmer hearing nightly the news of the world, the airplane pilot guiding his craft safely through the ocean of sky, the astronaut now in his capsule gathering in the whispers from space, the earthbound emergency crew contending with some mission of mercy or disaster, the army on the move and the man in his armchair, charmed or instructed for an hour by a great play, a symphony, a speech, a game of ball—all owe a debt to this man who in some forty years of high fidelity fashioned the instruments illimitably extending the powers of human communication. History in its long course is already beginning to correct many of the injustices beset him. FM is assuredly on its way to becoming the leading broadcasting system of the country and the world. And someday not too distant a people, grown wiser, will put down the arrogance of monopolies and insure to itself a radio-television system at least as free as its press. But when that day comes it will be well to remember that in this twentieth century as in all others, these advances were won only at great cost in blood and travail.[8]

Indeed, remembering is the *least* we can do. I'd prefer to see something done! When will the "put down" come?

NOTES

[1]Lorenzo W. Wilam, "Everything You've Ever Wanted to Know About Radio and Television (Which Your Friendly Local Broadcaster Would NEVER Tell You . . . ," *The Realist*, March, 1971, No. 89, p. 43.

[2]FCC, Address of George Henry Payne, Commissioner, at the University of the Air, College of the City of New York, December 19, 1936, Mimeo. No. 19289.

[3]*Ibid.*

[4]Editorial, *Broadcasting*, October 14, 1968, p. 96.

[5]Nicholas Johnson, "The Media Barons and the Public Interest," *The Atlantic*, June, 1968, p. 49.

[6]"The Cox-Johnson Beat Goes On," *Broadcasting*, November 18, 1968, p. 40.

[7]"The Tuned-out, Turned-off FCC," *Consumer Reports*, October, 1968, p. 533.

[8]Lawrence Lessing, "Edwin Howard Armstrong: Final Vindication," *FM Guide* (NY), February, 1969, p. 16.

BIBLIOGRAPHY

A. Books

Almstead, F.E., Davis, K. E., Stone, G. K. *Radio: Fundamental Principles and Practices.* New York: McGraw-Hill Book Company, Inc., 1944.

Barnouw, Erik. *A Tower in Babel: A History of Broadcasting in the United States: Volume I–to 1933.* New York: Oxford University Press, 1966.

Barnouw, Erik. *The Golden Web: A History of Broadcasting in the United States. Volume II–1933–1953.* New York: Oxford University Press, 1968.

Head, Sydney W. *Broadcasting in America.* Boston: The Riverside Press, 1956.

Lessing, Lawrence P. *Man of High Fidelity: Edwin Howard Armstrong, A Biography.* Philadelphia: J. B. Lippincott Company, 1956.

B. Magazines, Newspapers, Journals
(chronological)

Carson, J. R. "Notes on the Theory of Modulation." *Institute of Radio Engineers, Proceedings,* Vol. X, February, 1922.

Carson, J. R. "Selective Circuits and Static Interference." *Bell System Technical Journal,* Vol. IV, April, 1925.

McCormack, Alfred. "The Regenerative Circuit Litigation," *Air Law Review,* Vol. V, No. 3, July, 1934.

New York Times. June 10, 1934.

New York Times. July 1, 1934.

New York Times, July 8, 1934.

New York Times, April 26, 1935.

New York Times. May 8, 1935.

Crosby, Murray G. "Frequency Modulation Propagation Characteristics." *Institute of Radio Engineers, Proceedings,* Vol. XXIV, June, 1935.

Christian Science Monitor, November 18, 1935.

"Sarnoff Urges Against Radio Shakeup." *Broadcasting,* December 1, 1935.

New York Times. December 28, 1935.

New York Times. January 5, 1936.

New York Times. January 3, 1937.

Carson, J. M. and T. C. Fry. "Variable Frequency Electric Circuit Theory with Application to the Theory of Frequency Modulation." *Bell System Technical Journal*, Vol. XVI, No. 4, October, 1937.

Boston Sunday Globe, November 17, 1935.

"Revolution in Radio." *Fortune*, October, 1939.

"FCC Deplores Hint it Collaborated in Retarding Technical Advance." *Variety*, October 11, 1939.

Shepard, John. Editorial. *FM*, November, 1940.

"Revolution for Profit." *FM*, November, 1940.

Armstrong, Edwin H. "Evolution of Frequency Modulation." *Electrical Engineering*, December, 1940.

Armstrong, Edwin H. "Mathematical Theory vs. Physical Concept." *FM & Television*, August, 1944.

"We Don't Want a Successful Operation and a Dead Patient on Our Hands." *FM & Television*, February, 1945.

New York Times. February 25, 1945.

"FCC Allocates 88–106 mc Band to FM." *Broadcasting*, July 2, 1945.

Sleeper, Milton B. Editorial. *FM & Television*, August, 1945.

"Furore Caused by Porter Letter to Cosgrove." *Broadcasting*, August 27, 1945.

"RMA Asks FCC Action on FM Band." *Broadcasting*, September 3, 1945.

Jansky, C. M. Jr. "Opportunity for a 'Free Radio' Through FM." *FM & Television*, February, 1947.

"Armstrong of Radio." *Fortune*, February, 1948.

Armstrong, Edwin H. "A Study of the Operating Characteristics of the Radio Detector and Its Place in Radio History." *Radio Club of America*, *Proceedings*, November, 1948.

New York Times. April 21, 1949.

The World Telephone (Bloomington, Indiana). June 1, 1949.

Editorial. *Broadcasting*, December 19, 1949.

New York Times. December 25, 1949.

"FM Hours: Protests Mount to Proposal." *Broadcasting*, December 26, 1949.

"Checking Up on Audio Progress." *FM & Television*, July, 1951.

"BBC Scheme for VHF Broadcasting." *FM & Television*, April, 1952.

Sleeper, Milton B. "Report on Hi-Fi Business." *FM & Television*, April, 1952.

"Chicago: Big News was Hi-Fi." *FM & Television*, June, 1952.

Armstrong, Edwin H. and Bose, John H. "Some Recent Developments in the Multiplexed Transmission of Frequency Modulated Broadcast Signals." *Radio Club of America*, *Proceedings*, Vol. XXX, No. 3, 1953.

Dreher, Carl. "The Hero as Inventor." *Harper's Magazine*, April, 1956.

Gold, Hal. "FCC's Pep Shot for Nets: 50% Separate FM Slate." *Radio Television Daily*, July 27, 1964.

Lachenbruch, David. "New FCC Rules Seen as Boosting Sales of FM." *Billboard*, August 8, 1964.

Stofa, John. "Tragedy of FM's Father." *Omnibus* (Chicago), May, 1966.

Maynard, Harry. "Evolution of a Hi-Fi Broadcast." *FM Guide* (NY), October, 1966.

"The New Voices of FM." *FM Guide* (NY), January, 1967.

"FM Captures 25% in 7 Markets." *Broadcasters Daily*, April 1, 1967.

"FM Catching the Bridal Bouquet." *Broadcasting*, April 1, 1967.

"Auto FM Sets Way Out of Line Is Claim." *Broadcasters Daily*, April 3, 1967.

"Survey Costs Down, Audience Up." *Broadcasting*, April 3, 1967.

"FM Reaches New Plateau at NAB-time." *Sponsor*, April 3, 1967.

"Consumer Electronics." *Television Digest*, April 3, 1967.

"FM Set Sales at an All-time Peak; Kinship with AM Formats Also Rises." *Variety*, April 5, 1967.

"The Acceleration of FM Radio: Down a Road Paved with Gold." *Merchandising Week*, April 10, 1967.

"Global Satellites Will Speed FM in Stereo's Growth: FCC's Cahill." *Billboard*, April 15, 1967.

Canby, Edward Tatnall. "A Study in Greatness and Tragedy." *Audio*, June, 1967.

"PATENTS: An Inventor's Vindication." *Newsweek*, October 30, 1967.

Berger, Ivan B. "Hi-Fi." *Esquire*, November, 1967.

New York Times. April 1, 1968.

Johnson, Nicholas. "The Media Barons and the Public Interest." *The Atlantic*, June, 1968.

"The Tuned-out, Turned-off FCC." *Consumer Reports*, October, 1968.

Editorial, *Broadcasting*, October 14, 1968.

"The Cox-Johnson Beat Goes On." *Broadcasting*, November 18, 1968.

Lessing, Lawrence. "Edwin Howard Armstrong: Final Vindication." *FM Guide* (NY), February, 1969.

C. U.S. Government—Federal Communications Commission
(chronological)

U.S. Federal Communications Commission. Annual Report, Vols. 1–33, Washington, D.C.: Government Printing Office, 1936-1967.

————. Address of George Henry Payne, commissioner, at the University of the Air, College of the City of New York, December 19, 1936.

————. "Brief on Behalf of Panel 5 'FM Broadcasting' of the Radio Technical Planning Board." Docket 6651. In the Matter of Allocation of Nongovernmental Services in the Radio Spectrum from 10 Kilocycles to 30,000,000 Kilocycles, 1945.

————. *An Economic Study of Standard Broadcasting*, October 31, 1947.

————. Address of Paul A. Walker, vice chairman, Federal Communications Commission, a the First Convention of the FM Association, New York City, September 12, 1947.

————. Address by Wayne Coy, chairman, Federal Communications Commission, at the 20th Annual Convention of the Radio Manufacturing Association, Chicago, Illinois, June 8, 1950.

————. *FCC LOG: A Chronology of Events in the History of the Federal Communications Commission from Its Creation on June 19, 1934, to July 2, 1956* (compiled in a stapled booklet form by the FCC Office of Reports and Information, July, 1956).

————. Address of Robert T. Bartley, commissioner, Federal Communications Commission, before the Electronic Industries Association Symposium, New York City, June 26, 1962.

————. Address of E. William Henry, commissioner, Federal Communications Commission, before the Georgia Radio and Television Institute, Athens, Georgia, January 24, 1963.

U.S. Federal Communications Commission. Information Bulletin No. 2-B. *Broadcast Primer*, February, 1964.

————. Newsletter, Mimeo. No. 47668, February 20, 1964.

————. Docket 18110. FCC68-554, Mimeo. No. 15881, May 17, 1968.

————. Report and Order. FCC68-739, Mimeo. No. 1850, July 18, 1968.

————. News Release, Mimeo. No. 38130, December 19, 1939.

————. News Release, Mimeo. No. 41117, May 20, 1940.

————. News Release, Mimeo. No. 41119, May 20, 1940.

————. News Release, Mimeo. No. 41739, June 22, 1940.

————. News Release, Mimeo. No. 84329, August 21, 1945.

————. News Release, Mimeo. No. 87220, December 14, 1945.

————. News Release, Mimeo. No. 90423, March 5, 1946.

————. News Release, Mimeo. No. 92927, April 10, 1946.

————. News Release, Mimeo. No. 99555, October 23, 1946.

————. News Release, Mimeo. No. 2467, January 10, 1947.

————. News Release, Mimeo. No. 2468, January 19, 1947.

————. Public Notice, Mimeo. No. 66825, April 12, 1951.

————. Public Notice, Mimeo. No. 66152, July 13, 1951.

————. Public Notice, Mimeo. No. 98434, November 27, 1953.

————. Public Notice, Mimeo. No. 17282, undated (1954).

————. Public Notice, Mimeo. No. 67238, December 23, 1958.

————. Public Notice, Mimeo. No. 78365, September 23, 1959.

————. Public Notice, Mimeo. No. 95209, October 17, 1960.

————. Public Notice, Mimeo. No. 12337, November 8, 1961.

————. Public Notice, Mimeo. No. 23315, July 26, 1962.

————. Public Notice, Mimeo. No. 28747, December 6, 1962.

————. Public Notice, Mimeo. No. 35534, May 16, 1963.

U.S. Federal Communications Commission. Public Notice, Mimeo. No. 43720, November 21, 1963.

———. Public Notice, Mimeo. No. 58052, October 7, 1964.

———. Public Notice, Mimeo. No. 58084, October 9, 1964.

———. Public Notice, Mimeo. No. 80342, undated (1964).

———. Public Notice, Mimeo. No. 74940, October 22, 1965.

———. Public Notice, Mimeo. No. 81217, March 10, 1966.

———. Public Notice, Mimeo. No. 90562, October 18, 1966.

———. Public Notice, Mimeo. No. 10206, December 19, 1967.

———. Public Notice, Mimeo. No. 15796, April 25, 1968.

———. Public Notice, Mimeo. No. 17105, May 17, 1968.

———. Public Notice, Mimeo. No. 17470, May 29, 1968.

———. Public Notice, Mimeo. No. 19446, July 18, 1968.

———. Public Notice, Mimeo. No. 21260, August 28, 1968.

———. News Release, Mimeo. No. 27306, February 7, 1969.

D. OTHER
(chronological)

De Forest Notes: June, 1912. Privately published in 1914 for use in patent litigation trial.

Agreement A-1. Privately published legal agreement between General Electric Company, Radio Corporation of America, and Westinghouse Electric and Manufacturing Company, New York, November 21, 1932.

FM Broadcasting. New York: RCA, 1944.

25 Years of Radio Progress with RCA. New York: RCA, 1944.

Konecky, Eugene. Monopoly Steals FM From the People. New York: Provisional Committee for Democracy in Radio, 1946.

Newsletter. Capitol Radio Reporter. Vol. I, No. 46, October 18, 1947.

U.S. Congress. Senate. Committee on Interstate and Foreign Commerce, On Certain Charges Involving Development of FM Radio and RCA Patent Policies, Hearings, 80th Cong., 2d Sess., 1948.

U.S. President. Proclamation. "Title 47—Telecommunications, Chapter 1-Federal Communications Commission, Sixth Report and Order." Federal Register, XVII, No. 87, May 2, 1952.

33 Years of Pioneering and Progress: RCA. New York: RCA, 1953.

News Office Release No. 5329. New York: Columbia University, November 16, 1953.

Armstrong v. Emerson Radio and Phonograph Corp. (SD NY 1959), 179 F. Supp. 95.

Address of Frank A. Gunther, made at the Armstrong Memorial Research Foundation, Second Major Armstrong Awards Banquet, The Engineers Club, New York City, December 16, 1965.

Beard, Richard Lee. "Development and Utilization of the Frequency Modulalation Subcarrier as a Commercial Communications Medium." Unpublished Ph.D. dissertation, University of Illinois, 1966.

Warner, J. C. "Radio Corporation of America: Part I—The Years to 1938." *The Radio Corporation of America: Four Historical Views*, New York, RCA, 1967.

Armstrong v. Motorola, Inc. (CA, 7), 1967, 374 F.2d 764.

NAFMB News Release. New York: NAFMB, mimeographed sheet, April 26, 1968.

SRDS Spot Radio: Rates and Data. March 1, 1968.

Consumer Electronics 1968: An Annual Review of Television, Radios, Phonographs, Tape Recorders, and Players. Washington, D.C., Electronic Industries Association, 1968.

Broadcasting: 1968 Yearbook.

Radio Audience Measurement. American Research Bureau Newsletter, undated from 1968.

Ward's Automotive Report, November 2, 1970.

Wilam, Lorenzo W. "Everything You've Ever Wanted to Know About Radio and Televison (Which Your Friendly Local Broadcaster Would NEVER Tell You. . . ." *The Realist*, March, 1971.

INDEX